PATRIOT SAGE

PATRIOT SAGE

*George Washington and the
American Political Tradition*

Edited by
GARY L. GREGG II AND MATTHEW SPALDING

Foreword by
WILLIAM J. BENNETT

Afterword by
RICHARD BROOKHISER

ISI BOOKS
WILMINGTON, DELAWARE
1999

Cataloging-in-Publication Data

Patriot sage : George Washington and the
   American political tradition / edited by
   Gary L. Gregg II and Matthew Spalding ;
   foreword by Wiliam J. Bennett. —1st
   ed. —Wilmington, DE : ISI Books, 1999

       p.   cm.

   ISBN 1-882926-38-2
       1. Washington, George, 1732-1799. 2.
   United States—Politics and government—
   1775-1783. 3. United States—Politics and
   government—1783-1809. I. Gregg, Gary L.,
   1967- II. Spalding, Matthew.

   E302.5 .P37 1999   99-64472
   973.4—dc21   CIP

Published in the United States by:

ISI Books
P. O. 4431
Wilmington, DE 19807-0431
www.isi.org

Book design by Marja Walker

Printed in Canada

"Oh Washington! Thou hero, patriot sage, Friend of all climes, and pride of every age!"

— THOMAS PAINE

ACKNOWLEDGMENTS

December 14, 1999, marks the two hundredth anniversary of the death of George Washington. Events of recent history make this date an especially important and timely one to mark.

On June 11-12, 1999, the Intercollegiate Studies Institute and The Heritage Foundation brought together accomplished scholars, junior faculty, and top undergraduates from around the nation to discuss our first and greatest president. Held at Mount Vernon, Washington's beloved home, the conference was a joint project of ISI's Honors Program and The Heritage Foundation's Salvatori Fellowship Program. *Patriot Sage* had its origins in that conference. Together with a few additional outstanding essays, these contributions represent a considered evaluation of Washington's life and legacy.

A number of institutions and individuals deserve considerable thanks for their various roles in making this volume a reality. Jim Reese and the Mount Vernon Ladies' Association were generous and gracious hosts of the conference. Paul Rhein and Melissa Naudin did yeomen's work in making the conference run as smoothly as it did. Tina Chapman and Claudia Pasquantonio did considerable work on the manuscript, and Jeffrey Nelson, Brooke Daley, and Christopher Briggs provided crucial moral support for the project and brought their considerably honed skills to the manuscript.

We are grateful to everyone who contributed to helping us mark the two hundredth anniversary of the passing of Washington and hope the finished product is worthy of this important occasion in the life of our nation.

CONTENTS

FOREWORD

WILLIAM J. BENNETT

A t the end of the Revolutionary War, General George Washington observed that the "Citizens of America" are now the "Lords and Proprietors" of a great continent possessed of "all the necessities and conveniences of life." The citizens find themselves, he said, in a condition of "absolute freedom and Independency." Nothing better illustrated this condition than the "happy conjuncture of times and circumstances" under which America had declared its independence and status as a sovereign nation: "The foundation of our empire was not laid in the gloomy age of Ignorance and Superstition," he wrote in one of the most distinctive statements of the American Founding,

> but at an Epocha when the rights of mankind were better understood and more clearly defined, than at any former period; the researches of the human mind, after social happiness, have been carried to a great extent; the Treasures of knowledge, acquired through a long succession of years, by the labours of Philosophers, Sages and Legislatures,

are laid open for our use, and their collected wisdom may be happily applied in the Establishment of our forms of Government; the free cultivation of Letters, the unbounded extension of Commerce, the progressive refinement of Manners, the growing liberality of sentiment, and *above all*, the pure and benign light of Revelation, have had a meliorating influence on mankind and increased the blessings of Society.

One can hardly imagine a more auspicious beginning for the new nation or a statement more fitting to such optimism.

But then, with all the gravity of the situation, Washington added this concise and simple observation: "At this auspicious period, the United States came into existence as a Nation, and if their Citizens should not be completely free and happy, *the fault will be entirely their own.*"

With the war won, it was now up to the American people to decide for themselves whether they were to be "respectable and prosperous, or contemptible and miserable as a Nation." This was the moment when they would "establish or ruin the national Character forever." The choice they were to make would determine whether the Revolution would be seen as a blessing or curse not only for present and future generations of Americans but also for the rest of the world: "This is the time of their political probation; this is the moment when the eyes of the World are turned upon them."

One can almost hear the echo of Puritan John Winthrop's famous phrase that "we shall be as a City upon a Hill, the eyes of all people are upon us." Likewise, Washington's was a prelude to the more familiar opening passage of *The Federalist,* where Publius remarked that "it seems to have been reserved to the people of this country, by their conduct and example, to decide the important question, whether societies of men are really capable or not of establishing good government from reflection and choice, or whether they are forever destined to depend for their political constitutions on accident and force."

The American Founders were acutely aware of the many difficulties in forming a government based on the consent of the governed. They were close students of history and had learned how the tempestuous republics of Greece and Rome had been destroyed by convulsions and upheavals, vice and demagoguery. They knew of human weakness and designed America's political institutions to take human nature into account. The result was the United States Constitution, today the longest lasting, most successful, most enviable and imitated constitution man has ever known.

But while the institutional arrangements so carefully wrought by the Founders would be central to the success of our republic, they knew that these institutions would ultimately depend on the American people. Although the Constitution was absolutely necessary for good government, the Founders knew that good citizens were needed for the republic—and republican self-government—to survive.

"The preservation of the sacred fire of liberty, and the destiny of the republican model of government," Washington remarked in his First Inaugural Address, "are justly considered as deeply, perhaps as finally, staked on the experiment intrusted to the hands of the American people." In the end, the gritty and noble work of securing the American republic would have to be done not by government but by us—we, the people.

Left unsaid, however, was the need for extraordinary individuals who themselves would be models of citizenship and good character for the rest of the nation. The need, in other words, for men like George Washington.

From 1775 onward, Washington was the *de facto* leader of the colonial struggle and the personification of the American Revolution. At the darkest moments of the war he stood virtually alone in the pursuit of independent nationhood. He led a rag-tag army to victory against the strongest and best trained military force in the world. After the war he was the center of correspondence among the most thoughtful men of the day and was instrumental in bringing about a convention over which he presided to create a new constitution. The presidency, an office having been designed with him in mind, was an integral part of the process of forming the new government.

Speaking at Boston's Bunker Hill monument in 1843, Daniel Webster remarked that no matter what America had accomplished, it had given to the world Washington's example and that "if American institutions had done nothing else, that alone would have entitled them to the respect of mankind."

Lately, Americans have become worried about the state of our culture and, in my opinion, rightly so. A majority of Americans now cite moral decline as our chief malady. There is a growing agreement that we need to engage in a reassessment of things— to borrow Tom Wolfe's phrase, a great relearning. But as we restore the nation's sense of goodness, we also need to restore its sense of greatness. And in this project we would do well to remember George Washington. Not that we should blindly emulate him or even suggest that he was perfect. Nevertheless, there is much we can learn from his life, character and statesmanship.

Mason Locke Weems gave a rather mystical account of Washington's life in *The Life of George Washington, with Curious Anecdotes Equally Honourable to Himself and Exemplary to His Young Countrymen*. But Parson Weems's stories were the ones learned by school children the country over. When the story of Washington and the cherry tree was incorporated into McGuffey's *Third New Reader* for children, it became part of the fabric of our nation. At least one future statesman read a copy of Weems's book early in his childhood and still remembered its lessons years later. On his way to Washington, D.C. to become president, Abraham Lincoln recalled Weems's account of Washington and how the stories had fixed the battle of Trenton in his memory. "You all know, for you have all been boys," Lincoln noted (confirming Weems's purpose of inculcating the young), "how these early impressions last longer than any others." The early impressions eventually led Lincoln to conclude, as he wrote in his famed Temperance Address, that Washington was "the mightiest name on earth— long since mightiest in the cause of civil liberty, still mightiest in moral reformation."

At the time of Washington's death, John Adams wrote that "his example is now complete and it will teach wisdom and virtue to magistrates, citizens, and men, not only in the present age, but in future generations, as long as our history shall be read." Adams was right. Washington still teaches wisdom and virtue. It is our job to make sure that American history is read and learned. On the two hundredth anniversary of Washington's death, I can think of no better way to honor him than to study his thought and action anew, for doing so will help rekindle the sacred fire of liberty.

INTRODUCTION

GARY L. GREGG II AND MATTHEW SPALDING

George Washington's daily journal entry of December 13, 1799, records three inches of snow and northeasterly winds at Mount Vernon. That entry was his last. A sore throat, the result of riding in a cold storm to inspect his farms, quickly worsened, and by late the next night the great, but now aged, hero was no more.

The news of Washington's death spread quickly throughout the young nation. Every major city and most towns in America conducted official observances. Churches held services to commemorate his life and role in the American Revolution. Innumerable pronouncements, speeches, and sermons were delivered to lament his passing. From his death until his birth date two months later, some 300 eulogies were published throughout the United States, from as far north as Maine to as far south as Georgia and as far west as Natchez, on the Mississippi. Hundreds more were surely delivered but never published.

"Ancient and modern names are diminished before him. Greatness and guilt have too often been allied, but his fame is whiter than it is brilliant," read the official message of the United States Senate, addressed to President John Adams. "Let his countrymen consecrate the memory of the heroic General Washington, the patriotic statesman and the virtuous sage. Let them teach their children never to forget that the fruit of his labors and his example are their inheritance." Washington's successor answered in turn: "The life of our Washington can not suffer by a comparison with those of other countries who have been most celebrated and exalted by fame. The attributes and decoration of royalty could only have served to eclipse the majesty of those virtues which made him, from being a modest citizen, a more resplendent luminary.... For his fellow citizens, if their prayers could have been answered, he would have been immortal."[1]

In Europe, Napoleon Bonaparte ordered the standards and flags of the French army dressed in mourning crape. Calling for a statue of Washington to be erected in Paris, French Minister of Foreign Affairs Talleyrand wrote that "a proper veneration for all that is held dear and sacred to mankind, impel us to give expression to our sentiments by taking part in an event which deprives the world of one of its brightest ornaments, and removes to the realm of history one of the noblest lives that ever honored the human race."[2] In honor of Washington, the British Channel Fleet lowered its flags to half-mast.

To this day, Washington remains one of the most recognized figures in American history. His image adorns our currency and postage stamps, and innumerable counties, towns, schools, streets, squares, and parks bear his name. But popular conceptions of Washington indicate little familiarity with the man.

Consider the two most well-known images of the first president. The first image is Gilbert Stuart's famous Athenaeum portrait, which once hung in public buildings and schoolhouses across America: Washington here is solemn, impersonal, and humorless. He is the granite statesman, distant and obscure, perceived to be patriarchal and above the people. Mark Twain once quipped that if Washington were to return and not look like this well-known painting, he would be considered an impostor.

The second image is the one of folklore and legend, the subject of childhood stories and nursery rhymes. What is it that we remember about George Washington? As a boy he chopped down a cherry tree with his hatchet and could not tell a lie. As a man he prayed at Valley Forge, had wooden teeth, and naively thought honesty to be the best policy. Familiarity with these two lifeless images has left Washington as likely to be the subject of parody and farce as the object of esteem and veneration.

But George Washington was neither a monument nor a myth. He was a mere mortal and very ordinary in many ways. Undereducated and prone to anger, he was at different periods of his life a surveyor, a farmer, and a soldier. Washington never wrote a political tract or a philosophical treatise on politics. And yet his words, thoughts, and deeds as a military commander, as president, as patriot, and sage make him one of the greatest-perhaps the greatest-statesman in our history.

THE LIFE OF WASHINGTON—A BRIEF SKETCH

George Washington was born on his father's estate in Westmoreland County, Virginia, on February 22, 1732. He was the eldest son of a well-to-do farmer, Augustine Washington, whose grandfather had settled in Virginia in 1657.

Young Washington received most of his schooling from his father and, after his father's death in 1743, from his elder half brother Lawrence. As a boy Washington had a liking for mathematics, a discipline he found useful in acquiring a knowledge of surveying, a skill in great demand in a country full of people seeking new lands in the west. At seventeen years of age he was appointed surveyor of Culpepper County, Virginia, the first of several public offices he was to hold. In 1751 he accompanied an ailing Lawrence to the island of Barbados in the West Indies, an excursion that was his first and only experience of foreign lands. Lawrence died in 1752.

In that same year, Governor Robert Dinwiddie appointed George Washington adjutant of the southern district of Virginia. Major Washington's first military mission came during the summer of 1753. Reports of a French expedition from Canada establishing posts on the Ohio River had alarmed Virginia. In response to the threat, Dinwiddie had Washington carry a message to the French commander demanding an immediate withdrawal. The French refused. Upon his return Washington recommended that an English fort be erected at the forks of the Ohio before the French returned to that strategic position in the spring. Washington, now a lieutenant colonel, was sent back, and the resulting skirmishes between Washington's force and a French and Iroquois force turned out to be the opening engagements of the French and Indian War. The French ultimately forced him to accept surrender terms, but Washington had become famous back in Williamsburg for his bravery and leadership.

In 1754 the Virginia military was reorganized. Regular army officers coming from Britain now had command over officers who held colonial commissions. As this change meant that Washington might find himself reporting to officers he outranked and who had less experience, he resigned his commission. When a British force under Major General Edward Braddock arrived early the next year with orders to drive the French from Fort Duquesne at the forks of the Ohio, however, Braddock invited Washington, whose military reputation was high, to join the staff as a volunteer aide-de-camp. In a battle near Fort Duquesne, the French surprised and routed the British forces, and Braddock was mortally wounded. Washington did his best to rally the regulars and to use a few Virginia troops to cover the retreat. His coolness and bravery under fire further enhanced his reputation. In August 1755, Governor Dinwiddie appointed Colonel Washington commander in chief of all the colony's troops, and for the next three years he struggled with the endless problems of frontier defense.

After this tour of duty, Washington returned to the quiet life of a Virginia planter. In January 1759, he married Martha Dandridge Custis, a charming and wealthy young widow. From 1759 to 1774, he was a member of the House of Burgesses, the lower chamber of the Virginia legislature. As he prospered and his responsibilities grew in number, Washington became involved in the protests of Virginians against the restrictions of British rule. Convinced that the king's ministers and British merchants and financiers regarded Americans as inferior and sought to control, as he wrote, "our whole substance," he opposed such measures as the 1765 Stamp Act. It was clear to Washington that British policy was moving against self-government in America, and by 1774 Washington had become one of the key Virginians supporting the colonial cause. Elected to the First Continental Congress, Washington spent the winter of 1774 and 1775 organizing militia companies in Virginia. When Washington attended the Second Continental Congress in May 1775, just after fighting had broken out at Lexington and Concord, he appeared in the blue and buff uniform of the Fairfax County militia, colors later adopted by the army of the colonies.

On June 15, 1775, the Continental Congress unanimously elected George Washington as general and commander in chief of its army, and he proceeded to Boston, where the militia of the surrounding towns had besieged the only British army in the colonies. For the next six years, General Washington led a rag-tag and ill-supplied army through the rigors of war, from the daring attack on Trenton to the trying times of Valley Forge to the battle of Yorktown in 1781, the victory that ended the war. The peace treaty came two years later, on September 3, 1783, and in November, as the last British boats put off to their ships, Washington's victorious troops entered New York City. After taking leave of his principal officers at Fraunces Tavern—and stopping at Annapolis, Maryland, to surrender his commission—General Washington returned to Mount Vernon to remain, as he put it, "a private citizen...under the shadow of my own vine and my own fig tree...[and] move gently down the stream of life until I sleep with my fathers."

The Articles of Confederation had been ratified in March 1781, but many doubted the document could be a successful constitution for a continental government. Washington feared that the jealousy and bickering between the individual states and their petulant refusal to grant adequate powers to the federal government would eventually lead to the downfall of the new nation. Congress failed to act, and the states continued obstreperous. By October 1784, Washington concluded that the lack of energy in the federal government and the divisions between the states had severely weakened the national character and "brought our politics and credit to the brink of a precipice."[3] In March 1785, commissioners from Virginia and Maryland met in Alexandria to consider problems dealing with the navigation of Chesapeake Bay and the Potomac River. The commissioners quickly moved the meeting to Mount Vernon in order to avail themselves of the wisdom of Washington, who had long shown a keen interest in inland navigation. Given the success of the Mount Vernon Conference, the Virginia legislature invited all the states to meet in Annapolis to discuss their commercial relations. Only five of thirteen states sent representatives to the Annapolis Conference; nevertheless, these five took the radical step of adopting a statement (drafted by Alexander Hamilton) calling for a new convention at Philadelphia to discuss all matters necessary "to render the constitution of the Federal Government adequate to the exigencies of the Union."[4]

In late 1786, the Virginia legislature decided to send a delegation to the upcoming Convention and nominated Washington its head. For the next six months, while encouraging calls for the

Convention, Washington hesitated to accept the nomination—he
had doubts about the seriousness of the general reform effort.
When he did decide to attend, while deferring to James Madison
on the details of constitutional structure, Washington deliberately took the lead on the political front. He believed that fundamental reform should be proposed at the start of the Convention,
and that Virginia should sound the call. Washington recommended to Madison that the Convention adopt "no temporizing
expedient" but instead "probe the defects of the Constitution to
the bottom, and provide radical cures." Washington thought
that, regardless of whether such reforms were ultimately
approved, this thorough examination of the American political
order should be the aim of the Convention from the beginning:
"a conduct like this," he wrote to Madison, "will stamp wisdom
and dignity on the proceedings."[5]

Having been immediately and unanimously elected president of the Convention, Washington presided over it for the next
four months. With his ability to take part in the open discussion
limited by this role, he contributed to formal debate only once at
the end of the convention. But he worked where he could and
voted with his state delegation throughout the proceedings. An
examination of his voting record shows his consistent support for
a strong executive and expansive national powers—two issues on
which he was a leading advocate. The members of the Convention
so trusted Washington that they placed all the papers and notes
of the Convention in his care. Washington did not publicly participate in the ratification debate, but he staunchly supported the
Constitution. Indeed, his prestige and backing were crucial to its

eventual approval. "Be assured," James Monroe wrote to Jefferson, "his influence carried this government."[6]

Unanimously chosen by the presidential electors to be the first president of the United States, Washington took the oath of office on the portico of Federal Hall in New York City on April 30, 1789, in the presence of Vice President Adams and both houses of the newly organized legislature. When Congress authorized the creation of the first executive departments, Washington chose the individuals he thought most qualified for the jobs—Alexander Hamilton as secretary of the treasury, Thomas Jefferson as secretary of state, John Jay as chief justice of the Supreme Court, Henry Knox as secretary of war, and Edmund Randolph as attorney general.

The chief controversies of Washington's first term revolved around fiscal proposals made by Hamilton. Hamilton urged, that the national debt (both foreign and domestic) be funded at full value, that the federal government assume the liabilities incurred by the states during the Revolution, and that a system of taxation be established to pay the bills. Although the proposal to pay the foreign debt was virtually unopposed, the scheme to pay the domestic debt was highly controversial and led to the first suggestion of sectional political divisions in the new nation. Ultimately, the question was settled in a political deal that placed the national capital on the Potomac River. With the compromise agreed to by all sides, Washington hoped the simmering political divisions had been settled.

Hamilton also proposed a national bank. Washington initially supported the idea but later was troubled by objections

Madison had raised about the constitutionality of Hamilton's proposal. When the president turned to Attorney General Edmund Randolph and then Secretary of State Thomas Jefferson for their opinions, both cabinet members thought the bank unconstitutional. Jefferson, for instance, argued for a "strict construction" of the Constitution: a national bank was not, he argued, among the specific powers delegated to Congress.[7] When the president turned to Hamilton for a response, however, Washington received a long exposition that set forth a broad view of government based on a doctrine of implied powers. The bank, according to Hamilton, was perfectly constitutional as an implied means to the end of government's delegated powers and therefore within the compass of national authority.[8] Washington agreed with Hamilton and, convinced America needed a bank to the restore its finances, signed the legislation.

Toward the end of Washington's first year as president, the news of a revolution in France arrived in North America, beginning the first great foreign policy controversy of the young Republic. Like many in the United States, Washington was initially optimistic about events in France but soon had reservations about the revolution; his conservative temperament was averse to the extreme politics and philosophy of the revolution. Washington considered stepping down at the end of his first term in 1792. The members of his cabinet, however, argued strenuously against his retirement. In the end, Washington, in light of the nation's domestic affairs and the volatile international scene, agreed that his leadership was necessary to maintain a moderate and stable course in America. He would remain until, as Madison had urged, "public opinion, the character of the Govt, and the course of its administration shd be better decided, which could not fail to happen in a short time."⁹ Washington was inaugurated for a second term of office in March of 1793.

In the fall of 1792 and the spring of 1793, very disturbing news reached America: mobs had stormed the Tuileries, Lafayette had fled and had been captured, the monarchy had been abolished, and the king had been executed. Then France declared war on England, Spain, and Holland in February 1793, presenting the United States with the possibility of war under the Franco-American treaties of 1778, which implied a defensive alliance with France. Hamilton's sympathies lay with Great Britain (he wanted to repeal the treaties of 1778), but Jefferson favored France. Washington, however, chose a completely independent course and issued a strong proclamation calling for "a conduct friendly and impartial toward the belligerent powers."¹⁰ The controversy surrounding Washington's policy led to the very public and philosophically important debate between Hamilton, who adopted the pseudonym "Pacificus," and Madison, who adopted the pseudonym "Helvidius," over the president's constitutional authority in foreign policy.

Relations with the British, which had always been a difficult matter, became particularly dangerous with the outbreak of their war with France. During the summer and again in the fall of 1793, when the British adopted orders interfering with neutral American shipping, Madison and Jefferson proposed economic retaliation. Hamilton, when more news of maritime seizures reached America, proposed recruiting and fitting a federal army.

Washington knew that the nation must take the step of preparing for war, but at the same time he decided to send a special envoy to London—Chief Justice John Jay—to seek a negotiated settlement. The resulting treaty (November 19, 1795) and the controversy surrounding it created the second foreign policy crisis of the Washington administration.[11] The treaty was far from perfect, but Washington supported the agreement: he believed that Jay's Treaty did settle a few important questions and prudently postponed a number of others. Above all, it prevented war at a point when America was weak and could ill afford a protracted struggle with a world power.

Jay's Treaty put an end to the foreign occupation of American territory north of the Ohio River. In the Treaty of San Lorenzo (October 27, 1795), Spain recognized the United States' boundaries of 1783 (the Mississippi in the west and the thirty-first parallel in the south) and gave Americans free navigation of the Mississippi River.[12] These treaties went far in achieving Washington's goal of removing from the North American continent those powers he considered hostile to the United States.

All told, Washington's foreign policies allowed a young nation the time and protective space to strengthen its constitutional order, thus perpetuating the cause of republican government in North America.

In the last years of his presidency, the emerging party struggle between Hamilton's Federalists and Jefferson's Republicans dominated the public mind and, Washington feared, threatened to undermine the structure of government. It came as no surprise, then, that when he decided to retire, Washington gave as one of the reasons a disinclination to be attacked by the "set of infamous scribblers" who wrote for the party presses.[13]

Washington had performed his duty to his nation and now, finally, could return home. As his lasting legacy to his country, he issued his famous Farewell Address in 1796. Washington recommended commercial relations with other nations but as few political entanglements as possible. Often overlooked is his sage advice concerning issues like federal union and the Constitution, faction and political parties, the separation of powers, religion and morality, and public credit. While seeming to focus only on immediate concerns, the Address presented Washington's understanding of the principles and policies most conducive to the long term safety and happiness of the American people.

In 1799 Washington made the last journeys of his life. The first was to the army camp at Harper's Ferry, Virginia (now West Virginia) and the second was to Philadelphia to consult on army matters. In 1789 President John Adams appointed Washington head of a provisional army during the period of tensions with France. The aged hero who had given so much to his country, and who had longed for nothing more than the peaceful life of the farm, again had responded to the call of sacrifice. Washington died on December 14, 1799, and his body was laid to rest in the hillside overlooking the Potomac river at his beloved Mount Vernon.

AN OVERVIEW OF *Patriot Sage*

Generations of American's knew well the history of Washington's life and the greatness of his character—they had learned about him in their copy books, in their classrooms, and in their homes.

More recently, we seem to have lost our understanding of Washington, both the man and his character. Marking the two-hundredth anniversary of Washington's death, *Patriot Sage* is our effort to help the American people comprehend once again their Founding Father.

America and the world have changed dramatically since the end of the eighteenth century. Is Washington still relevant to America? Does he speak to the challenges of the twenty-first century as he did to the nineteenth? Forrest McDonald opens *Patriot Sage* by arguing convincingly that Washington remains today, as he was during the nation's formative years, the indispensable man. The rest of the essays collected here explore, in roughly chronological order, the various aspects of Washington's life, thought, and character, and collectively make the same point: that Washington has many things to teach us. Each essay, while representing scholarship of the first order, is written with an eye toward the needs of contemporary America.

Washington did not form an upright character simply by reading books; mainly forged it in a life on the farms of rural Virginia and under fire in combat. In his own day, Washington was often compared to the heroes of the classical world, most famously to Cincinnatus, the Roman hero who, called from his field and made dictator to save the Roman army, promptly resigned his powers once he had completed his task. Bruce Thornton and Victor Hanson's essay illuminates the importance of the agrarian life and service in the military to the formation of Washington's character. These two accomplished classicists also raise important questions for contemporary America—an America where the rural life has largely disappeared and where fewer and fewer of our national leaders have the character-forming experiences of military service.

Focusing on Washington's talents as a military strategist, Mackubin Owens further explores Washington's experience as a leader in war. General Washington has come under considerable criticism lately by historians who argue that he was not a successful military commander, and that his position and his actions were not essential to the success of the American cause. Professor Owens analyzes the record in light of established principles of military strategy and makes the case for Washington's place among the best military leaders—not only because Washington achieved victory, but also because he executed the war in a manner that prevented a struggle for independence from becoming a devastating civil war.

Washington's retirement from military service simply marked a new chapter in his service to his country. In the intervening years between war and the presidency, as the inadequacies of the Articles of Confederation became clear, Washington kept abreast of political developments. William B. Allen makes a strong case that it is to Washington that we owe a considerable debt for the development and the success of America's Constitution. According to Allen, Washington played a key role in the development and adoption of our fundamental law. And as the first president, he would serve to give life to the Constitution and infuse the Union with legitimacy. Rather than remembering him for the fictional cherry tree episode, Allen concludes, we should remember Washington for his constitutional legacy-a legacy that still stands today as a majestic oak in human history.

Washington was the first president, but he was more. He was, in fact, the very reason a strong presidency could have been created at all after the colonists had thrown off George III's rule. The office was not much more than an outline of powers on parchment when Washington assumed office. He therefore had the awesome task of shaping the presidency and determining its lines of development. There were no precedents to follow, no institutions to inherit, no experts to consult, or former office-holders whose advice he might solicit. He would, in effect, create the office as he went along. As Mark Rozell demonstrates, Washington, well aware he was setting precedents, exhibited a chastening concern for the propriety of his actions; and the success of the office these past two hundred years has been due largely to its first occupant's conscientious attention to duty and decorum. This last fact is usually overlooked by professional historians and political scientists, who often treat Franklin Roosevelt as the first president worthy of serious consideration.

As Ryan Barilleaux points out in his essay, Washington set particularly important precedents in his role as first commander in chief and chief diplomat. He did not shrink from exerting his constitutional authority in the realms of military policy and diplomacy. Whether dealing with Indian tribes on the frontier or insurgents during the Whiskey Rebellion, or overseeing military preparations, Washington was an engaged commander in chief. He also used his power to direct foreign policy and negotiate treaties, thereby shaping America's role in the world.

Yet the presidency is more than power and command. Symbols are an essential part of human life and politics, and in the American political system there are no more important wielders of political and cultural symbolism than presidents. The presidency is a place of symbolism and ceremony, of moral leadership, and civic education. Washington inherited an office with no expectations, no set of required behaviors, no approved modes of conduct, and no established etiquette. In his contribution, Gary Gregg explores the important symbolic aspects of Washington's presidency and their meaning for the American regime. Washington understood the importance of his actions and his rhetoric and, as Gregg points out, by means of them, always strove to set the proper tone and convey the proper lessons to the American people. In other words, Washington understood what few do today-that executive leadership is about more than policies, legislation, and economic growth. The constitutional principles and devotion to duty our presidents embody-or do not embody-should be of central importance in gauging the success of our nation's highest officeholders.

Washington is too often seen simply as a man of action; as a doer, not a thinker. His words are often overlooked or simply dismissed by scholars interested in those Founders considered to be intellectually more sophisticated. But Washington's letters and speeches deserve much more of our attention. Virginia Arbery explores Washington's Farewell Address and finds it to be an effort to root in the American imagination the basic principles of the American Founding. Through the rhetoric of that address, Washington aimed to encourage in the citizens a proper attachment to constitutional government. Favorably comparing Washington's rhetoric to Jefferson's, Arbery makes us wonder what happens when our presidents misunderstand the nature of the American union and their place in it.

Arbery does a close textual analysis of the Farewell Address, but Matthew Spalding casts his net wider and finds Washington concerned, throughout his life, for the integrity of his own character and the character of his fellow citizens. Realizing the regime would be successful only to the degree that the character of the citizenry matched the needs of republican self-government, Washington sought to embody, encourage, and form an American character. He understood that America's success would depend more upon the conduct and lives of the American people than upon any parchment barrier or particular scheme of power distribution. To the end, Washington remained concerned that his words and his deeds taught the virtues required for ordered liberty.

Whether we remember his greatness or not, Washington is still very much a part of American life. His portrait no longer adorns as many classrooms in America as it used to, but his likeness appears regularly in our culture. Placing it on currency and in advertisements and political cartoons, Americans have made Washington's image a part of their daily routines. Art historian Mark Thistlethwaite explores the history of our artistic portrayal of George Washington, whom we have depicted as civic icon, as national hero, as family man, and as farmer. Washington's image, Thistlethwaite concludes, has been resilient enough to have survived many interpretations. And it has remained, through it all, at the center of our national identity.

Washington has often been portrayed by artists in various religious scenes—from kneeling in prayer at Valley Forge to ascending Christ-like into heaven—but what were his own religious beliefs? Was he a devout Christian, as some have claimed? Or was he a Deist, an atheist, or an agnostic? John West explores these questions in his essay and provides some answers. Washington left us very few solid clues to his own creedal commitments, but he clearly believed in a creator God who actively intervened in human affairs—it would be difficult to read his private letters and public statements and conclude otherwise. According to West, Washington also believed that religion was essential to the perpetuation of morality, that revelation and reason cooperated at the level of the moral law to guide men in their actions, and that religious liberty was meant to strengthen, not weaken, religion in the public square. In sum, Washington thought religion should be the guiding hand in the life of the nation.

Patriot Sage concludes with the official eulogy for George Washington and an Afterword by a man who has perhaps done more than anybody in modern America to rekindle the public's affection for our Founding Father. On December 26, 1799, in Philadelphia, Congressman Henry (Lighthorse Harry) Lee delivered John Marshall's majestic tribute before an assembled Congress. The eulogy, standard reading in American textbooks well into the current century, cannot but move the spirit and inspire the imagination. In soaring prose, Marshall summarized the qualities that made Washington "First in war, first in peace, and first in the hearts of his countrymen." Regrettably, school children no longer read this edifying portrait of our greatest national hero.

Richard Brookhiser's *Founding Father* has been credited with significantly contributing to what interest there is today in George Washington and his legacy. In his Afterword, Brookhiser explores some of the forgotten qualities of Washington's character that remain vitally important for modern America to recognize, remember, and emulate. Brookhiser discusses Washington as a charismatic leader, a gentleman, a hero, a politician, and a thinker.

Lately, we are fortunate that there has been somewhat of a renaissance of Washington scholarship—a trend that has been encouraged by many of the contributors to the present volume. The matter is by no means settled, of course; skeptics of Washington's greatness and critics of the Founding in general still dominate mainstream academic opinion. Nevertheless, it is instructive to note that, after rigorous examination of vast stores of primary documents, neither Douglas Southhall Freeman nor James Flexner, Washington's two great modern biographers, could discard the Washington of patriotic lore. Freeman wrote in the introduction to his work that "the transformation of the quiet Virginia planter into the revered continental commander is beyond explanation." Washington, Freeman concluded, was, and always had been, exactly what he appeared to be.[14] Flexner concluded similarly: "My labors have persuaded me that he became one of the noblest and greatest men who ever lived. He was not born that way.... He perfected himself gradually through the exercise of his own will and skill."[15]

The two-hundredth anniversary of Washington's death gives us all good reason to reconsider the life and legacy of our first president. *Patriot Sage* is not intended to be a comprehensive account of the statesmanship of George Washington, and the authors are mindful that no one book can provide a final estimate of his contributions to the cause of liberty. Nevertheless, it is hoped that the essays in this book will contribute to the renewal of Washington's rightful authority in our political tradition. If the legacy of the man is not to be forgotten, such a renewal is needed, but it is absolutely necessary if Washington is ever again to be "first in the hearts of his countrymen."

ONE

Today's Indispensable Man

FORREST McDONALD

The men who established the American republic were acutely aware that they lived in a pivotal era in human history, and they eagerly rose to the occasion. They were all impelled by a love of liberty, but a large number were, in addition, driven by a desire for immortal Fame—the grateful remembrance of a distant posterity. To put it simply, they wanted to remain alive and be cherished in your memory and mine.

It may be that the Founders were as unlucky in their choice of posterity as they were lucky in their choice of time in which to live, for the American people are notoriously lacking in a knowledge of the past. But until Goals 2000 ensures that our children will learn nothing of our past, we still can assume that there is one American of the Founding generation whose name everybody knows: George Washington. And yet, knowledge of just what he did is far from widespread. Beyond the cherry tree episode (which never happened) and the fact that he was the first president, most Americans do not know why they should remember and cherish him. What I propose to do is to describe what he was like and thereby help us cherish his memory.

Let us begin with an overview. No historian doubts that Washington was the indispensable man of the epoch. By sheer force of character he created the Continental Army and held it together, under extremely adverse circumstances, for the eight years it took to win independence. His awesome prestige created the atmosphere in which the Philadelphia Convention of 1787 could draft a constitution that the states would ratify; and it is certain that the office of president was created only because he was available to fill it. Moreover, he never abused or sought to aggrandize his power, and he voluntarily surrendered power when a job was done, though he might easily have held it for life.

On the opposite hand, no scholar who has studied Washington would maintain—as schoolchildren used to be taught—that the man was flawless. As a soldier he was capable of rashness and poor judgment. He was addicted to gambling, indulged in a good deal of wenching, and was said to be a "most horrid swearer." He was vain, a bit pretentious, and hot tempered; and though he was a perfect gentleman in public, he was sometimes not one in private.

Yet he was respected, admired, even revered by his countrymen, and he was the most trusted man of the age. What is more, and different, he was the most trustworthy man. Why he was so trusted, and why he came to be so trustworthy—in revolutionary circumstances of a kind that almost invariably breed Caesars, Cromwells, Castros, and Stalins—are questions that must be examined if we are to understand Washington's true legacy.

In regard to his being trusted, it is easy to overlook a crucial ingredient, that Americans sorely needed someone to trust. Partly this need arose from the perilousness of the undertaking on which they embarked in 1776. They had no way of knowing whether they would be founders or failures: the winners in such circumstances are called Patriots, the losers are hanged as traitors. But there is more to it than that. Difficult as it may be to imagine, Americans were a monarchical people, a people who loved their kings. George III had been especially beloved, and when he betrayed Americans by making war on them, they reacted by embracing republicanism and by refusing to entrust executive power to anyone. And yet the craving for a symbol to embody the nation remained. In this diverse new entity—the United States of America—it was not enough to have leaders, no matter how virtuous or capable; there had to be one above all others. As Americans had earlier referred to George III as the Father of his People, they now needed someone to call the Father of his Country, if there were to be a country, and not thirteen separate countries.

Washington satisfied this need, and not least because he looked the part. Tall and powerfully built, he was "the most graceful figure...on horseback," as Thomas Jefferson put it, and was instantly recognized as the commander in chief even by soldiers who had never seen him before. When Abigail Adams finally met him in 1789 she was moonstruck. She gushed, as had the Queen of Sheba when first setting eyes on Solomon, "the *half* was not told me."

His physical appearance was complemented by an aura, not merely of strength, but of invincibility. His immunity to gunfire seemed almost supernatural. Early in his career a treacherous guide fired at him from point-blank range—and missed. Once he rode between two columns of his own men who were firing at one another by mistake and struck up their guns with his sword—the musket balls whizzed harmlessly by his head. Time and time again during the Revolutionary War musket balls tore his clothes, knocked off his hat, and shredded his cape; horses were killed under him; but he was never touched. What mortal could refuse to entrust his life to a man whom God obviously favored? What country could refuse to do so?

But if it was his natural gifts that made others prone to trust him, there remains the question, how did he come to be worthy of trust? The answer is, he made himself that way. To understand how he did it, we must turn to the prevailing ideas about the nature of the human animal. Virtually every American at the time believed in God—the God of both the Old Testament and the New—which meant that, while they believed in the possibility of redemption in the hereafter, they also believed in original sin, in the inherent baseness of man.

And yet, though man could not escape his nature, there were a number of ways he could improve himself. All of them rested on the premise that the social instinct is a primary force; the desire to have the approval of one's peers ranked with the physical appetites in motivating people. A perceptive person could turn this instinct into an engine for self-improvement, which is what Washington did. As a child he devoutly wished to become a country gentleman (a status he was by no means born to) and toward that end he recorded and followed *110 Rules of Civility and Decent Behaviour in Company and Conversation.* These rules were a manual of etiquette for circumstances ranging from being at the dinner table ("Being Set at meat Scratch not neither Spit Cough or blow your Nose—except there's a Necessity for it") to being "In Company of those of Higher Quality than yourself."

Notice the adolescent Washington's phraseology: "those of Higher Quality than yourself." Eighteenth-century Virginia society was highly stratified, as was society throughout Europe. Washington was acutely conscious of his own social position, for as a teenager he had been taken under the wing of a wealthy, titled family, the Fairfaxes. From watching them, and also from a play he saw for the first time in his late teens, he learned to aim higher than just seeking the approval of his peers. The play was Joseph Addison's *Cato*, and its message was clear: Addison advised young Washington to follow precisely the opposite course from that recommended by Shakespeare's Polonius. In Hamlet, Polonius says: "This above all: to thine own self be true, and it must follow, as the night the day, thou canst not then be false to any man." Shakespeare put those words in the mouth of a prattling fool, and Addison's message is that, for public men, they are foolish words. Rather, he says: Do not trust in your own righteousness. Instead, be true to others; seek the esteem of the wise and the good, and it follows that you cannot then be false to yourself—or to your country.

Washington made that a guiding star for his own conduct. Later, when circumstances and his achievements made it possible, he aimed his sights even higher, and he sought by conscious design to earn the esteem of posterity, of generations of discerning and virtuous people yet unborn.

That was one way Washington improved himself. Another was through the concept of character. The term "character" was rarely used in the eighteenth century as we use it, to refer to internal moral qualities. Rather, at least in polite society and among people in public life, it referred to a persona or mask that one deliberately selected and always wore: one picked a role, like a part in a play, and sought to act in that role unfailingly, ever to be in character. If one chose a character with which one was comfortable, and if one played it long enough and consistently enough, it became a "second nature" that in practice superseded the first. One became what one pretended to be.

The results, for good or ill, depended upon the character or characters chosen and upon how well one acted the part. Washington chose to play a progression of characters, each grander and nobler than the last, and he played them so successfully that he ultimately transformed himself into a man of almost extrahuman virtue.

The first character to which he aspired was that of the country gentleman. This entailed becoming a successful commercial farmer. Washington's inheritance was small, but he worked skillfully as a tobacco planter and steadily increased his holdings. It did not hurt that he married a wealthy widow, whose property was greater than his. (As an aside I must point out that Washington, like his neighbors, employed slave labor. At the time, slavery was legal in almost every country on earth. Washington's duty, he believed, was merely to treat his slaves humanely. He gradually changed his mind, however, and in his will he freed his slaves. Though many other Virginians, including Jefferson, talked about the evils of slavery, none followed Washington's example. Moreover, Washington made provision for supporting his former slaves who were too old to support themselves. His estate was paying pensions to them as late as 1833.)

The key to Washington's success as a farmer was that, in an age in which scientific farming was in its infancy, he became the scientific farmer par excellence. He read every book and journal on the subject, and he exchanged letters with experts throughout Europe. He conducted endless experiments and made endless calculations (my favorite is that he determined that there were 13,411,000 grains in a bushel of timothy). He invented a plough that automatically dropped seeds in the furrows. He was his own architect in the construction of Mount Vernon. He conducted time and motion studies a century and a half before efficiency experts introduced the concept into American manufacturing. And he became an immensely wealthy man by the time of the Revolution.

Already, however, he had aspired to and succeeded in his first public character, that of a military hero. At the age of twenty-two he was entrusted with the command of Virginia troops sent to the back country in what turned out to be the beginnings of the French and Indian War. He took to warfare enthusiastically. "I heard the bullets whistle," he wrote to a younger brother, "and, believe me, there is something charming in the sound." He made mistakes, but in the crucial Battle of the Wilderness, he offered his commanding British general advice which, had it been followed, would have saved the day. Instead, the British employed conventional tactics—and were slaughtered. Washington emerged as a hero and was regarded throughout the colonies as a man destined to do great things.

His opportunity came twenty years later, when the Continental Congress convened to defend American liberties against British encroachments. Washington was the obvious choice for commander in chief, partly because he was the only American with an inter-colonial reputation as a fighting man, partly because as a Virginian in charge of New England troops he would give the army a "national" flavor. However, lest Congress overlook the obvious, Washington attended its sessions dressed in a splendid general's uniform designed especially for the occasion. On the motion of John Adams, he was given the command.

Washington and his men drove the British out of Boston early in 1776, but soon thereafter things began to go badly. The Americans failed to defend New York, and Washington's army was forced to retreat to Pennsylvania. Part of the army disbanded; the remainder was a shambles. Making everything worse was that large numbers of civilians, upon seeing the British, suddenly lost their taste for independence and went over to the enemy. (Indeed, Washington's mother was a Loyalist.)

Washington headed off disaster by a bold stroke. On Christmas night, 1776, he crossed the ice-choked Delaware River and successfully attacked the British garrison in Trenton. Popular morale improved, and many volunteers joined the army. Yet by the summer of 1777 Washington knew that he would never have enough strength to defeat the British head-on. Instead, he would have to maneuver carefully and wait, possibly for years, until the British made a blunder that would enable him to strike the deci-sive blow.

But the waiting game required patience and discipline—

traits that the Americans did not have and that Washington himself would have to teach them. Moreover, it cost a great deal of money to keep an army in the field, and the Congress had very little. Congress raised funds by printing paper money, backed merely by a vague promise to repay some day; the paper rapidly lost its value until it was worth nothing at all (giving rise to the expression "not worth a continental").

In the fall of 1777, General Horatio Gates won a major victory in upstate New York, but out of jealousy of Washington he declined to cooperate with the main army, and as a result the enemy took Philadelphia. Washington's army retreated to Valley Forge, where it endured a winter quite as dreadful as legend depicts. A single brushstroke conveys the whole: Congress declared a day of "Continental Thanksgiving" and ordered that each soldier be fed a special "dinner" consisting of "half a gill of rice and a tablespoon full of vinegar."

Somehow, by one means and another, Washington kept the army together for three more years—a task made more difficult by his refusal to commandeer supplies from civilians. The British, meanwhile, steadily expanded the territory under their control. The low point came on January 1, 1781, when 2,400 veterans of the Pennsylvania line rose in mutiny. With difficulty they were persuaded to return to their duties. Then after ten more anxious months Washington got his opportunity. The British general Cornwallis made the blunder of encamping in Yorktown, with his back to the sea and without naval cover. A combined American and French force besieged the town, and Cornwallis had no option but to surrender. Suddenly the war was won.

Even so, danger persisted. A peace treaty had to be negotiated, and the army was held in Newburgh, New York, in readiness to fight again if the negotiations failed. The soldiers were
restless and eager to go home, but they had not been paid in years
and did not want to disband without some of their overdue pay
or their promised bonuses. Grumbling increased alarmingly and
reached a climax early in 1783, when anonymous pamphlets were
circulated among the officers calling for a meeting where "plans"
would be made to seek "justice." This was a perilous situation,
one that could easily end in a military dictatorship.

To the surprise of the mutinous officers Washington showed
up at the meeting. He had written a short speech, and when he
took it from his coat pocket, he also drew out a pair of eyeglasses,
which only his aides and closest friends knew he needed. He began,
"Gentlemen, you will permit me to put on my spectacles, for I have
not only grown gray but almost blind in the service of my country." He went on to shame the officers for betraying the Revolution,
and reduced them, literally, to tears. The mutiny dissolved.

When Washington was finally able to retire to his beloved
Mount Vernon, he was the most famous man in the Western
world. He was idolized by his countrymen, praised throughout
Europe, regarded as the greatest man of the age even in Britain.
But Washington had considerable cause for uneasiness, nonetheless: he now lived in a goldfish bowl, as it were, with all eyes
upon him, and he had to live up to the almost impossibly high
standards that he had set for himself.

His situation was made doubly uncomfortable by the ongoing
current of public affairs. Upon retirement, he had announced that

he would never again emerge from private life. He was greatly concerned, however, that the Union was likely to fall apart. To prevent
that, he sent a circular letter to Congress and the governors of the
states, urging that the Articles of Confederation be altered to create
a central government adequate to the nation's needs. Otherwise, he
predicted, the states would drift into anarchy.

The drift toward anarchy was already under way, and it
increased with a rush during the winter of 1786-1787, when
Shays' Rebellion erupted in Massachusetts. The rebellion was
actually a taxpayers' revolt, but it was generally perceived as an
uprising of desperate debtors who threatened a redistribution of
all property. It was beginning to appear that the Father of his
Country would soon have no country to be father of.

It was mainly in response to the news of Shays' Rebellion that
Congress and the state legislatures called the Philadelphia
Convention of 1787—and that Washington agreed to serve as a
delegate from Virginia. James Madison thought it amazing that
Washington would attend and thereby place his reputation in
jeopardy, for it was by no means certain that a convention would
accomplish anything. But Washington, being the man he had
become, realized that what was at issue was the grand question
whether a people could govern themselves by a reasonable process
of deliberation, rather than by the violent force of arms to which
every other government on earth owed its origins. In a sense, the
Constitutional Convention would be legislating for all mankind.

Washington was not an especially active member of the
Convention—constitution making and abstract political theory
were not his dish of tea—but he was indispensable to its success-

ful outcome in at least three ways. The first had to do with cred-ibility. Eighteenth-century Americans intensely distrusted cen-tralized power and had an almost paranoid fear of conspiracies against their liberties. Washington's widely publicized participa-tion in the Convention as its president gave it a legitimacy it oth-erwise could not have had. Americans were willing to give a convention meeting behind closed doors a chance because they trusted Washington.

Washington's second vital contribution had to do with the force of his personality among the delegates. Justly celebrated as the Framers have been for their wisdom and prudence, there were hot-heads among them, and prima donnas and schemers. Washington's dignity and overpowering aura, however, made it impossible to behave in a mean-spirited, improper, or uncivil way when he was around. He kept his fellow delegates on their best behavior.

The third contribution pertained to the creation of the pres-idency. Most of the delegates had learned from experience that a government without an executive branch is not a government at all, but fear of executive power persisted. More than a third of the delegates supported a proposal for a plural executive—consisting of three to five persons—and a few others wanted a single execu-tive checked by an executive council. A majority would support a one-man presidency only because Washington would be the man, but few were confident about giving the president more than ceremonial functions; and it is doubtful that Washington would have accepted the office under such restrictions.

The main sticking point was that Washington could not live forever, and no one could think of a safe way to choose his successor. Today it might seem that the solution would be to elect the president by popular vote; but given the primitive technology in communication and the fear of direct democracy, that was not an option. Objections ruled out any decentralized form of election—by the state governors or the state legislators, for instance—and that meant the choice must be placed in Congress. But congressional election would make the executive dependent upon the Congress, not a separate branch, and would encourage outside powers and special interests to corrupt the process.

For these reasons, the delegates were unwilling, as late as two weeks before the end of the convention, to endow the presidential office with substantive powers. Then somebody proposed the electoral college—a complicated, cumbersome, one might say cockamamie scheme—that overcame all the objections, and it was adopted.

Properly, at that point, the whole draft constitution should have been gone over again to separate the executive powers from the legislative. But that would have been a painstaking process, and the delegates, tired after nearly four months of tedious labors, were anxious to be done and go home. So they hastily made some changes in their draft: they made the president commander in chief of the armed forces, and they made the conduct of foreign relations the joint concern of president and Senate (instead of, as in the draft, exclusively the affair of the Senate). Otherwise, they simply stated that "the executive power shall be vested in a president." This amounted to a blank check for Washington to fill in as he saw fit. The precedents he would set in office would determine just what the executive power was to be.

In my *American Presidency*, I consider in detail the enduring precedents that he set; here let me mention but a few. Washington made the president responsible for relations between the United States and foreign governments. We take that for granted, but constitutionally the "advice and consent" clause would have permitted the Senate a major role. After a couple of fruitless efforts to consult with the Senate in person, Washington and the senators agreed that, thenceforth, advice and consent should come after, not before, the president acted.

A related matter has to do with the tensions between Congress's exclusive authority to declare war and the president's exclusive power as commander in chief. When the wars of the French Revolution broke out, Washington wanted to issue a neutrality proclamation. Secretary of State Jefferson objected that since only Congress could declare war, only it could declare neutrality. But Washington in his capacity as commander in chief prevailed. In another exercise of the power as commander in chief, Washington sent the army to wage war against the Indians in the Ohio country—without asking for a declaration of war. He did so on additional occasions thereafter. The vitality of these precedents will be appreciated when I point out that although Congress has declared war five times in our history, presidents have sent American troops into combat, not counting the Indian wars, more than 200 times.

Others of Washington's major precedents include the use of departmental heads as a cabinet, the two-term tradition, and the practice of initiating the budget-making process.

The last part of Washington's legacy is the most subtle, and it may be the most important. He was acutely aware that he had become a legend in his time, a true myth, and he recognized that the presidency made possible the institutionalization of the role he had been playing. That is to say, he endowed the presidency with the capacity—and the awesome responsibility—to serve as the symbol of the nation, of what it is and what it can aspire to be.

In the following passage from his First Inaugural Address, Washington specified our founding principles. It was imperative, he said, that "the foundation of our national policy be laid in the pure and immutable principles of private morality,...there is no truth more thoroughly established than that there exists...an indissoluble union between virtue and happiness;...[and] that the propitious smiles of Heaven can never be expected on a nation that disregards the eternal rules of order and right;...the preservation of the sacred fire of liberty and the destiny of the republican model of government are justly considered, as deeply, perhaps as finally, staked on the experiment intrusted to the hands of the American people [Washington's emphasis]." Those words are as true and as relevant today as they were when Washington uttered them in 1789.

TWO

"The Western Cincinnatus": Washington as Farmer and Soldier

BRUCE S. THORNTON AND VICTOR DAVIS HANSON

L ord Byron, in his "Ode to Napoleon," was hardly original when he called George Washington the "Western Cincinnatus." To the classically educated contemporaries of Washington, his resignation of his commission at Annapolis in 1783, along with his well-known love of the farming life, immediately evoked thoughts of the Roman hero who in 458 B.C. was called from his plough to be voted dictator in order to save the Roman army from the Aequi, and who then promptly returned to his farm once the danger passed, giving up the dictatorship and its powers after a mere fifteen days, and becoming for the Romans the exemplar of simple rural virtue and the republican citizen-soldier animated by duty rather than power.[1] So it was that the same year as Washington's resignation Philip Freneau, in a poem entitled "Cincinnatus," wrote with enthusiasm: "In Vernon's groves you shun the throne,/Admir'd by kings, but seen by none." Artists found the equation useful as well: two paintings, now lost, by John Trumbull and Charles Willson Peale, as well as sculptures by Jean-Antoine Houdon and Antonio Canova depict Washington as the Roman hero.[2]

The popularity of identifying Washington with Cincinnatus is not hard to explain. In the figure of the Roman hero, eighteenth-century Americans could economically communicate the important political ideal Washington embodied: the citizen-farmer and citizen-soldier whose republican virtues were created by and nourished on the farm and were expressed actively in a just war, a war fought not for private glory or national aggrandizement, but for freedom and autonomy.

For many reasons, agrarianism was the fertile soil in which American republicanism flourished.[3] The most obvious and mundane reason is that 90 percent of the people alive at the time were farmers, including the first several presidents. The life, experiences, and most importantly the virtues of farming—frugality, simplicity, hard work, duty over self-indulgence, self-sufficiency and autonomy—pervaded the material and intellectual milieu of the Founders. In addition, the Romans, the primary historical model for republican virtue, were for much of their history small farmers and citizen-soldiers who explicitly linked the virtues of farming to their political ideals. So too eighteenth-century American agrarianism connected farming to freedom and order. As Meyer Reinhold summarizes this link, "American agrarianism was, like its classical antecedent, politico-ethical in nature: an agricultural base for the republic with availability of freehold land was deemed by most of the Founding Fathers to be a prime safeguard for liberty and stability. The virtuous farmer, and the purity and simplicity of his life, were widely invoked."[4] Writers like Richard Price, Timothy Dwight, James Madison, John Taylor, even Alexander Hamilton, and of course Thomas Jefferson and George Washington all assumed, as James Madison put it, that "the classes of citizens who provide at once their own food and their own raiment, may be viewed as the most truly independent and happy. They are more; they are the best basis of public liberty and the strongest bulwark of public safety."[5] Such ideas were ubiquitous in late eighteenth-century America, uniting private property, farming, republicanism, and freedom into one coherent political philosophy.

As well as fostering republican values, ancient farming could be lucrative, a form of gain that united the benefits of moral improvement with a greater financial security than that enjoyed by merchants. In American agrarianism, too, an emphasis on profit and wealth, and their usefulness for ensuring the nation's autonomy, occurs repeatedly. All farmers are necessarily concerned with profit, the material counterpart to moral improvement and freedom. Early Americans lived in an uncertain, harsh world that brought home the truth of Aristotle's statement that "it is impossible or at least not easy to perform noble actions if one lacks the wherewithal."[6] The Founders, including George Washington, knew that material prosperity was necessary for supporting the nation's freedom and autonomy, and the agrarians among them saw farming as the best way to achieve such prosperity, avoiding as it does the evils attendant on manufacturing, the entangling dangers of trade, and the dependency inherent in wage labor.

Another utilitarian aspect of eighteenth-century agrarianism is its reflection of the Enlightenment ideal of rational improvement. The application of Baconian New Science to agricultural practice culminated in what was called first the New Husbandry and then the Agricultural Revolution, which comprised innovations in farming theory, technique, and technology.[7] The English agricultural improver most significant for American agrarianism was Arthur Young (1741-1820), who published widely on agricultural improvement and corresponded with Washington and Jefferson. Young promoted hands-on experimentation and trial-and-error as the means of improving agricultural practice, and he encouraged the dissemination of the results so that progress could spread as widely as possible. The benefits to society and political order were obvious: improving agriculture would increase productivity, creating wealth both private and public, and hence eliminate hardship and want, those perennial seeds of political disorder. Independent citizen-freeholders, prosperous and productive through the rational improvement of their own land, could then form the bulwark of a self-sufficient, autonomous republican government. This link of farming, prosperity, and republican freedom defended by citizen-militias defines the agrarianism Washington's life exemplifies.

Washington's formative years were spent on his father's two farms: the Ferry Farm on the Rappahannock River, and then Epsewasson, later Mount Vernon, on the Potomac River. Washington spoke little of his less-than-genteel childhood, but we can gather from the realities of frontier farming in colonial America that he would have learned much from his experience.[8] Though covering thousands of acres, the Washington farms were not the elegant plantations of later times. Rather, in the mid-eighteenth century they were tenuous islands of order carved by hard work out of the surrounding frontier forests still inhabited by Indians, whose smoke fires Washington could see from the farm. Stephanie Grauman Wolf writes that American pioneer farmers like Washington's father "stood on the agricultural frontier of strange land, unfathomable weather, and previously unknown plants and animals."[9] Difficult in the best of environments and climates, American farming required from people qualities such as hard work, persistence, duty, independence, hard-headed practicality, and a wide range of skills in order to survive the harsh conditions. As he accompanied his father Gus on the latter's rounds of tasks and chores required by the tobacco and mining operations, Washington no doubt absorbed by experience and precept the very virtues—a powerful sense of duty, a fierce love of freedom, and an impressive physical prowess—that would contribute to his military abilities and political philosophy.

Certainly from Washington's later statements we can see the importance he gave to farming not just for personal but for political reasons as well. Throughout his life he expressed in his correspondence his love of farming. In a letter to Arthur Young he described agriculture as "among the most favourite amusements of my life," and toward the end of his life he wrote to the Earl of Buchan that farming was "at all times the most pleasing occupation of my life."[10] Usually Washington linked his love of farming to his natural disposition: "No pursuit," he wrote to Doctor James Anderson, "is more congenial with my nature and gratification, than that of agriculture; no more I so much pant after as again to become a tiller of the earth."[11] Perhaps the most famous of Washington's encomia to farming occurs in a letter to Alexander

Spotswood: "I think with you that the life of a Husbandman of all others is the most delectable.... To see plants rise from the earth and flourish by the superior skill, and bounty of the laborer fills a contemplative mind with ideas which are more easy to be conceived than expressed."[12] This life-long expression of his love of farming convinces us of Washington's sincerity when after his second term he asserted, using a well-known Biblical metaphor for the peace and contentment of country life, "I am once more seated under my own vine and fig tree, and hope to spend the remainder of my days...making political pursuits yield to the more rational amusement of cultivating the earth."[13]

Yet Washington's love of farming was no mere private taste. Farming produced benefits for everybody, not just the farmer. Writing to Arthur Young, Washington linked his personal affection to the larger good an improved agriculture could produce: "The more I am acquainted with agricultural affairs the better I am pleased with them. Insomuch that I can no where find so great satisfaction, as in those innocent and useful pursuits. In indulging these feelings, I am led to reflect how much more delightful to an undebauched mind is the task of making improvements on the earth, than all the vain glory which can be acquired from ravaging it.... [Farming is] an employment, which is more congenial to the natural dispositions of mankind than any other."[14]

As the key words "useful" and "improvements" suggest, Washington was an "improving" farmer, one who believed that superior technique based on scientific knowledge would increase productivity and profits. Among the books in the library at

Mount Vernon are many works of prominent eighteenth-century proponents of the New Husbandry such as Jethro Tull, Thomas Hale, and Edward Weston.[15] His letters to his London agents frequently requested the "newest, and most approved Treatise of Agriculture," books with frankly utilitarian titles like *A New System of Agriculture*, or *A Speedy Way to Grow Rich*,[16] and he was grateful when Arthur Young sent him his complete works, canceling the order he had put in for them.[17] Washington was eager for the latest agricultural theory not just for his own improvement but to end, if only by successful example, the sloppy and wasteful practices of many American farmers, "exceedingly unprofitable, but so destructive to our lands," as he put it, and "as unproductive to the practioners as it is ruinous to the land-holders."[18] The waste of America's natural bounty—the "blessings of nature," as he called them[19]—through old-fashioned or irrational farming practices reduced both the United States' wealth and its autonomy; hence Washington was eager to rationalize agricultural production to make it as profitable as possible, and thus a contributor to the political and material well-being of the United States. As he wrote in 1786, agricultural improvement "is in my opinion, an object of infinite importance to the country; I consider it to be the proper source of American wealth and happiness"—the "only source," he wrote to another correspondent, "from which we can at present draw any real or permanent advantage; and in my opinion it must be a great (if not the sole) means of attaining to that degree of respectability and importance which we ought to hold in the world."[20]

The political and private benefits of an improved agricultural practice are explicitly recognized and linked by Washington in a letter to Samuel Chamberline: agricultural improvement should be fostered "not only as promoting the interest and lessening the labor of the farmer, but as advancing our respectability in a national point of view; for, in the present state of America, our welfare and prosperity depend upon the cultivation of the lands and turning the produce of them to best advantage."[21] This view of farming's political significance was consistent throughout Washington's life. In the seventies he inquired into the possibility of settling Palatine immigrants from Holland as tenants on his Ohio Valley lands, a scheme he said was "founded on interested as well as political views."[22] The latter no doubt included the recognition that settling the American West with small farmers, who lived on the land they rented and worked and eventually could own outright, would form the civic as well as economic bedrock of the young, expanding Republic. The same sentiment is apparent in President Washington's desire to introduce husbandry to the Indians: "Humanity and good policy," he wrote to Timothy Pickering, "must make it the wish of every good citizen of the United States, that Husbandry, and consequently civilization should be introduced among the Indians."[23] Clearly, farming was seen as a necessary precondition to integrating the Indians into the new Republic, as Washington told the Cherokee Nation in 1796, linking the political benefits to the nation to the Indians' own self-sufficiency and autonomy.[24]

Repeatedly in Washington's writings the political and material goods of an improved agriculture are recognized and promoted. Like Jefferson, Washington believed the availability of western land would ensure that successive waves of cultivators could expand the nation, increase its prosperity and hence autonomy, and underwrite its political virtue both by inculcating the virtues necessary for the Republic and by avoiding the manifold evils of manufacturing and trade. In an undelivered address to Congress written in 1789, Washington expressed his confidence that Americans "shall not soon become a manufacturing people. Because men are ever better pleased with labouring on their farms, than in their workshops." The innate desire for freedom and self-rule makes farming the activity most suited to human nature. "Even the mechanics who come from Europe," Washington writes, "as soon as they can procure a little land of their own, commonly turn Cultivators." As long as this natural human desire for independence can be expressed in farming, and as long as the profits of farming allow "finer manufactures" to be purchased from abroad rather than made in American factories, a critical mass of yeomen will exist to nurture and pass on the republican virtues that guarantee freedom:

> As their [Americans'] remoteness from other nations in a manner precludes them from foreign quarrels: so their extent of territory and gradual settlement, will enable them to maintain something like a war of posts, against the invasion of luxury, dissipation, and corruption. For after the large cities and old establishments on the borders of the Atlantic, shall, in the progress of time, have fallen a prey to those Invaders; the Western States will probably long retain their primeval simplicity of manner and incorruptible love of liberty.[25]

No Roman could better express the economic, political, and moral benefits accruing from citizens owning and working their own lands.

The ideas expressed in Washington's proposed address are perhaps best summarized in an earlier letter to Thomas Jefferson, where one can see linked the various strands of American agrarianism:

> For our situation is such as makes it not only unnecessary, but extremely imprudent for us to take a part in their [Europeans'] quarrels; and whenever a contest happens among them, if we wisely and properly improve the advantages which nature has given us, we may be benefitted by their folly, provided we conduct ourselves with circumspection and under proper restrictions, for I perfectly agree with you, that an extensive speculation, a spirit of gambling, or the introduction of any thing which will divert our attention from Agriculture, must be extremely prejudicial, if not ruinous to us. [B]ut I conceive under an energetic general Government such regulations might be made, and such measures taken, as would render this Country the asylum of pacific and industrious characters from all parts of Europe, would encourage the cultivation of the Earth by the high price which its products would command, and would draw the wealth, and wealthy men of other Nations, into our bosom, by giving security to property, and liberty to its holders.[26]

Here we see encapsulated the agrarian ideal Washington's own life as a farmer exemplified: the natural abundance of America, cultivated by a rationally improved agriculture, could create the wealth and autonomy that would insulate the United States from the destructive wars of the European elites. Moreover, the freedom and opportunity of America would ensure a steady stream of hard-working immigrants who could take advantage of the abundant land to further improve and expand the nation. Finally, the sober values and simple virtues learned on and reinforced by the farm would provide the moral underpinnings of the Republic, creating citizens who would be committed to freedom and independence rather than power and gain alone. In this agrarian vision, material, moral, and political goods are all intertwined and mutually reinforcing.

Every bit as important in classical literature as the yeoman-farmer was the idealization of the citizen-soldier, and especially the notion of the battlefield commander as a man of the people, a general by his own choice and by statute subject to the oversight of civilian peers. In classical Greece and Rome, civic militarism operated around a core of widely shared beliefs. The general, or *stratêgos*—an elected officer in most of the city-states—had a clearly prescribed tenure. He was responsible for sending written communications either to an elected assembly or a civilian board of overseers, and he was to fight alongside his men and to share firsthand their ordeal. Indeed, in the entire history of the classical Greek city-state, it is difficult to find a single infantry battle in which the general survived the fighting when his army lost the general encounter. Equally important, generals were to enter and leave military life with great frequency; the entire idea of a permanently professional military man is a post-classical phenomenon that arose during the Hellenistic Age (323-146 B.C.) and again during the Roman Empire (31 B.C.-A.D. 476).

In contrast, every great Hellenic statesman of the city-state—Miltiades, Themistocles, Pericles, Lysander, and Epaminondas—at some point in his career was both elected general and then subsequently fined, exiled, removed of command, or threatened with court proceedings.

Finally, the general in the classical mind was to be one with his men, and yet not part of the formal military apparatus of the state; just as his soldiers were subject to military justice meted out by their commander while in the field, so their commander in turn was subject to a quite different code of behavior set by the capricious consensus of the elected leaders of the state, if not the assembly of citizens itself. Clearly, the aim of the ancients was to create military commanders who embodied the egalitarian principles of elected government, and who were unable, despite the enormous power and prestige put into their hands, to translate military success into political aggrandizement.

When the Continental Congress met in June 1775 to select a commander in chief of the motley forces of revolution, Washington was nearly a unanimous choice. His long military service and distinguished record in the French and Indian Wars, his Virginian ancestry and quasi-aristocratic background as a plantation owner, and his well-known reluctance to campaign for the post—he purportedly ducked into an adjoining library when he learned of the discussion of his appointment—made him the ideal choice to the squabbling and deeply suspicious delegates. In his acceptance speech Washington noted briefly that he did not think himself "equal to the command I am honored with," and then finished by stating clearly that he would refuse any compensation for his services despite the loss of his "domestic ease and happiness" that such enormous responsibilities entailed.[27]

Washington was immediately plagued with the paradox that historically had faced both commander and enlisted man in all citizen-armies composed of amateurs: how to impose very necessary and undemocratic methods of discipline on highly individualistic and stubborn groups of revolutionaries; and, when and if successful in inculcating such standards of military regimen, how to allay suspicions that the new disciplinarian and his crack troops might soon loom too large for their suspicious congressional masters. Washington despaired of the task and wrote to a friend of the squabbling among his officers and the lawlessness of his men:

> Such a dearth of public spirit, and want of virtue, such stock-jobbing, and fertility in all the low arts to obtain advantages of one kind or another in this great change of military arrangement, I never saw before, and pray God I may never be witness to again.... Could I have foreseen what I have, and am likely to experience, no consideration upon earth should have induced me to accept this command.

But from his actions and formal speeches and reports, it is clear that Washington immediately sought a middle and sometimes impossible course of instilling discipline without playing the martinet, of demanding freedom to create ex nihilo an army that could crack English professionals without threatening a revolutionary Congress. Thus at times he forgave the first offense of desertion, while on other occasions he condoned hanging—and submitted complete reports of his actions to Congress.

Unlike some revolutionaries such as General Charles Lee, who called for "a popular war of mass resistance," Washington realized that such utopian visions were impossible. Despite the rhetoric, America could never rely on a spontaneous uprising of Patriots to defeat a professional British army in a sustained war that would last many years. Wisely, he sought to impose a Prussian type of discipline on his troops, with formal rules of enlistment and obedience, thus crafting an army more Roman than Greek. For more than six years (June 15, 1775–October 17, 1781), Washington would fight bitterly with his men, suffer mutinies, threaten to resign, outfox cabals of jealous peers eager to displace him, resist congressional intervention into his authority in the field, be generally ridiculed and compared unfavorably to most of his subordinates—Europeans believed that Benedict Arnold was the far greater general—and yet win the war without once exceeding his legal authority or extending his own pre-scribed tenure.[28]

In his first year of command, he was astounded at the general disorder among his some 16,000 newly enlisted recruits. Drunkenness was common; soldiers left the army at will; fighting and brawling were regular occurrences. After instituting a strict regimen of cashierings, court-martials, and public whippings, Washington remarked that the general level of chaos was perhaps due to the inherent nature of the democratic experiment itself, which infected his troops with "the leveling spirit." Yet throughout 1775 and 1776, Washington slowly forged a new army precisely in accordance with that "leveling spirit," found qualified officers, distributed uniforms and weapons, and created a new American strategic doctrine of mobility and maneuver without reliance on entrenchment. Again, for all his complaining, at no point in his inaugural years did Washington request greater powers, appoint officers illegally, or demand control of public funds without congressional oversight. Before he took command, Washington outlined his views of the proper role of the new commander in chief of the Continental Army:

> On a general in America, fortune also should bestow her gifts, that he may rather communicate lustre to his dignities than receive it, and that his country in his property, his kindred, and connexions, may have sure pledges that he will faithfully perform the duties of his high office, and readily lay down his power when the general weal requires it.[29]

After his initial victory in Boston, Washington quickly lost control of New York City and requested permission in the fall of 1776 to burn the city down, both to deny the British occupiers supplies and to punish the large number of Loyalists. Congress overturned his decision.[30] Only twice did Washington obtain dictatorial power—after the American collapse in New Jersey during November and December 1776, and again in September 1777—and Washington neither requested nor welcomed the added responsibilities given him by Congress.[31] In April 1779, on orders of a congressional commission, Washington led an inquiry into the behavior of his finest general, Benedict Arnold. Washington was able simultaneously to postpone a trial on the trumped-up charge of financial malfeasance and resist pressures by Arnold's supporters to elevate him in command.[32]

Between September 1777 and March 1778, half of all Washington's troops became casualties to enemy action, disease, and the weather, or simply deserted, emboldening a number of critics both in the army and Congress itself to fashion plans to ensure his ouster. Some wanted to take command of the armies away from Washington and create an unwieldy "Board of War" in its place; in any case, Congress continued to appoint political generals and to foist them upon Washington's command, prompting him to complain, "It will be impossible for me to be of any further service if such insuperable difficulties are thrown in my way." Things came to a head with a cabal launched by Thomas Conway, who schemed among both military officers and Congress to dismiss Washington and install himself as commander in chief. It is often forgotten that Washington was surrounded by fellow officers who felt they deserved supreme command and who often had strong supporters in Congress; in addition, Loyalist sympathy was strong among the aristocratic officer corps. At times, Washington felt that in addition to the British, he had enemies among Congress and his own fellow officers. Yet, we hear of no extraordinary measures taken to ensure his tenure; and, in general, he reported his apprehensions publicly in formal letters to Congress.[33]

During the later Benedict Arnold crisis, Washington took proper steps that British officer John André, Arnold's personal emissary who was caught red-handed with papers outlining Arnold's treason, be tried in a formal court-martial, overseen by fourteen high-ranking generals. After the execution, Washington systematically weeded out disloyal officers until at war's end he was surrounded by only two officers who were with him in 1776, Henry Knox and Nathanael Greene. In most modern armies, such high treason and rank insubordination would have led to wide-scale courts of inquisition accompanied by a general paranoia in the army; yet Washington's temperance ensured that the American army continued to function as usual despite having one of its top generals defect to the British.

In general, Washington proved more sensitive to civilian concerns than was Congress. He proved a forceful advocate for officers' complaints that Congress had not paid their full salaries in accordance with their contractual terms of enlistment, and argued vehemently for complete payment of soldiers' pensions at war's end. On the controversial question of requisitioning civilian stores to provision the army—an American complaint against British troops for most of the eighteenth century—Washington proved himself far more reluctant to take from the people than was Congress itself.[34]

At the conclusion of the war, Washington had voluntarily given up eight years of pay totaling $48,000; and unlike many of his wealthier high officers who pressed the new government to make good on its promises of bounties (which Washington supported), Washington himself never went back on his word that he would serve his country without compensation. In addition, throughout the war, he used his personal wealth for supplies for his army and lost over $5,000 a year at Mount Vernon through his absence; in total, Washington lost half his net worth during the Revolution.[35]

No American army had ever been disbanded before, and once

again Washington took the initiative in discharging his men in April 1783, with the announcement that they were "to preserve a perfect unvarying consistency of character through the very last act, to close the drama with applause, and to retire from the military theatre with the same approbation of angels and men, which has crowned all their former virtuous actions." With congressional approval he then discharged them—on the proviso they could keep their military accoutrements and arms.

After his victory march through New York in November 1783, Washington wanted to quickly retire from the army and return to Mount Vernon as a private citizen. On December 23, before the national Congress then meeting in Annapolis, Washington gave a brief farewell address, praising his officers and men, and then concluded:

> Having now finished the work assigned me, I retire from the greater theater of action and, bidding an affectionate farewell to this august body, under whose orders I have so long acted, I here offer my commission and take my leave of all the employments of public office.

Of course the presidency and a second appointment as commander in chief of the armed forces in 1798 still awaited him.[36]

As America's first commander in chief of its armies and later as the first president, Washington established the proper balance between civilian and military authority, specifically the legal and moral relationship between a commanding general and his civilian board of auditors. Previously no modern nation had attempted to wage a war under the complete auspices of a democratically elected Congress. Thus Washington established a number of precedents that would characterize American military practice for the next two centuries.

We should keep in mind that by the end of the war Washington had achieved near divine status, and an appreciative country wished to grant him all sorts of extraconstitutional powers from permanent executive office to kingship. Yet Washington replied to Colonel Lewis Nicola's suggestion of monarchy with the following warning: "Let me conjure you then if you have any respect for your Country, concern for yourself or posterity, or respect for me, to banish these thoughts from your Mind, and never communicate, as from yourself, or anyone else, sentiments of a like nature."[37]

Washington established the American principle that all major campaigns of the army must be approved by civilian authorities; moreover, to his frequent chagrin, he agreed that Congress, not the commander in chief, has the right of final approval of all promotions and military appointments. This interference Washington never questioned. Also, the commander in chief is to seek retirement from the armed services at war's end, and in all matters financial, it is critical that a general not profit from war.

While his most obvious exemplar was that of a successful military hero going on to become president of the United States—Andrew Jackson, Zachary Taylor, Ulysses S. Grant, and Dwight D. Eisenhower would follow—Washington was careful to ensure that such political aspirations were at the conclusion of hostilities and followed from a successful rather than controversial tenure. Through the darkest days of the Civil War and the Cold War, American commanding generals would respect Washington's precedent; those who did not and openly flouted federal authority in the midst of warring—George B. McClellan and Douglas MacArthur are good examples—would be urged to resign or be relieved of command. Despite their own enormous popularity, neither figure would ever overcome that loss of confidence to go on to be president.

Since the dark days of the declining Roman Republic, the presence of a popular military hero at the cessation of war had always raised the spectacle of insurrection and revolution. Yet for the American Republic, no victorious general while still in command has threatened Congress with his own military power. Indeed, the Washingtonian idea that a successful general should relinquish command immediately upon the successful conclusion of war is a precedent followed by a number of American generals, from William Tecumseh Sherman to Norman Schwarzkopf.

Finally, Washington taught Americans how generals should behave in the public realm following the war. The natural temptation since ancient times has been for retired commanders to watch domestic affairs carefully and to use the specter of their influence among the military to sway both public opinion and legislative bodies themselves in matters political. In this regard, Washington's tenure as first president of The Society of the Cincinnati, a fraternal association of Revolutionary officers who met to honor and perpetuate the traditions of military command and aristocratic chivalry, is illustrative. Once Washington sensed opposition to the society from popular spokesmen like Aedanus

Burke and Thomas Jefferson, he took steps to assure critics that he would not allow the society to threaten the republican foundations of the new nation. His orders to the new group reflect his own strong republican sympathies and perhaps echo the common suspicion of such aristocratic military clubs that had survived from classical antiquity:

> Strike out every word, sentence, and clause which has a political tendency. Discontinue the hereditary part in all its connexions, absolutely, without any substitution which can be construed into concealment, or a change of ground only, for this would, in my opinion, encrease, rather than allay suspicions. Admit no more honorary Members into the Society.... Abolish the General Meetings altogether.[38]

Washington's military model, then, was Cincinnatus, not Caesar; and his real legacy as a general was not so much his military accomplishments—though they can be defended, as in Mackubin Owen's essay in this collection—but rather his demeanor and attitude toward civilian command in a republic. Much of that notion of a citizen-general who is directly responsible to civilian overseers and is careful not to confuse military command with political power derives from his own knowledge of classical antiquity, and perhaps from his own cherished occupation as a gentleman-farmer who had a full life outside of both war and the state.

Washington's public life, shaped as it was by farming and military service, invites modern Americans to reflect upon societal changes that have made our world so different from the

America in which Washington's character was formed. Americans have, by and large, left the small farms that from classical Greece to the Founding comprised the great bulk of life and formed the character of 98 percent of the population. With the all-volunteer army and general demographic trends in our armed forces, it is more and more likely that our political leaders will also not share Washington's defining experiences under fire.

Washington's life, actions, and words were shaped by a profound understanding of the tragic limits of human life—limits both farming and war bring home every day—the knowledge of which can keep many ill-advised social schemes at bay. In the current era, such a profoundly human understanding is too often supplanted by the therapeutic language of political leaders who profess to "feel your pain."

But Washington, living as he did in a harsher world substantially unchanged from the world of the Greeks and Romans, perforce learned from experience the truth of the tragic vision of human life, a truth every farmer and every soldier experiences on a daily basis: the world is a hard and dangerous place; nature and man's passions are destructive if unchecked; and only duty, self-sacrifice, hard work, and a willingness to "see life steadily, and see it whole," as Matthew Arnold said of Sophocles, can ensure our survival both materially and politically. At the end of the millennium, it is sobering to ask ourselves whether we moderns—we who are ignorant of the classical tradition that enshrines the tradition of republican citizen-farmers that animated the Founders—can survive without that tragic knowledge that shaped the character of Western leaders from Cincinnatus to Washington.

THREE

General Washington and the Military Strategy of the Revolution

Mackubin Owens

...[P]ossessing an energetic and distinguishing mind, on which the lessons of experience were never lost, his errors, if he committed any, were quickly repaired; and those measures which the state of things rendered most advisable, were seldom, if ever, neglected. Inferior to his adversary in the numbers, in the equipment, and in the discipline of his troops, it is evidence of real merit that no great or decisive advantage was ever obtained over him, and that the opportunity to strike an important blow never passed away unused. He has been termed the American Fabius; but those who compare his actions with his means, will perceive at least as much of Marcellus as of Fabius, in his character.

—John Marshall, *The Life of George Washington*[1]

Everything in strategy is very simple, but that does not mean that everything is very easy. Once it has been determined, from the political conditions, what a war is meant to achieve and what it can achieve, it is easy to chart the course. But great strength of character, as well as great lucidity and firmness of mind, is required in order to

follow through steadily, to carry out the plan, and not to be thrown
off course by thousands of diversions. Take any number of outstanding men, some noted for intellect, others for their acumen, still others
for boldness or tenacity of will: not one may possess the combination
of qualities needed to make him a greater than average commander.

—Carl von Clausewitz, *On War*[2]

The American Founders rightfully took pride in establishing
a constitution for governance based on "reflection and
choice," rather than "on accident and force."[3] But to create such a
constitution, it was necessary for the Americans to achieve success
on the battlefield. To paraphrase Thomas Hobbes, the high principles upon which America declared its independence were but
words without the sword. Had the principles of the American
Founding not been vindicated on the battlefield, they would have
been stillborn.

Despite the critical role of arms in establishing the American
Republic, military historians do not pay a great deal of attention
to the War of American Independence or the generalship of
George Washington, who developed and implemented the strategy that led to ultimate American success. There are several reasons for this lack of interest. First, the War of American
Independence was a transitional war, lying between the dynastic
conflicts of the eighteenth century and the French Revolution,
which has shaped war ever since. It preceded too closely the revolution in war associated with that epochal conflict, which swept
away everything that had gone before it.

Second, the modern American army is founded on the vision

of General Emory Upton, hero of the Civil War, protégé of William T. Sherman when he was General in Chief of the U. S. Army, and military reformer. Upton sought to create a professional force along Prussian lines: a large, well-trained, long-term army designed to fight large-scale wars.[4] For the Uptonians, the lessons of the Revolution were negative: Washington was forced to fight a defensive struggle using inexperienced, poorly trained regulars supplemented by militia.[5]

Third, Washington was a defensive strategist whose approach did not appeal to later students of war who looked to the Napoleonic model of warfare, characterized by the *offensive à outrance* and the battle of annihilation. For advocates of what Russell Weigley has called the "American way of war," the battle of annihilation promises quick results, an outcome superior to a protracted struggle. They find little of interest in a long, drawn-out affair in which the chief American strategist's goal seemed to be to avoid battle.[6]

Washington's generalship is usually examined through the prism of administration, organization, and his ability to inspire his subordinates and soldiers. He has not often been studied as a strategist, and when he has, his reputation usually has not fared very well.[7] To even the most fair-minded, Washington as military leader seems less interesting than Frederick the Great, who epitomized eighteenth-century warfare, or Napoleon Bonaparte, who came to represent the acme of generalship during the nineteenth century. Those who study the U. S. military tradition prefer the Civil War or World War II. For most, Grant, Lee, Pershing, Marshall, Eisenhower, and Patton, not Washington, epitomize the American military tradition.

And in reaction to the filio-pietistic tradition of praising Washington, many recent and contemporary historians have come to view him as a general of, at best, only mediocre military talents. Thus George Athan Billias remarks that "Washington's gifts as a general were more political than military and that his unique contribution to the Continental army resulted not from his grasp of strategy and tactics but rather from his skill in handling America's military leaders."[8] Marcus Cunliffe claims that "grand strategy was not [Washington's] forte."[9] Richard Ketchum asserts that "he was less than a brilliant strategist...his method can only be described as persistence."[10] And finally John Alden contends that he was "not a consistently brilliant strategist or tactician."[11] Still others have argued that Washington was able to prevail in the struggle only because his adversaries were somehow incompetent.[12]

These views do a great injustice to Washington. Examining his conduct of the war in light of the modern understanding of strategy reveals a different story. Washington was indispensable to American success. The principles of the Revolution had to be vindicated on the field of battle, and it was mostly Washington's strategic sense that made this vindication possible.

ON STRATEGY

The word "strategy" was not employed in Washington's day. The division of the art of war into *tactics* (the use of military forces for the purpose of winning individual battles) and *strategy* ("the theory of the use of battles for the object of war") did not occur until the time of the great interpreters of Napoleon, Carl von

Clausewitz and Henri Baron Jomini.[13] The closest term available to Washington was "stratagem," a ruse or a gambit to achieve an advantage through surprise. But just because the term had not been invented did not mean that strategy did not exist.

Strategic studies and the modern conception of strategy originated with Clausewitz, who understood strategy to be the art of assembling and employing forces in terms of time and space.[14] Within time and space, strategy does three things.

First, strategy links ends and means, ensuring that there is not a mismatch between the two. Second, strategy helps to establish a priority among ends. Since means are limited, not everything can be done. Strategy ensures that choices are made among competing ends. As Frederick the Great observed, "he who tries to defend everything ends up defending nothing." Finally, strategy helps to conceptualize resources as means. In other words, it translates raw inputs such as men and money into the divisions and fleets that will be employed for the object of war. To carry out a strategy, one must have the right tactical instrument. Even the best-conceived strategy will fail unless it can rely on the right instrument to implement it.[15]

Strategy is both a process and product. As such, it is dynamic. It must be adapted to changing conditions, e.g., geography, technology, and social conditions.[16] A strategy that works under one set of conditions may not work under different ones. To develop and execute a strategy requires that one be able to comprehend the whole and bring the right instrument to bear at the right time and in the right place in order to achieve the object of the war. In Clausewitz's words,

> Strategy is the use of the engagement for the purpose of the war. The strategist must therefore define an aim for the entire operational side of the war that will be in accordance with its purpose. In other words, he will draft the plan of the war, and the aim will determine the series of actions intended to achieve it: he will, in fact, shape the individual campaigns and, within these, decide on the individual engagements.[17]

Strategy thus can be seen as a species of prudence. Like the prudent man, the strategist never loses sight of the proper end. But he must be able to adapt to particular conditions.

Before we can evaluate Washington's strategy, or for that matter, anyone else's strategy, we must articulate criteria for making our judgment. These can be seen as a series of questions.

- Was the strategy adequate for achieving the end? Did it fit with the character of the war?
- Did it take account of the strengths and weaknesses of the enemy and tactical, operational, logistical, and geographical constraints?
- Were the means appropriate to the political objective?
- Did attainment of the military objective translate into the achievement of political objectives?
- Did the actual conduct of the war correspond to the strategic conception at the beginning of the war?
- Was the strategy in accord with social conditions, i.e., did it fit the "genius" of the people; how was public support for the war and the chosen strategy maintained; and could the social and political factors withstand the shock of war?

- What were the costs and risks of pursing the strategy?
- *Were there better alternatives than the one chosen?*

When we apply these criteria to Washington's strategic sense, especially considering the paucity of his means, we begin to see how unfair many previous assessments of his generalship have been.

WASHINGTON'S STRATEGIC SENSE

Strategy is a plan of action for using available means to achieve the ends of policy. Although at least at the beginning of hostilities, some Americans entertained the possibility of reconciliation with Britain, the goal of the war as Washington understood it by the end of 1775 was the *independence* of the United States as a *republican union* not hemmed in *geographically* by other powers. But as Clausewitz observes, war is the violent clash between two opposing wills.[18] Thus Washington's strategy had to take account of not only American goals, but also the strategy of the British.

BRITISH GOALS AND STRATEGY

The Americans faced an adversary in possession of a multitude of advantages. First among these was Britain's sea power, which enabled British forces to strike at will anywhere along America's substantial coast and inland as far as deep-draft ships could navigate. The second was a well-trained and disciplined army of long-term professionals, both British regulars and German mercenaries. These soldiers were competent practitioners of eighteenth-century tactics, which involved intricate battlefield maneuvers designed to gain a positional advantage over an adversary, or if necessary, close with the bayonet. Third, no matter how divisive the conflicts resulting from party factions in British politics may have been, George III and his ministers possessed a unity of effort that the Americans in Congress and the States could only envy.

The British, of course, faced problems of their own. To begin with, they had to overcome the "tyranny of distance." Despite its naval supremacy, the projection of power by Britain into North America required a major effort. Second, to win, the British had to occupy all of the colonies. However, the expanse of territory and low population density of North America made it difficult to maintain armies in the field anywhere away from the major population centers. When operating in the American interior away from their naval support, e.g., British General John Burgoyne at Saratoga, British armies were at a major disadvantage. Some understood this from the outset. William Pitt (the Elder), architect of Britain's victory in the Seven Years' War and now Earl of Chatham, warned that "[y]ou cannot conquer America."

Third, British commanders fought the war with a sword in one hand and an olive branch in the other, believing that popular support for the war was minimal. This often prevented British commanders from delivering the *coup de grace* when they had the opportunity. A case in point is the Long Island–New York campaign of the summer and fall of 1776, during which General William Howe failed to exploit several opportunities to annihilate Washington's force.

Fourth, economic reality and the need to address its other security problems limited the resources Great Britain could bring to bear against the American insurgents. This reality affected the way British commanders fought in North America: they could not afford to accept high casualties because losses could not easily be replaced. This problem of allocating resources was exacerbated when France entered the war in 1778.

Finally, British strategy was constrained by the dictates of eighteenth-century warfare. Battles fought according to the tactics of the time could be costly. Because these casualties could not be replaced, British commanders usually sought to avoid battle, attempting instead to maneuver their adversary into hopeless situations, in which the latter's only options were surrender or dissolution of the army.

AMERICAN GOALS AND STRATEGY

A successful strategy always focuses on the object of the war. For America, the *political* objective was to maintain the cause of liberty and secure the independence of the American colonies. It quickly became apparent to Washington that to achieve this political object he must achieve a *military* object as well, which was not the defense of places, but the maintenance of the army as an effective force. This was because of the failure of Americans to act according to the tenets of republican theory.

Theoretically at least, one of the most important means for achieving the American goal was the will of the American people to be free. The Americans were, by and large, the armed independent proprietors and freeholders who, according to republican theory and radical Whig doctrine, constituted the militia for the common defense of public liberty and personal property.[19] But following a brief surge of *rage militaire* during 1775, public

enthusiasm for the war waned as subsequent British military success rendered the outcome questionable.[20]

Washington believed that more than republican virtue and
moral ardor would be required to defeat the British. He did not
believe that patriotism or republican virtue alone would survive
sustained campaigns against trained British regulars.
Accordingly, his primary means for achieving the ends of policy
was not the people as a whole or the militia, but the Continental
Line: well-trained and well-disciplined citizen-soldiers under
national control rather than the control of individual states. But
this was easier said than done: national control ultimately resided
in the Continental Congress, which could not act without the
approval of the individual states, each of which was jealous of its
own sovereignty and prerogatives.

In general, there are two types of war-fighting strategies:
strategies of *annihilation* and strategies of *attrition* or *exhaustion*.
Strategies of annihilation focus on the cataclysmic battle and are
usually associated with Hannibal, Napoleon, and Moltke (the
Elder). Strategies of attrition can be further subdivided into attrition by strategic *offensive* (the American Civil War and the U. S.
approach to World War II) and attrition by strategic *defensive*
(Pericles and Fabius Maximus).

A paucity of means forced Washington to assume the strategic defensive for most of the war. While it may have been the
only alternative open to him given the circumstances he faced,
this strategic choice created a dilemma for him and the
Revolution. The fact that neither the militia nor the Continental
Line was able consistently to defeat the British in the open field

meant that he had to avoid combat except under the most favorable circumstances. By thus protracting the war, he hoped to wear the British out before they achieved success.

But there was always the danger that this strategy would cause the Americans to give out first. A strategy based on constant avoidance of battle and ceaseless retreat risked an adverse psychological impact on the American people at large. "On every side there is a choice of difficulties," Washington complained at one point. He recognized the dilemma he faced: if he fought and lost his army, he could lose everything, but if he refused to fight, he could still lose everything as the people he defended lost heart.

Washington's strategy is often described as Fabian in character. But while Fabius Maximus Cunctator always avoided battle with Hannibal when the latter invaded Italy, Washington sought to deliver an offensive stroke whenever possible, as he did at Trenton, Princeton, and Monmouth. Yet he consistently took pains to ensure that when he did fight he would be able to disengage to fight another day.

It should be noted that Washington shared with Congress the responsibility for the conception, if not the execution, of strategy during the War of American Independence. During the early years of the war, Congress generally deferred to Washington, but after the setbacks of 1776, it attempted to take on a more active and assertive role. Washington, cognizant of republican fears of a standing army and the possibility of an American Cromwell, went out of his way to allay the concerns of Congress and to inform that body of his actions.

By 1778, Washington had once again begun to take the lead

in developing as well as implementing American strategy, with Congress focusing on providing Washington what he needed. The division of labor matched the pattern described by Clausewitz as "preparation for war" (Congress) and "war proper" (Washington).[21] By the end of the war, economic problems and the weakness of the Articles of Confederation had combined to render Congress nearly impotent. As one writer notes, one of the most remarkable ironies of the war was that "the Congress which had begun the war with such a dread of a military takeover was at the end of the war saved by the very general it feared. And—this is the crux of the irony—it was protected largely from itself."[22]

It is possible to divide the War of American Independence into four periods: (1) April 1775–June 1776—*From Rebellion to Revolution and Independence;* (2) July 1776–December 1777—*Defending American Independence Against Superior Force;* (3) January 1778–October 1781—*The American War Becomes World War;* and (4) November 1781–December 1783—*Winning the Peace.*[23] During each period, Washington kept the ultimate goal in view but, balancing potential outcomes against possible risks, adapted his strategy to meet changing conditions.

FROM REBELLION TO REVOLUTION AND INDEPENDENCE

The first fourteen months of the War of American Independence may be called the revolutionary period. This was the war's *offensive* phase as well, during which the Revolutionaries successfully seized control of the institutions of governance and ejected British power and authority. In most respects, it was a spontaneous uprising of the people in which the militia played the prominent role. Militia engaged the British regulars at Lexington and Concord; it was militia that subsequently surrounded the British in Boston, and it was militia under Ethan Allen and Benedict Arnold that seized Fort Ticonderoga and other British posts on Lake Champlain.

The magnitude of the popular uprising against the British in New England surprised even the most ardent American Revolutionaries. Most were simply swept along by the tide of events. The Continental Congress created the Continental Army in June, appointing Washington as commander in chief. But in keeping with the character of this phase of the war, before Washington could assume command of the newly created army around Boston, the militia had precipitated another battle. The British drove the rebels off Bunker (Breed's) Hill, but at a staggering price. This Pyrrhic British victory had important consequences for the future—British commanders rarely again risked a frontal assault against even untrained American forces.

Washington realized that the situation prevailing in the summer of 1775—with the British bottled up in Boston—was unlikely to improve. He hoped that by acting quickly and decisively and by threatening to make a costly and protracted war, the Revolutionaries could deter British military action and convince Britain to recognize the colonists' "rights as Englishmen."

Those accustomed to thinking of Washington as a Fabian strategist are struck by the aggressive tenor of his correspondence during this period. During the last five months of 1775 alone, he organized expeditions to Bermuda; he considered a campaign against St. Augustine in Florida; he organized privateers to strike at British shipping; he attempted to forge alliances with Indian tribes in the west; he launched an invasion against Canada; and he harassed the British in Boston, waiting for the right time to attack in force.

Many of the plans he developed for attacking Boston involved risky operations probably beyond the capabilities of his untrained army. One option, however, enabled him to take offensive action against the British without the risk associated with the other alternatives: moving captured artillery from Fort Ticonderoga to Boston. Once the guns were emplaced on Dorchester Heights, the British position in Boston became untenable.

The British evacuated Boston in March 1776, leaving no forces in the American colonies. Since, for the most part, Revolutionaries also had seized colonial governments and ousted and defeated Loyalists, the Americans had achieved important military objectives, despite their one major failure in Canada. But the primary political objective—acceptance by the British of American demands—remained elusive. George III refused to budge from the principles he had established in his August 1775 "Proclamation for Suppressing Rebellion and Sedition" in the colonies.

Washington's strategy during this period was strongly influenced by his certainty that time would not improve the situation for the Revolutionaries around Boston. British power, he believed, could only increase. Thus, Washington had an incentive to act quickly and decisively in order to maintain the advantage.

Another factor that caused him to proceed aggressively was the fact that most of his soldiers had enlisted for short terms and that many of these enlistments would be up before sustained operations realistically could be undertaken. This accounts for his offensive-mindedness despite the precariously low level of military supplies and equipment and what many commentators consider to be the rash nature of some of his plans, e.g. his idea to attack Boston across the harbor had it frozen.

Short enlistments also played a major role in the failure of the expedition against Canada. Despite atrocious weather, two small American columns under General Richard Montgomery and Benedict Arnold were able to reach the walls of Quebec. The season being late, the British defenders could not expect reinforcements until spring. Had the Americans, now combined into one force under Montgomery, been able to invest the city, it is likely that Quebec would have fallen into American hands before the spring, and Canada would have become the fourteenth state.

But the enlistment terms of Montgomery's soldiers were nearly up and they made it clear they intended to go home. Montgomery felt he had no choice but to launch an attack before his force melted away. The assault, launched in a blinding snowstorm on December 31, 1775, was repulsed. Montgomery was killed and Arnold wounded. The American plan came close to success, but not close enough. Washington and others considered the assault against Quebec another bitter consequence of the Americans' commitment to a policy of short-term enlistments.

The failure in Canada notwithstanding, the first fourteen months of the war generally favored the American cause. The decision by General Howe, the British commander in America, to concentrate his available forces in Boston stripped Loyalists in the remaining northern colonies of the Crown's protection, leaving them at the mercy of the Patriots. The Loyalists in the South were able to put up more resistance, but Patriot militia soon overthrew them as well. By the time the British evacuated Boston, the Revolutionaries had seized the institutions of power in all thirteen colonies.

DEFENDING AMERICAN INDEPENDENCE

During the second phase of the war, three major elements changed. First, the political goal of the war changed from reconciliation—the insistence that Britain merely recognize the Americans' equal rights as Englishmen—to the demand for independence. Second, the magnitude of the British effort increased substantially. Finally and consequently, the British took the offensive, actively trying to suppress the rebellion in America. Washington was forced to adapt his strategy to these changing circumstances.

The Americans initially justified armed resistance to Britain on the basis of the demand that the Crown and Parliament recognize their equal rights as Englishmen. But as it became increasingly difficult for the Americans to war against British forces while maintaining their allegiance to the Crown, they had, for the most part by the summer of 1776, changed their political goal in the war to outright independence. This was important for Washington, because in order to raise the volunteer recruits necessary to man the Continental Army—the instrument he needed to implement his strategy—the political goal had to be seen by veterans and potential recruits alike as worthy of considerable effort and risk.

In his General Orders of July 2, 1776, Washington invoked the new circumstances to exhort his troops to greater levels of exertion.

> The time is now at hand which must probably determine, whether Americans are to be, Freemen, or Slaves; whether they are to have any property they can call their own; whether their Houses, and Farms, are to be pillaged and destroyed, and they consigned to a state of Wretchedness from which no human effort will probably deliver them. The fate of unborn Millions will now depend, under God, on the Courage and Conduct of this army....We have therefore to resolve to conquer or die: Our own Country's Honor, all call upon us for a vigorous and manly exertion, and if we now shamefully fail, we shall become infamous to the whole world. Let us therefore rely upon the goodness of the Cause, and the aid of the supreme Being, in whose hands Victory is, to animate and encourage us to great and noble Actions—The eyes of all our Countrymen are now upon us, and we shall have their blessings, and praises, if happily we are instruments of saving them from the Tyranny mediated against them. Let us therefore animate and encourage each other, and shew the whole world, that a Freeman contending for Liberty on his own ground is superior to any slavish mercenary on earth.[24]

Seven days later, he had the Declaration of Independence read to the troops. He expressed the hope that "this important Event will

serve as a fresh incentive to every officer, and soldier, to act with
Fidelity and Courage, as knowing that now the peace and safety
of his country depended (under God) soley on the success of our
arms: And that he is now in the service of a State, possessed of sufficient power to reward his merit, and advance him to the highest Honors of a free Country."[25]

But Washington recognized that while patriotism was necessary, it was not sufficient if America was to vindicate its independence on the battlefield. As he wrote to John Bannister in 1778:

> Men may speculate as they will; they may talk of patriotism; they
> may draw a few examples from [an] ancient story, of great achieve-
> ments performed by its influence; but whoever builds upon it, as a
> sufficient Basis for conducting a long and [bloody] War, will find
> themselves deceived in the end. We must take the passions of Men as
> Nature has given them, and those principles as a guide which are
> generally the rule of Action. I do not mean to exclude altogether the
> Idea of Patriotism. I know it exists, and I know it has done much in
> the present Contest. But I will venture to assert, that a great and last-
> ing War can never be supported on this principle alone. It must be
> aided by a prospect of Interest or some reward. For a time, it may, of
> itself push Men to Action; to bear much, to encounter difficulties;
> but it will not endure unassisted by Interest.[26]

The sort of army he would need to outlast the British was a long-
term force of regulars who would have to be compensated for
their service.

Washington and a committee of the Continental Congress

had assumed that the British would send a force of about 23,000 soldiers to America, 10,000 to Canada, and the remainder to New York, which Washington assumed to be the British objective. Given the expected superiority of trained British troops over an American force, their "net assessment" projected a requirement for a force twice the size of the invader's army.

Unfortunately, Congress overestimated its own ability to raise troops and underestimated the ability of the British to do the same. In particular, they did not count on the Crown's access to German soldiers, 30,000 of whom eventually were employed in America.

By the end of the summer of 1776, General Howe commanded the largest expeditionary force that Britain had ever sent anywhere up to that time: 30,000 British and German troops, with 5,000 more Hessians on the way, backed by a fleet of seventy warships and hundreds of other vessels under his brother, Admiral Richard Howe. To defend New York, Washington could muster fewer than 10,000 troops, most of whom were new recruits. Appeals to Congress and nearby states doubled the force by the time Howe attacked in August.

British strategy for 1776 centered on controlling the Hudson River and eliminating the rebellion in New England, where it appeared to be strongest. To do this required Howe to seize New York and, if possible, destroy the Continental Army. Because Washington was slow to modify his strategy to take account of the new conditions, Howe nearly succeeded.

To be fair to Washington, his choices during the New York campaign of 1776 were severely constrained by political considerations. Foremost among these limitations on his freedom of action was the demand by Congress that he defend New York, despite British operational advantages. Nonetheless, Washington remained committed to an offensive posture long after it should have been clear that the tactical instrument he possessed did not meet the requirements of this posture.

During the New York campaign of the summer and fall of 1776, Washington rashly invited head-to-head engagements with the British. As a result of his aggressiveness, he nearly was trapped on Long Island and Manhattan when Howe used the mobility afforded by the Royal Navy to sail up the Hudson River and interdict Patriot communications with New Jersey. He subsequently was surprised and outflanked by Howe on Long Island and his forces routed. When Howe prepared to besiege Washington's entrenchments on Brooklyn Heights, Washington executed a skillful withdrawal to Manhattan. But twice more, Howe almost trapped him on Manhattan, once on the southern end of the island and again at Harlem Heights. He refused to abandon Fort Washington after he finally evacuated Manhattan. This failure cost the Patriots 3,000 troops killed or captured.

At this point, Washington recognized that because he could not prevail against a force the size of Howe's possessing the mobility it was afforded by the Royal Navy, he needed to change his strategy. Political considerations had required that he at least attempt to defend New York, but strategic necessity now required that he give it up or the cause might be lost. Nathanael Greene had provided the rationale for this strategy:

The City and Island of New York are no objects for us; we are not to bring them into competition with the general interests of America. Part of the army has already met with a defeat; the country is struck with a panick; any capital loss at this time may ruin the cause. 'Tis our business to study to avoid any considerable misfortune, and to take post where the enemy will be obliged to fight us; and not us them.[27]

Washington accepted the thrust of Greene's argument and laid out in a letter to Congress the strategy he would pursue for the remainder of the year:

In deliberating on this question it was impossible to forget that history, our own experience, the advice of our ablest friends in Europe, the fears of the enemy, and even the declarations of Congress demonstrate that on our side the war should be defensive. It has even been called a war of posts. That we should on all occasions avoid a general action, or put anything to the risque, unless compelled by a necessity into which we ought never to be drawn, [is evident].... when the fate of America may be at stake on the issue; when the wisdom of cooler moments and experienced men have decided that we should protract the war if possible; I cannot think it safe or wise to adopt a different system when the season for action draws so near a close.[28]

This was Washington's blueprint for the Fabian phase of his strategy.

Though Howe and his subordinates tried to bring him to battle, Washington adhered to his strategy. He maintained constant contact with Howe's army, retreating when Howe advanced, advancing cautiously when he fell back. In the late fall, Washington abandoned New York and retreated into New Jersey. As winter approached, he informed Congress that he would have to retreat beyond the Delaware River, causing panic in Philadelphia.

Howe originally had no intention of driving as far as the Delaware. He had waged a cautious campaign, achieving most of his strategic objectives. The flame of revolution was barely flickering as the bedraggled Continental Army retreated just ahead of Howe's pursuit. But then Howe made an error that undid all that he had accomplished up to that point. Giving in to his more aggressive subordinates, he authorized an advance to the Delaware. According to one commentator, "Howe's major overall failing in 1776 had been his overcautiousness; ironically, his single greatest error was in not adhering to that prudent policy at the very last moment."[29] Howe was now overextended, exposing himself to a counterstroke, which Washington delivered with stunning suddenness against the Hessian outpost at Trenton on Christmas night and a British brigade at Princeton less than a fortnight later.

Battles must be judged not only according to tactical outcome, but also in terms of their strategic and political effects. This is the case with Trenton and Princeton. In less than two weeks, an army on the verge of disintegration won two unexpected victories, forced Howe to abandon New Jersey, and revived the revolutionary cause teetering on the brink of extinction. Strategically, Howe was back where he had started in the summer—holding bases at New York and Newport, but little more.

For reasons long debated by historians, British strategy for 1777 was hopelessly muddled. Ultimately, a column under General Burgoyne attempted to move down the Hudson from Canada. From New York, Howe could have marched north to meet Burgoyne, and had he been successful, he might have gained control of the Hudson River and isolated New England. As it turned out, Howe chose not to link up with Burgoyne but to invade the middle colonies instead.

Meanwhile Washington positioned his army where it could respond no matter what Howe did. Moving into the hills of northern New Jersey and the Hudson highlands, Washington took up a position that was easily defended, easily resupplied, and most importantly, sat astride Howe's communications in New Jersey. No matter whether Howe moved north toward Albany or south toward Philadelphia, Washington, by holding the Hudson, could counter his thrust by taking advantage of interior lines of operation. He explained his rationale in a letter to Major General Philip Schuyler, commanding general of the northern department:

> It is of the greatest importance to the safety of the country involved in a defensive war to endeavor to draw their troops together at some post, at the opening of a campaign, so central to the theater of war that they may be sent to the support of any part of the country the enemy may direct their motions against.... Should the enemy's design be to penetrate the country up the Hudson River, we are well posted to oppose them; should they attempt to penetrate into New England, we are well stationed to cover them; and besides, it will oblige the enemy to leave a much stronger garrison at New York.[30]

In order to maintain his strategic advantage, he vociferously opposed Congress's attempt to force him to disperse his force along the Delaware River.

Washington's strong strategic position was probably one factor that influenced Howe's decision to move by sea to the middle colonies rather than up the Hudson to support Burgoyne. The prospect of rooting Washington's forces out of their defenses in the Hudson highlands could not have appealed to Howe, "in whose mind was indelibly etched that horrible scene on Bunker Hill."[31]

Earlier in the year, Washington had advised Schuyler concerning how to deal with Burgoyne, backing up his advice with troops from his own command to reinforce Schuyler's force. Horatio Gates, who replaced Schuyler, followed Washington's advice, letting the woods do the fighting against Burgoyne, who was operating inland where the British fleet could not support him. Gates's Continentals, augmented by swarming militia, surrounded Burgoyne, forcing the capitulation of his army at Saratoga. Meanwhile Washington moved to delay Howe's army as it approached Philadelphia, fighting sharp clashes at Brandywine Creek and White Horse Tavern, and then attacking a part of Howe's force at Germantown. Though all were tactical setbacks for the Americans that failed to prevent Howe's occupation of Philadelphia, the strategic effect of the campaign as a whole was to convince Howe to end the war effort for 1777.

Indeed, the strategic outcome of the second phase was to make it increasingly clear to the British that they could not prevail against the Patriots. As 1777 ended, the British had nothing to show for their effort but enclaves at New York, Newport, and Philadelphia. Meanwhile, the cost had been ruinous: Burgoyne's entire army and a third of Howe's irreplaceable troops had become casualties. Most importantly, by maintaining his army intact and delivering a blow whenever possible, Washington's strategy helped to create the conditions that convinced France to join the war on the side of America. France's entry completely changed the character of the war, and once again Washington adapted his strategy to fit the circumstances.

THE AMERICAN WAR BECOMES WORLD WAR

The French alliance had a number of effects, not the least of which was to neutralize Britain's greatest single advantage over the Americans—sea power. "Next to the loan of money," wrote Washington, "a constant naval superiority on these coasts is the object most interesting.... This superiority, with an aid of money, would enable us to convert the war into a vigorous offensive."[32]

When France entered the war, it initiated the fourth of five Anglo-French Wars that stretched from 1689 until 1815.[33] In the previous round, The Seven Years' War, Britain had been able to take advantage of continental allies to tie down French armies, permitting the Royal Navy free reign at sea. This freedom at sea enabled Britain to project substantial expeditionary forces against the French in North America and India. Pitt (the Elder) aptly described the essence of British strategy during the Seven Years' War when he observed that "America was conquered in Germany."

The 1763 Treaty of Paris led to a substantial increase in the size and geopolitical importance of the British Empire, especially in America. France renounced all territories and claims in Canada and the Ohio Valley, and all territory east of the Mississippi except New Orleans.

But as Clausewitz observes, the results of war are never final. "The defeated state often considers the outcome merely as a transitory evil, for which a remedy may still be found in political conditions at some later date."[34] Accordingly, France had entertained dreams of revenge ever since the humiliation of 1763 and had refurbished its military, especially the navy, in hopes of evening the score.

Since Britain had allowed its naval arm to atrophy, the French navy was actually superior to the Royal Navy in material terms (number of ships, weight of armament). But more importantly, unlike the Seven Years' War, this time Britain had no continental allies to tie down the French in a European land war that would absorb resources and limit the aid France could send to an isolated America. Indeed, in 1779, Spain and the Netherlands, both harboring resentment against Britain's arrogance, entered the war on the side of France.[35]

With France's entry into the war, North America became an "economy-of-force" theater for the British. Britain was now forced to follow a policy of limited liability, hoping to pacify the colonies but refusing to commit any more resources to the effort. Sir Henry Clinton, who had replaced Howe at the end of 1777, was ordered to abandon Philadelphia, and even New York if need be, in order to free up troops for operations elsewhere.

Clinton evacuated Philadelphia on June 18, 1778, and began

a march north to New York. He was hounded along the way by Washington's army, which had improved greatly under the tutelage of the Prussian captain Friedrich Wilhelm von Steuben during the winter at Valley Forge. The Continentals fought splendidly at Monmouth Court House, and by July, Washington was back where he had started two years earlier, but this time in an offensive posture.

Shortly thereafter, a French fleet under the command of the Comte d'Estaing bottled up the British fleet in New York harbor. Washington saw an opportunity to annihilate the British in conjunction with the French fleet, but d'Estaing demurred. He did agree to support an attack against Newport, but to the disappointment of Washington and the commanders of the Continental force designated to conduct the campaign, this effort also fell through. D'Estaing subsequently departed North American waters for the West Indies, leaving his American allies frustrated and angry.

In the fall of 1778, Washington attempted to divine Clinton's moves for the campaign season of 1779. He concluded that his adversary had only three options: attempt to destroy Washington's army, attempt to defeat the French fleet, or attempt to seize West Point on the Hudson. In fact, Washington was wrong, for once. Clinton had in mind a southern campaign, descending on Savannah at the end of December 1778.

Significantly, given his preference for offensive action, Washington argued at this time against a proposed French and American invasion of Canada. Indicative of his strategic foresight, he was concerned lest the price of cooperation with the

French would be the reintroduction of France into Canada and an America subsequently hemmed in by a combination of Europeans and Indians. As he wrote to Henry Laurens:

> France acknowledged for some time past the most powerful monarchy in Europe by land, able now to dispute the empire of the sea with Great Britain, and if joined with Spain, I may say certainly superior, possessed of New Orleans, on our right, Canada on our left and seconded by the numerous tribes of Indians on our Rear from one extremity to the other, a people, so generally friendly to her and whom she knows so well how to conciliate; would, it is much to be apprehended have it in her power to give law to these states.[36]

The year 1779 was a year in which political and economic problems outweighed military ones. Inflation was rampant, speculation was widespread, and political factions were emerging to make Congress even less effective than it had been previously. Financial problems limited the military options. Washington and Congress decided on a punitive expedition against the Iroquois, standing on the defensive elsewhere unless a French fleet should appear.

D'Estaing did enter American waters again in September but, as before, accomplished little. However, his presence and limited American successes at Stony Point and Paulus Hook caused Clinton to contract his defenses around New York and abandon Newport altogether. The expedition against the Iroquois was successful and George Rogers Clark conquered the Old Northwest.

Issues of war termination began to take center stage by the end of 1779. France made it clear that it would not support American claims to territory beyond the original thirteen states that were not in American possession at the beginning of peace negotiations. It became apparent that if America were not to be hemmed in by other powers, it would have to expand its territory.

If 1779 was a generally good year for the Americans, 1780 was a disaster. British troops launched a vigorous campaign in the South, seizing Charleston and inflicting the bloodiest defeat of the war on the Americans at Camden. British forces overran Georgia and the Carolinas and threatened Virginia. Worst of all, Benedict Arnold, America's best-known combat commander, turned traitor and nearly succeeded in betraying West Point to the British. Because of economic paralysis and political infighting, Washington was unable to organize a summer campaign. Additionally, Patriot morale reached a low point in 1780.

But there was some good news, delivered by the Marquis de Lafayette. A French expeditionary force, including a ground force, was en route. Given that the Patriot cause was teetering on the brink of collapse, Washington immediately began to plan a major combined-force effort against the British. "Every view of our own circumstances ought to determine us to the most vigorous efforts...," he wrote to Joseph Reed.[37]

New York was his preferred objective, but circumstances combined to prevent the necessary preponderance of force to ensure success. He laid out the general conditions that would have to prevail if the allies were to defeat the British. The most important of these was naval superiority. "In any operation, and under all circumstances, a decisive naval superiority is to be considered as a fundamental principle, and the basis upon which every hope of success must ultimately depend."[38]

Despite his efforts, there was not to be a major combined offensive in 1780. But Washington recognized that the perilous state of the American cause required activity somewhere. Accordingly, Washington looked south, sending Nathanael Greene, his most aggressive subordinate, to the Carolinas to try to redeem the situation there in the aftermath of Gates's debacle at Camden.

Greene, of course, was a proponent of the strategy of protracted war practiced by Washington and put that strategy into action immediately. "Few generals," Greene wrote, "[have] run oftener or more lustily than I have done. But I have taken care not to run too far, and commonly have run as fast forward as backward to convince our enemy that we were like a Crab that could run either way."[39] Greene never won a battle in the South, but the strategic effect of his campaign was to force the British to abandon the Carolinas because they could not afford the casualties they suffered in gaining their tactical successes.

Meanwhile, the French decided to increase their effort in America. Louis XVI dispatched a fleet under the Comte de Grasse and provided the financial support that would permit the Americans to sustain a major effort against the British. De Grasse was instructed to cooperate with Washington and the French army under Rochambeau.

Washington and Rochambeau agreed to attack the British wherever the prospects for success were greatest. Washington still preferred to attack New York, but when de Grasse informed him of his intention to sortie into the Chesapeake Bay and remain there from early September through mid-October, Washington seized this opportunity to destroy the British army in Virginia.

In a flawless operation, coordinated with Rochambeau, he executed a march from New York to Virginia before the British could react. His well-known preference for an attack on New York worked to his advantage, permitting him to deceive the British about his intentions until it was too late. A feint at Staten Island fixed Clinton in place until the main body of the combined force had cleared Philadelphia on its way to its rendezvous with de Grasse on the Chesapeake.

Cornwallis's position at Yorktown, Virginia, was invested by Washington and Rochambeau, and de Grasse fought off a British fleet in the Battle of the Capes, sealing the British commander's fate. On October 17, Cornwallis asked for terms. Benjamin Franklin later described the interaction of skill and fortune. It was astonishing, he wrote, that the allied force

> should with such perfect concord be assembled from different places by land and water, form their conjunction punctually without the least regard for cross accidents of wind or weather or interruption from the enemy; and that the army which was their object should in the meantime have had the goodness to quit a situation from whence it might have escaped, and place itself in another from whence an escape was impossible.[40]

By ending British efforts to subdue the colonies and thereby ensuring the independence of the United States, the Yorktown campaign ranks as one of the most decisive in history. It was also a tribute to Washington's persistence in pursuit of his strategic vision.

Winning the Peace

Euphoria swept the country after Cornwallis's surrender. The end of the war at last seemed to be at hand. But Washington understood that the war was not yet won and that a relaxation of vigilance could undo all that had been accomplished over six years of war. Indeed, the period from Yorktown to the Treaty of Paris was a time of great peril for the new Republic.

Washington had to hold the Continental Army together to ensure that the peace would favor the United States. At the same time, he had to ensure that this army would not become an instrument for overthrowing the Republic. The obstacles he faced in achieving these goals were substantial.

Immediately after Yorktown, Washington proposed a swift campaign against the British in Charleston or Wilmington. De Grasse demurred, leaving Washington angry. Had de Grasse cooperated, Washington wrote to Lafayette, no one could doubt "the total extirpation of the British force in the Carolinas and Georgia."[41]

New York remained the main strategic objective for Washington. Sending forces south to reinforce Greene, Washington himself rejoined the forces he had left to guard the Hudson. Washington continued to hope for French cooperation and began to plan for a subsequent campaign.

It is well he did. Despite what his countrymen may have thought, the war was not yet over. George III had no intention of giving up his claim to the colonies. The King's ministers proposed a return to a strategy based on naval blockade, supported by Loyalists and regulars. Washington divined the British approach: they would cease operations in the South, hold a minimal number of bases, and "take up the desultory naval war." But a series of reverses in the Caribbean, at Minorca, and in South Florida finally convinced the King that he should cut his losses in America.

As peace negotiations progressed, Washington pursued a "conciliatory war," never letting down his guard and treating every British proposal with skepticism. After de Grasse was defeated at the Battle of the Saintes in April 1782, and Rochambeau's army embarked at Boston for the Indies in the fall, Washington was once again left to his own devices. He proposed to concentrate his forces against the British in New York.

While there were to be no more campaigns, it seems clear that Washington's vigilance helped to ensure a favorable outcome in the peace negotiations. "There is nothing," Washington wrote to James McHenry, "which will so soon produce a speedy and honorable peace as a state of preparation for war, and we must either do this or lay our account for a patched up, inglorious peace after all the toil, blood, and treasure we have spent."[42] The American diplomats, led by Benjamin Franklin, deserve tremendous credit for their negotiating skill, but the fact that the Americans gained both independence and generous territorial concessions can be attributed in part to Washington's refusal to permit the military situation to deteriorate. He had won the war, and his vigilance now strengthened the hand of the American negotiators, enabling them to win the peace.

Washington had one more task: to ensure that an independent America became a republic and did not descend into military dictatorship. With peace at hand, many concluded that an army was no longer necessary. But Congress was broke and there was no money to pay the soldiers. The resulting mood of the army was dangerous for a republic. "The temper of the Army is much soured," wrote Washington, "and has become more irritable than at any period since the commencement of the war." What most concerned Washington was the attitude of the officers, "who always before had stood between the lower order of the soldiery and the public." [43]

Although renegade soldiers did chase Congress from Philadelphia in 1783, Washington's moral authority was sufficient for the most part to keep the army reined in. This moral authority was most on display when he addressed his officers at Newburgh, where he reminded his disaffected officers that he had "been their constant companion and witness of their distress" during their long service. Acknowledging their legitimate grievances, he promised to pursue remedies with Congress. [44] Then with dramatic effect, he fumbled to put on reading glasses that few knew he used. "Gentlemen, you will permit me to put on my spectacles, for I have not only grown gray but almost blind in the service of my country." [45] The military threat to the Republic dissolved before the moral authority and humility of their leader.

Had he not pitted his moral authority against the penury of Congress and intrigue and self-pity within the army, the latter might well have been destroyed. Who knows what would have followed, perhaps a coup or civil war. At the least, the position of the negotiators in Paris would have been weakened, making it unlikely that the United States could have achieved anything like the generous terms it did.

Before resigning his commission and returning to his beloved Mount Vernon, Washington reminded his countrymen how close a thing the War of American Independence had been. In his Circular to the States, he enumerated the steps he believed were necessary to ensure the security and tranquillity of an independent American republic. "According to the system of policy the states shall adopt at this moment, they will stand or fall and, by their confirmation or lapse, it is yet to be decided whether the Revolution must ultimately be considered a blessing or a curse—a blessing or a curse, not to the present alone, for with our fate will the destiny of unborn millions be involved."[46] Many of the ideas he expressed in this communication would later find their way into the Constitution.

CONCLUSION

There is often a tendency to treat the outcome of events as inevitable. Since we know how things turned out, we conclude that they could not have turned out any other way. But such reasoning is fallacious. History is not predetermined. Indeed, there would seem to be an infinite number of possible outcomes, all dependent on prior events.

The War of American Independence is a case in point. Its outcome was far from inevitable. Washington was not infallible. He made mistakes, especially early in the war. Many of these, especially during the Long Island campaign of 1776, could have been disastrous to the cause of American independence. Additionally, one can point to any number of small events that could have changed the results of the war.

But while one can argue that, even with Washington, America might have failed to win its independence, could America have won it *without* Washington? At the risk of being consigned to the category of filio-pietistic writers on Washington, I would argue that the answer is no. Two relevant questions come to mind: If not Washington, who? If not Washington's strategic approach, what?

Several years ago, the historian John Shy raised the clearest challenge to Washington and his strategy. Writing in the aftermath of the Vietnam War, Shy suggested that a "peoples' war" might have offered a viable alternative to Washington's strategy. This possibility, argued Shy, was recognized most clearly by Charles Lee, a former professional British army officer who took up the Patriot cause and who regarded his own military judgment superior to Washington's.

In contrast to Washington, wrote Shy, Charles Lee "envisioned a popular war of mass resistance, a war based on military service as an obligation of citizenship" using the same tactics "the free men at Lexington and Concord had instinctively employed."[47] Shy argued that there were several factors that led to the rejection of Lee's strategic vision.

The first of these was "provincialism"—the colonial elite's love-hate relationship with Britain that led its members to wish to emulate the British at the same time as they feared and resented them. "Nothing better illustrates American 'provincialism'…," argued Shy, "than George Washington's vain effort to get a regular commission in the British army." The second, of course, was the dissipation of popular enthusiasm after 1775 and the internal divisions and conflicts of late colonial America.[48] But "if Washington's strategy had failed, as it almost did in 1776, then the Revolution would have collapsed or turned sharply left." Had this occurred, Lee "might have had a chance to translate his vision into reality."[49]

What was wrong with this vision? Shy provides a good answer on Washington's behalf: "He would have recoiled with horror from such an idea" because such a strategy would have changed "the war for independence into a genuine civil war with all its grisly attendants—ambush, reprisal, countereprisal. It would [have torn] the fabric of American life to pieces." Shy also suggests that Washington was afraid that such a strategy would have undermined the political process and thrown "power to a junta—a committee of public safety with a Lee, not a Washington, as its military member."[50]

There is another objection to the idea that a "peoples' war" could have succeeded alone. Washington in effect had the army equivalent of a "fleet in being": the Continental Army forced the British always to concentrate their forces. Had it not been so, the British could have dispersed their forces to track down partisan bands, as Colonel Banastre Tarleton did with great success in the South. Tarleton's success against partisan guerrillas indicates that, without the necessity to concentrate their main forces to check Washington's conventional force, the British probably could have dealt with a "peoples' war."

Many factors contributed to America's success in gaining its independence. Not the least of these is Washington's often-denigrated abilities as a strategist. He always kept the political object foremost in his considerations. He always seemed to examine his alternatives in terms of the whole strategic picture. Learning from his early mistakes, he constantly adapted his strategy to the circumstances. Recognizing the defects of his tactical instrument, he never asked too much of it. These are the marks of a great strategist and help explain why Washington was indeed "first in war," the successful termination of which was necessary for all that followed.

FOUR

George Washington
and the Standing Oak

WILLIAM B. ALLEN

The George Washington of cherry tree fame might better be associated with a standing oak. Our Constitution is like a mighty oak tree; and this would be a better association because, as I hope to show in the following essay, George Washington sought in every way to give the United States a Constitution with the right structure and with roots in the right soil, so that it could stand with all the might and permanence an oak tree suggests. For example, Washington's efforts can be seen in a letter to James Madison in May 1789: "[A]s you have begun, so I could wish you to finish, the good work in a short reply to the Address of the House of Representatives...that there may be an accordance in this business.... As the first of everything *in our situation* will serve to establish a precedent, it is devoutly to be wished on my part, that these precedents may be fixed on true principles." In these passages, President Washington referred to the fact that he had called upon Madison to draft the first inaugural address which had actually been delivered just the week before, and he therefore wished Madison also to draft a response to the return address from the House. Such care was ever the hallmark of Washington's life.

To understand Washington's efforts and influence, however, we need unveil it beneath that characteristic diffidence noted throughout his career, whether in the military or upon installation of the new government. It was universally believed that the Constitutional Convention settled on the design it did, above all the strong executive, because of the expectation that Washington would be the first president. Nevertheless, just as he had been at length persuaded to attend the Convention he had done so much to produce, at length he had to be persuaded to accept the presidency. Washington seemed honestly uncertain whether events were unfolding around him or whether he was in fact producing them, giving credibility to his opinion that "a greater drama is now acting on this theatre than has heretofore been brought on the American stage, or any other in the world." Whether he was merely acting—or directing—the climactic act in this drama was his inauguration on April 30, 1789.

On April 14, 1789, Charles Thomson, secretary to Congress, had handed Washington a letter from John Langdon, president pro tempore of the Senate, stating that Washington had been unanimously elected president of the United States. He had left Mount Vernon on April 16, 1789, bid farewell to his friends and neighbors in Alexandria, Virginia, and arrived in New York City on April 23.

The Senate and the House of Representatives had completed the plans for the inauguration and ceremony on April 27. The event followed on the thirtieth. Shortly after noon, on the balcony of Federal Hall in front of the Senate Chamber, Robert R. Livingston, chancellor of the state of New York, administered the oath of office. Washington then addressed his assembled countrymen.

The First Inaugural Address focused almost exclusively upon the responsibilities of the officers of government. As the years passed, however, and corresponding with the growth of political parties and increasing dissension, Washington devoted greater attention to addressing the general public, including the much remarked 1794 State of the Union passage in which he condemned the "self-created democratic societies" that had become implicated in the Whiskey Rebellion and that seemed to him so strikingly like those nurseries of terror spawned in the French Revolution.

Washington organized the new government with exquisite attention to the significance of every word and deed for subsequent practice. At one point, for example, he determined to advise and consult with the Senate on a matter involving negotiations with Indian tribes. Washington, accompanied by Secretary of War Henry Knox, presented himself before the Senate while the clerk read off the main points that concerned him—seeking the point-by-point "advice and consent" of the Senate. After cooling his heels while what was to become the world's greatest deliberative body debated how to proceed, the president turned on his heels—never to return personally before the Senate for such purposes—and initiated the strong executive, who would present his accomplishments for "advice and consent" *after* rather than *before* the fact.

As president, Washington seemed very much the "delegator."

He gathered around him able minds whom he trusted to investigate, debate, and recommend. Though he reflected much (and wrote a great deal), in councils he was rather spartan, generally preferring to entice others to consider options and reserving for himself the job of deciding among them. He seemed throughout his life to follow the advice he gave to his nephew in 1786, namely that the secret in democratic politics is to "speak seldom but always to effect." The most dramatic instance—which I will explain later—occurred in the Constitutional Convention of 1787. In the presidency, there were numerous such instances, from the debate over the national debt and the location of a national capitol, to the stratagems for bringing the United States safely through the perils of European wars.

President Washington was at Mount Vernon early in April 1793, when news reached America of a declaration of war against Britain by the Republic of France. He cut short his Virginia vacation and returned to Philadelphia (the temporary national capital) to confer with his cabinet as to the best means to protect the United States in the crisis. Washington sent inquiries to the secretaries and to the attorney general, asking them to consider what measures would be proper for the United States to observe, especially in light of the defensive treaty of alliance consummated with the French monarchy during the American Revolution. He ultimately determined that the United States would follow a neutral course, desiring to give neither belligerent cause for complaint. Accordingly, he issued the Proclamation of Neutrality on April 22, 1793. In doing this, Washington led rather than followed Congress—and perhaps led popular opinion as well.

His efforts to establish healthy precedents speak for themselves, but Washington's administration of the government under the Constitution was not untroubled. During those eight years, the Founding itself was consummated; yet during that same time, Americans witnessed the birth of what ultimately became the system of political parties. Washington's unanimous election to the presidency was never to be repeated, as statesmen of the founding era discovered room to contest the "administration" of the government within the protective confines of the Constitution. He became the tacit head of the Federalist Party, direct heir to the Federalists, who prevailed in the struggle over adoption of the Constitution.

The opposition party, the Democratic-Republican Party, was headed by James Madison and Thomas Jefferson. In the last six years of Washington's administration, growing party discord was the most significant and most pressing political development. The country witnessed the emergence of party presses and party organizations. Most significantly, however, the parties divided the administration itself; for the parties' chief spokesmen, apart from Madison, were members of Washington's own cabinet. Alexander Hamilton, secretary of the treasury, managed the Federalists, while Thomas Jefferson spearheaded the opposition party, the Republicans, even while he was secretary of state. Madison, whose 1791–1792 essays in the *National Gazette* laid out the Republican platform, had been the principal Federalist spokesman in Congress. To all appearances, therefore, the cemented union for which Washington had so long labored was being fractured in a contest over the spoils of victory. While maintaining the principle of energetic government, Washington sought to contain the damage of division, praying that "the cup which has been presented may not be snatched from our lips by a discordance of action." The fact that this discord was ultimately contained "within the walls of the Constitution" is perhaps the single greatest achievement of the Founding.

With a presidential election and the prospect of a third term of office looming before him, Washington determined upon a definitive retirement in 1796. He devoted considerable thought to the appropriate manner in which to effect his retirement so as to render it, too, an advantage to his countrymen. On May 10, 1796, he asked Alexander Hamilton to help in preparing a vale-dictory address. Washington sent to Hamilton a draft, parts of which had been authored by James Madison, upon whose offices Washington had called four years earlier, prematurely as it turned out. After four months of correspondence, Washington's objective had been achieved, and he published the Farewell Address on Monday, September 17, 1796—Constitution Day—in *Claypoole's American Daily Advertiser*.

Washington confidently speaks of "the happy reward of our mutual cares, labors, and dangers" in his Farewell Address. He would leave the office of the presidency with no less pleasure than he had resigned his military commission earlier. On the earlier occasion, he had declared that he resigned "with satisfaction the appointment he accepted with diffidence." The spontaneous and universal acclaim that welcomed him home from the Revolutionary War in 1783 would be duplicated on this occasion. This time, however, he had completed a much more trying task, the increasingly bitter party strife having made even him an open target. Not only had the country been solidified and its finances put in order, but the ominous threats of war that loomed over his last five years in office had been greatly lessened, even as the country had been strengthened to meet any eventuality. At the same time, his resignation removed him from that unfamiliar position of being held up to public scorn and ridicule by "infamous scribblers."

In testing Washington's contribution to the United States and his character in the presidency, it is absolutely necessary to weigh his last years against the backdrop of his early years. He had ended his military career with a poignant farewell to the officers who had served faithfully under him. Woodrow Wilson noted that, in the final years of the war and "the absence of any real government, Washington proved almost the only prop of authority and law." How this came to be was displayed fully in Fraunce's Tavern on November 23, 1783. The British departed New York, and the general took leave of his men. In an emotional moment, at a loss for words, Washington raised his glass: "With a heart full of love and gratitude, I now take my leave of you." He extended his hand to shake the hands of his officers as they filed past him. Henry Knox stood nearest to Washington and consequently was first in line. As Knox held out his hand, Washington impulsively embraced and kissed his faithful general. There in perfect silence, he so embraced each of his officers as they filed by, and then they parted.

This dramatic signature to eight years of hard travail testifies how far Washington conquered the hearts of his men and his countrymen still more decisively than he conquered the armies of the enemy. The odyssey, the development of thoughts and principles, which brought Washington to this moment that began at least thirty years earlier and would not end for nearly fifteen years more. His story can be found, in his own words, through nearly fifty volumes of correspondence, memoranda, and diaries.

When young George Washington accepted the command of Virginia militia that had enlisted in the service of King George, he seemed already singularly self-possessed. This more than any other trait is perhaps that which has so often inclined biographers and historians to describe him as a "born aristocrat." He was only eleven years old when his father died of pneumonia. During those eleven years, he had lived with his family first at Bridges Creek, then at Hunting Creek, and finally near Fredericksburg, all in Virginia. It was at Hunting Creek, which was later rechristened Mount Vernon, where Washington lived from three to seven years of age and where he seemed to undergo the strongest influences on his life. Throughout the rest of his life, Mount Vernon served as a compass point.

In the long career that followed, Washington always centered his labors on the expectation of returning to Mount Vernon. Still, this planter-manager devoted more time—if not more thought—to the salvation of his country than to the care of his own estate.

From the first moment of the Revolution, if not earlier, Washington had a thoughtful appreciation of liberty and its political significance. Further, it is clear that the idea of a strong American Union motivated him throughout the thirty years (1769–1799) of active citizenship in which he guided his countrymen. At the same time, Washington was the original creator of the most pervasive myths about his person and character, above all the idea that he somehow lacked full intellectual power. His self-possession was rivaled by his habitual self-effacement. He never accepted a public charge without forswearing any opinion that he was "the man for the job," at least after his intense and successful lobbying for his first office as commander of Virginia militia. When he closed his life in 1799, requesting to be put away "without parade or funeral oration," he insisted for the last time that, in his view, his merit in no way exceeded that of his ordinary countrymen.

A fragment of an early letter written by Washington and rescued from a fire bears the following tantalizing dictum: "Law can never make just which in its nature is unjust."[1] From the fragment, which consists of only sixty-nine words, we can surmise only that it was certainly written prior to the ratification of the Constitution and probably during a period of currency instability during the Revolution. In the fragment, Washington speaks of imbibing "the true principles" and rails against attempts to depreciate currency by law as being an unjust infringement of contracts.

Washington's characteristic attitude—that is, punctiliousness in matters of just respect—culminated in his being named commander in chief of the Continental Army in 1775 and made a very large contribution to his developing political ideas. He assumed his command in the immediate aftermath of the Battle of Bunker Hill. The first task to confront him, therefore, was to dislodge the British force from Boston. That event set in motion

a train of events that would find the main army, with
Washington, running from battle to battle.

General Washington urged the notion of an American Union
prior to the signing of the Declaration of Independence—as early
as 1775. The progress of the war made his appeals ever more stri-
dent and more insistent. In the final two years of the war, despite
the enormous labors required to maintain his position in the face
of a powerful and determined enemy, his appeals reached the
status of virtual demands. Even as the Articles of Confederation
were finally being ratified by the last state (Maryland held out
until March 1, 1781), Washington was trying to convince legislators and others of the need for a stronger national union. His
opinion was the fruit of sad experience: "We must take the passions of Men as Nature has given them, and those principles as a
guide which are generally the rule of Action."

Victory did not bring an end to Washington's troubles. The
British would remain in place on American soil for two more
years. Further, it had become doubly difficult to preserve due
prudence and readiness in the face of general expectations of the
end of conflict. Similarly, there was a very real possibility of the
soldiers' countrymen simply dismissing them with thanks and
forgetting the fact that they had served dutifully through great
trials without compensation. Instead of elation, therefore,
Washington's attitude in the face of the triumph was to preserve
in his men and himself the sense of a "duty to bear present trials
with fortitude."

These events would soon be followed by Washington's
famous Circular Address to the Governors of the Thirteen States.

Written in 1783, the letter constitutes the centerpiece of his statesmanship, carrying directly to his countrymen a coherent vision of the unfinished work that lay before them in the aftermath of peace. His view of that work was that "we have a national character to establish." That greater victory yet eluded the Americans, even in the aftermath of peace.

Washington returned in 1783 to a Mount Vernon in considerable disrepair, to resume the domestic arts for which he had so long pined. Martha Washington had visited with him in the army's camp when occasion permitted, and she shared with him and his men their many privations. Her ministrations to the soldiers were a source of reinforcement for them and for George Washington. He had returned home but once during eight years of war, making a brief stop there at the time of the victorious Yorktown campaign. He could already see at that time the labors that lay before him to bring Mount Vernon back to its former glory. But it would be two more years before he could undertake the work. He could also see all that could not be restored, Martha's son, Jack Custis, having died just after the Yorktown victory. Both her children were now gone, and they had none of their own.

Though Washington plunged back into the tasks of managing his estates, public concerns still pressed in on him. Everyone, it seemed, required his opinion, and he disappointed none. He resumed his prewar efforts to produce a waterway connection between the Trans-Appalachians and the Potomac River, as much for reasons of state—"to cement the union"—as for reasons of commerce. Further, he continued to press for a strengthening of the Union. Between the end of 1783 and 1786, Washington managed to draw a coterie of reform-minded men around him, men whose efforts at length gave hope of a general reform of the Confederation.

The expectant air of Washington's correspondence during this period justifies his observation that "the present era is pregnant of great and strange events." The role he himself played in these events is critical in constructing an accurate view of his life and of his political ideas. In the Constitutional Convention, he played a pivotal though quiet role. He was elected to preside and did not participate in the debates, with one notable exception on the final day. The influence that was visible on that singular occasion was exercised invisibly throughout the course of the Convention, as Washington had maintained regular though informal conversation with the diverse delegates.

The single, compelling example of Washington's influence occurred on the last day of the Convention. At that moment, the Constitution had been completely agreed on, and only needed to be signed. It had been engrossed and was at hand, waiting for the delegates to determine how they wished to close the Convention. In spite of the spirit of accomplishment that filled the air, however, the delegates remained a parliamentary body. Motions were still in order. Massachusetts's Gorham rose to move for an alteration in the formula for representation. He urged a reduction in the scale of representation from 1:40,000 to 1:30,000. Rufus King of Massachusetts and Daniel Carroll of Maryland "seconded and supported" his idea, despite the fact that the delegates had reaffirmed the rule of 1:40,000 on a motion of James Madison more than a month before (August 8, 1787) and had undergone numerous discussions prior to that time. If anything had been settled, this was it. Indeed, Madison's motion had been that, considering the future growth of population, the rule of 1:40,000 would produce too large a representation, and therefore the provision should read, "not exceeding one for every 40,000." The Convention at that time accepted it *nemine contradicente*.

The only remarks recorded by Madison on this day came from George Washington, though Madison indicates that King and Carroll did indeed say something. In any case, the last substantive speech of the Convention was made by its president, his only recorded contribution to the debates. Madison described the scene as follows:

> When the President rose, for the purpose of putting the question, he said that although his situation had hitherto restrained him from offering his sentiments on questions depending in the House, and it might be thought, ought now to impose silence on him, yet he could not forbear expressing his wish that the alteration proposed might take place. It was much to be desired that the objections to the plan recommended might be made as few as possible—The smallness of the proportion of Representatives had been considered by many members of the Convention, an insufficient security for the rights & interests of the people. He acknowledged that it had always appeared to himself among the exceptionable parts of the plan; and late as the present moment was for admitting amendments, he thought this of so much consequence that it would give much satisfaction to see it adopted.

Following this appeal no voice of opposition was raised, and the measure passed unanimously. Washington thereby clearly left his mark on the Constitution; whereas theretofore, he had silently worked to assure that an adequate structure, capable of governing, would be erected by the delegates. In this display, we behold an instance of Washington's power within the Convention.

This example of Washington's enormous influence justifies our questioning whether Washington, as opposed to James Madison, should be called the father of the Constitution. I would argue that only someone who has laid down the fundamental law for a people could, fully and properly, be called a founder. Thus, not his great personal attributes but only his legislation could make Washington a founder.

That is the difficulty we have with Washington, knowing how great he was really. We cannot broach that question fully here, although we must at least give a nod to it. This would be required, if for no other reason, because of the wealth of materials that have been produced to call the matter into question. In general, these are works stretching back at least a century, that portray Washington as a symbol rather than as an accomplished human being. While recent publications seem happily to have departed from that pattern, in the 1980s historians such as Gordon Wood and sociologists such as Barry Schwartz have repeated the doubts. Schwartz's work was blunt indeed: "It is the range and significance of Washington's shortcomings that make it difficult to understand his veneration on the basis of personal qualities alone."[2] We find a glancing contrast in Forrest McDonald, who does not refute that Washington had shortcomings but offers substantial discussion of Washington's "self-conscious" attempt to construct and preserve his "character."[3]

Nothing highlights Washington's determination and intent so clearly as his efforts toward union on the last day of the Convention. There he foreshadowed the claim he would make to Lafayette in 1789, that "I see a path, as clear and direct as a ray of light," to the ultimate political happiness and prosperity of the United States.[4] For us, however, it remains true that no one to date has told the whole story with the compelling clarity it demands, and which, perhaps, Washington expected to obtain only at the hands of some American Homer.[5]

Washington was perfectly esoteric in his conduct regarding the development of an American republic. He published no treatises in his own name and founded no societies. Indeed, following the close of the war, he did not even hold any public office. Nevertheless, compared with others, he worked no less—and perhaps even more—assiduously toward the goal of a national union.

In the period from March 1787 to 1788, the Circular Address—the *locus classicus* for his ideas—was widely cited and reprinted in newspapers and pamphlets across the country.[6] So far as we can tell, this phenomenon was entirely spontaneous. The address had been immensely popular when originally issued in 1783, and now it was clear that it was being largely understood as Washington had intended—as a blueprint for founding.

Washington almost never relented in his private labors to encourage a strengthening of the national government. He maintained an extensive private correspondence devoted largely to this purpose; he pursued schemes such as the Potomac-Ohio Canal specifically with the view in mind of strengthening the Union; and he lost no chance to further opportunities to build the powers of the Confederation or, ultimately, to call a new convention. He virtually hovered over the 1785 Alexandria Conference (which turned into the Mount Vernon Conference) on trade, maintained an active interest in the subsequent Annapolis Conference (which grew out of the former), and consulted with its leading participants to secure the calling of the Philadelphia Convention. Even when his projects and activities seemed private and economic, they also seemed to him "big with great political, as well as commercial consequences to these States."[7]

Such an ambition required, over and above the vague hope of union, some specific notions of the form to be instituted. That it must be republican was the first level of specificity. That this general goal was in need of further refinement is suggested by Washington's continued development of it throughout the war. From Valley Forge he wrote: "If we are to pursue a right system of policy, in my opinion, there should be none of these distinctions. We should all be considered, Congress, Army, etc. as one people, embarked in one cause, in one interest; acting on the same principle and to the same end."[8] This *end* entailed not only the framing of a specific constitution, but a constitution understood as creating a regime—a characteristic way of life. Washington and his troops were struggling "for every thing valuable in society" and "laying the foundation of an Empire."[9] Not surprisingly, therefore, he had considered long before what that would entail:

To form a new Government, requires infinite care, and unbounded attention; for if the foundation is badly laid the superstructure must be bad, too much time, therefore, cannot be bestowed in weighing and digesting matters well. We have, no doubt, some good parts in our present constitution; many bad ones we know we have, wherefore no time can be misspent that is employed in sep[a]rating the Wheat from the Tares. My fear is, that you will all get tired and homesick, the consequence of which will be, that you will patch up some kind of constitution as defective as the present; this should be avoided, every man should consider that he is lending his aid to frame a con-stitution which is to render millions happy, or miserable, and that a matter of such moment cannot be the work of a day.[10]

Washington gave this advice to his brother in the middle of Virginia's efforts to repair its constitution and at a time when continental efforts to draft a constitution were just beginning. That he saw Virginia's work as part of a national effort may be gathered from his invocation of the fate of future "*millions*." That it would take time, and frequently renewed considerations, was the lesson of the years to follow.

In the Circular Address, Washington made clear that the conditions for achieving the status of "a people" in the United States hinged completely upon the establishment of a rule of jus-tice, not only within the institutions, but within the souls of the people. At the close of the address, Washington wrote that the precondition for self-government is the accomplishment of that prayer, for a disposition in the citizens "to do justice, to love mercy, and to demean ourselves with that charity, humility and pacific temper of mind." A spirit of moderation, understood as a moral proposition—the acceptance of self-government as an objective not only in institutional terms but within the soul of each—is that without which "we can never hope to be a happy nation." The accomplishment of such a spirit, however, turned upon the efforts of those who would supply the policy and institutions of the nation—it turned upon statesmanship.

We have a clear picture of the ideas with which Washington entered the Convention. Washington had exchanged a detailed correspondence with such coadjutors as Henry Knox, Alexander Hamilton, John Jay, and James Madison. He had read their sketches of possible plans, and he had even gone to the length of copying out in his own hand the essential points of those plans that detained his attention. As seen in one particular letter to Madison, he had also delivered his watchword: "...my wish is the convention may adopt no temporizing expedients, but probe the defects of the constitution to the bottom, and provide radical cures; whether they are agreed to or not; a conduct like this, will stamp wisdom and dignity on the proceedings, and be looked to as a luminary, which sooner or later will shed its influence.[11] Washington's use of the term "constitution" to refer to the Articles of Confederation plainly shows the extent of his ambition and, more importantly, his fundamental understanding of the terms of founding.

As the Convention opened, the first question pending was that of who should preside. All attention focused on Washington and Benjamin Franklin. Franklin diverted all hesitation by nominating Washington. With his elevation to the chair, Washington fell silent, at least according to all of our written records. This pattern conforms generally to what most biographers have recorded of his service in the Virginia House of Burgesses. He spoke there but seldom, though apparently with effect.

I should note that the apocryphal record suggests that Washington did speak more during the Convention, though Madison did not record it. Gouverneur Morris, in his eulogy of Washington, records an eloquent speech near the opening of the Convention, and another tale reports Washington rebuking (in general) a fellow delegate who had incautiously dropped his copy of the proceedings, potentially jeopardizing their secrecy. In each of these cases, the apocrypha emphasize an authority peculiar to Washington, whereby his words bear the weight of authoritative deeds in the eyes of his fellows.

Unlike many of the nationalists, Washington did not undertake a general campaign on behalf of the Constitution—at least not directly. True to his past experience, his private expressions of opinion had the facility of finding their way into the press. According to Henry Knox, "Washington's opinions, even rumors of them, were too good copy to be passed over even at his desire."[12] Nevertheless, he held to his resolve "not to appear as a partisan in the interesting subject." He wished, rather, that the Constitution would convey its own claims, as he urged in letters to friends, particularly distant friends such as Catherine MaCaulay-Graham and the Marquis de Lafayette. To Lafayette, for example, he could boast that the Constitution "is provided with more checks and barriers against the introduction of tyranny, and those of a nature less liable to be surmounted, than any government hitherto instituted among mortals hath possessed."

We seek, however, a more programmatic expression of Washington's views on the Constitution, especially a public expression. Unfortunately, the most helpful source for this task is partially lost. I refer to the Discarded Inaugural Address. Even in its defective form, however, it is a manifest contribution to our understanding of how far Washington's understanding, as opposed to his image, informed the founding of the United States. One example is his assertion, in the document, that "I presume now to assert that better may not still be devised." This is clearly Washington's retrospective judgment of the work of the Convention; and beforehand he had warned many of the delegates to aim not for the most that is acceptable, but for the best possible. Washington appraises the work of the Convention as that of his colleagues *and* his own:

> Although the agency I had in forming this system, and the high opinion I entertained of my Colleagues for their ability and integrity may have tended to warp my judgment in its favour; yet I will not pretend to say that it appears absolutely perfect to me, or that there may not be many faults which escaped my discernment. I will only say that, during and since the session of the Convention, I have attentively heard and read every oral and printed information on both sides of the question that could be procured. This long and laborious investigation, in which I endeavoured as far as the frailty of nature would permit to act with candour has resulted in a fixed belief that this Constitution, is really in its formation a government of the people; that is to say, a government in which all power is derived from, and at stated periods reverts to them—and that, in its operation, it is

purely a government of Laws made and executed by the fair substi-
tutes of the people alone.

Note the emphasis in this draft on both his agency in forming the
system and his continued effort to assure himself as to its nature.
The potential address considers all of the structural components
of the Constitution from the perspectives of both their republican
safety and of their efficiency. He judges its superiority to most
constitutions which "have existed in the world" on three grounds:
first, it has adequate powers to perform the task of governing;
second, it has no greater power than is requisite to accomplish the
"safety and happiness of the governed;" and, third (as he had said
to Lafayette), never before has any government so efficaciously
guarded itself against degeneration into oppression.

In this address, Washington places the Constitution in the
context of the Revolution, to show it as an accomplishment of the
Revolution rather than a latter-day departure. Washington
undertakes to define the character of the regime as such, as he put
it, "to express my idea of a flourishing state with precision; and
to distinguish between happiness and splendour." In making that
distinction, he returned to the animating theme of the Circular
Address: self-government understood as a spirit of moderation.
Now, however, he adds to it a spirit of "magnanimity," a spirit
that becomes possible for a people truly moderate once they enjoy
the blessing of a genuine regime. This is the same "magnanimity" that he praised and encouraged in the Farewell Address. This
theme returned Washington to the meaning of the Declaration of
Independence: "I rejoice in a belief that intellectual light will

spring up in the dark corners of the earth; that freedom of enquiry will produce liberality of conduct; that mankind will reverse the absurd position that the many were, made for the few; and that they will not continue slaves in one part of the globe, when they can become freemen in another."

Washington then aims to undertake the presidency with a sense of duty. He has explained earlier that he has no posterity to advantage by his conduct. He aims to do so in the company of his fellow citizens, entering a path that would yet prove "intricate and thorny," but that would "grow plain and smooth as we go." It would grow so, he held, because of their adhering to that "eternal line that separates right from wrong."

As we read such sentiments, we cannot fail to see that there is no other central participant in the Founding who spoke so comprehensively about the mission of founding the United States.

To Washington, the work of the Convention enabled the pursuit of a political course that vindicates self-government understood as the capacity of man to guide himself by the light of moral claims. The affirmation hinged on the twofold condition of accomplishing such a political structure as would preserve to individuals the opportunity to pursue that course at the same time as men in general proved capable of doing so. They would qualify for self-government, in the sense of free institutions, in proportion as they qualified for self-government in the sense of being able to govern themselves by the light of reason. Insofar as Washington's efforts within the Convention were directed toward that end, our assessment of his influence must be governed by the need to discern that principle at work. We have already suggested the basis for such judgment. It bears repeating, however, that Washington's final contribution to the Convention testifies as well as anything that he, at least, judged at the end that he had accomplished his goal. The time to make a bow to democracy was precisely at that moment when judgment held that democracy had been safely hedged in with appropriate checks and guides. This was surely Washington's way of joining in Franklin's recognition of the sun carved on the back of the president's chair in Independence Hall as a rising, not a setting, sun.

George Washington actively shaped not only the American presidency but also the work of the Constitutional Convention. To note this adds no lustre to his name, but rather advances our own understanding of the accomplishment of the Founding. We cannot embellish his epitaph, which was written in the characteristic form of that Socratic irony that proved immensely valuable to him in accomplishing the task he undertook (and to which he adhered in discarding the temptation to declare himself openly in the draft of his first inaugural address).

Washington lived only three years beyond his resignation from the presidency. He returned once again to a fallen Mount Vernon, which this time his labors could not hope to restore. Nevertheless, he plunged back into his favorite pursuits of agricultural development and experimentation and the design and organization of Mount Vernon. He was again to find himself under a constant press of correspondence and visitation. Even his enemy George III wrote of him as "the greatest" statesman alive. Indeed, he was even summoned back as a commander of American military forces at a time when war with France seemed an imminent prospect. That passed, however, and with it Washington's countrymen's claims upon him. His claims upon them, however, would reach beyond his death, and the deaths of generations of countrymen, through a Constitution that stands out in human history like a majestic oak in the middle of an orchard of cherry trees.

FIVE

Washington and the Origins of Presidential Power

MARK J. ROZELL

The Constitutional Convention of 1787 formally created the American presidency. George Washington put the office into effect. Indeed, Washington was very cognizant of the fact that his actions as president would establish the office and have consequences for his successors. The first president's own words evidence how conscious he was of the crucial role he played in determining the make-up of the office of the presidency. He had written to James Madison that "[a]s the first of everything, *in our situation will serve to establish a precedent*, it is devoutly wished on my part that these precedents be fixed on true principles."[1] In May 1789, Washington wrote that "[m]any things which appear of little importance in themselves and at the beginning, may have great and durable consequences from their having been established at the commencement of a new general government."[2]

All presidents experience the burdens of the office. Washington's burdens were unique in that only he had the responsibility to establish the office in practice. The costs of mis-

judgments to the future of the presidency were great. The parameters of the president's powers remained vague when Washington
took office. The executive article of the Constitution (Article II)
lacked the specificity of the legislative article (Article I), leaving
the first occupant of the presidency imperfect guidance on the
scope and limits of his authority. Indeed, it may very well have
been because Washington was the obvious choice for first occupant of the office that the Constitutional Convention left the
powers of the presidency vague. Willard Sterne Randall writes
that "[n]o doubt no other president would have been trusted with
such latitude."[3] Acutely aware of his burdens, Washington set out
to exercise his powers prudently, yet firmly when necessary.

Perhaps his greatest legacy to the presidency was his substantial success in establishing the office for the future. He was a
model for the office at that time when a model was most needed.
Indeed, as the historian Forrest McDonald has written, "the office
of president of the United States could scarcely have been created
had George Washington not been available to become its first
occupant."[4]

It is well established that Washington was a reluctant first
occupant of the office. He loved private life and wished to fulfill
his days tending to the business of agriculture at Mount Vernon.
But duty had called on the nation's most famous and admired citizen in the past, and he had always answered the calls. He had
sworn off attending the Constitutional Convention; but when
others placed his name as a participant and implored him to go,
he did. Although he had misgivings about certain provisions of
the Constitution, he lent his support to the document, under-

standing that his say carried clout and that the future of the nation depended on a strong government. He expressed his wish that some other qualified person would come forward to assume the presidency, but he knew that no one else had the nearly universal esteem of his people. As Forrest McDonald points out in his contribution to this volume, Washington was the indispensable man. Washington left the private life he desired to answer the call of duty. He determined that the well-being of the young nation had to override his personal preference for the comforts of private life.

Although Washington was careful to distinguish his own political interests from those of the nation, he recognized that for many Americans, he personally embodied the office of the presidency. He traveled to every state of the young nation so that the people could see their president, and this action fostered the notion of democratic governance. He resisted calls for elaborate titles and ill-founded advice that he close himself off to the people and remain aloof except to a select few. He opened the doors to the president's home during selected hours to meet with regular citizens; and although he found the exercise at times exasperating, he continued. Washington on the one hand wanted to be the president of the people. On the other hand, he understood the need to imbue the office of the presidency with the dignity needed to command the respect of the nation and of foreign nation-states.

Through his two terms, Washington took care to exercise his powers properly. He deferred to Congress where appropriate, but he was not at all reluctant to protect the powers of his office. He often took his constitutionally based powers quite literally, as when he went to the Senate in person to seek the "advice and consent" of its members on a proposed treaty. He learned from this experience that perhaps the Constitution need not be interpreted so precisely, as he found the meeting with the senators a counterproductive one at which he became visibly angry and reportedly left the room saying that he would be "damned" if he ever returned. Washington never repeated the experience of seeking the Senate's advice or consent prior to making such a decision. In this action, Washington helped establish an important precedent of the independent power of the presidency to act in foreign affairs *before* seeking the legislature's input.

On a host of matters, Washington, in a sense, "filled in the blanks" of Article II. He established the presidential power to remove executive branch officials, a position that some attacked as an intrusion on the authority of Congress. If the president has to seek advice and consent to appoint, some reasoned, then he should not have the unilateral power to remove officials. During a lengthy House debate on the issue in May 1789, some members argued that the necessary and proper clause of Article I of the Constitution empowered the legislature to ultimately control all departments and officers. Yet both houses of the Congress ultimately sided with Washington's interpretation of exclusive presidential power to fire top-level executive branch officers.[5] Washington's action also helped to establish in practice the principle of a truly independent executive branch of government.

Similarly, Washington established in practice the independent power of the president to act in foreign policy when he issued the controversial Proclamation of Neutrality. Congress had been in the midst of a debate over the proper U.S. position in the war between France and Great Britain. By acting alone and issuing the Proclamation, the president settled the issue. Although many in Congress protested, they lacked the authority to challenge Washington's action. Many presidents since have claimed that the executive holds the upper hand in the making of foreign policy, and the courts generally have sided with presidents in such disputes (that is, in those cases where the courts have decided the issue and not instead declared such disputes political questions).

Washington established a British-style system of cabinet government with appointed secretaries (with Senate approval) leading the Departments of State, War, and Treasury. The Senate gave wide deference to the president to have the cabinet secretaries of his own choosing, which established another long-standing precedent. The practice of "senatorial courtesy" also originated with Washington when he appointed an officer to command a Georgian naval port and the state's two senators protested. Washington deferred to the senators and withdrew the appointment. Hence he established the precedent that for federal appointments within a state the president must consult the state's senators. (In the modern era of party competition, that practice is modified to include the senior senator of the president's own party within the state.)

Not every precedent that Washington established succeeded or stood the test of time. He believed that Congress properly was the chief lawmaking branch of the government and that the executive did not share the legislative power. Consequently, he would veto legislation only on constitutional grounds, a practice that presidents mostly followed until the Andrew Jackson era. Today, of course, the veto is a policy instrument allowing the executive to share in a part of the legislative power.

In appointing officials to government posts, Washington generally applied merit-based criteria. Constitutional scholar Henry Abraham praises the first president for using merit as the sole criterion for nominations to the Supreme Court and for his strict avoidance of the pernicious modern practice of various litmus tests.[6] Although admirable, that practice did not last long.

Washington similarly appointed cabinet secretaries and key presidential advisers based on their qualifications. He perhaps created the only truly bipartisan and merit-based cabinet. Yet Washington's experiment in merit selection did not appeal to his successors. He relied on the advice of three leading figures— Alexander Hamilton, Thomas Jefferson, and James Madison— who were prodigious and independent thinkers destined to battle one another. Scholars Sidney M. Milkis and Michael Nelson praise the line-up as generally successful, despite the acrimony.[7] Washington of course had warned against the establishment of party competition in the United States, and the nation did not long heed that call. The political scientist Woodrow Wilson would later characterize the president's twin roles of nation's head and leader of a political party as not altogether compatible. Although modern presidents occasionally invite a member of the other party into their cabinet (President Bill Clinton's choice of the former Republican Senator William Cohen as defense secretary is a more recent example), the established practice is far from Washington's precedent.

Perhaps Washington's best known precedent was the two-term limit—an informal practice broken only once in our history, but then later foolishly amended into the Constitution. Washington surely could have served a third term. The Constitutional Convention delegates had ultimately favored indefinite re-eligibility for the president, in part because of the widespread expectation that Washington would hold the office. In this case, the well-being of the young Republic and Washington's personal wishes converged. It is not clear that Washington had actually acted in this case out of concern for establishing a good precedent. Edward S. Corwin wrote that Washington made this decision "purely on grounds of personal preference." But as Corwin correctly added, the effect was the same: Jefferson followed in Washington's footsteps and in so doing he emphasized Washington's precedent.[8]

Washington established numerous other precedents, one of which was the exercise of presidential secrecy. A more detailed examination of Washington's actions in this area serves to reveal how he balanced respect for Congress's authority with the need to establish certain prerogatives of his office. The Constitution is silent about presidential secrecy. Washington did not aggressively seek to grab a new source of power for himself. He nonetheless recognized the need for secrecy in certain circumstances, and he was careful to ground his defense of the practice in constitutional principles and not mere utility.[9] Ultimately Washington established the practice of what we today call executive privilege.

Executive privilege is the right of the president and high-level executive branch officers to withhold information from those who have compulsory power: Congress and the courts. Unfortunately, unlike Washington, not all presidents have exercised that power with the same care for the rights of the coordinate branches and the people. The purpose of what follows is to demonstrate Washington's prudence in exercising his powers and the extent to which he went to take care that he establish sound precedents. As such, the following is a more in-depth case analysis that nicely illustrates the major conclusions of this essay.

WASHINGTON AND EXECUTIVE PRIVILEGE

In what follows, I describe and analyze the exercise of executive privilege in the Washington administration. Washington's actions—indeed fixed on firm constitutional principles—established the legitimacy of this presidential power for future administrations. His exercise of executive privilege is germane to the contemporary exercise of this constitutional power and therefore can appropriately be regarded as a model for modern presidents.

The phrase "executive privilege" actually did not exist at the time of the Washington presidency. That phrase was not coined until the Eisenhower administration. Nonetheless, on several occasions Washington contemplated or exercised what we today call executive privilege, and his actions established important precedents for the exercise of this constitutional power by his successors.

The first such action concerned a congressional request to investigate information relating to the failure of a November 1791 military expedition by General Arthur St. Clair against

Native Americans. The military expedition had cost hundreds of lives as well as the total loss of supplies. The event was an enormous embarrassment to the administration.

The House of Representatives established an investigative committee on March 27, 1792, to call for such persons, papers and records, as may be necessary to assist their inquiries.[10] The investigating committee requested from the president testimony and documents regarding St. Clair's expedition.

Washington convened his cabinet to determine how to respond to this first ever request for presidential materials by a congressional committee. The president wanted to discuss whether any harm would result from public disclosure of the information and, most pertinently, whether he could rightfully refuse to submit documents to Congress. Along with Alexander Hamilton, Henry Knox, and Edmund Randolph, Thomas Jefferson attended the April 2, 1792, cabinet meeting, and he later recalled the group's determination:

> We had all considered, and were of one mind, first, that the House was an inquest, and therefore might institute inquiries. Second, that it might call for papers generally. Third, that the Executive ought to communicate such papers as the public good would permit, and ought to refuse those, the disclosure of which would injure the public: consequently were to exercise a discretion. Fourth, that neither the committees nor House has a right to call on the Head of a Department, who and whose papers were under the President alone; but that the committee should instruct their chairman to move the House to address the President.[11]

Washington eventually determined that public disclosure of the information would not harm the national interest and that such disclosure was necessary to vindicate General St. Clair. Although Washington chose to negotiate with Congress over the investigating committee's request and ultimately to turn over relevant documents to Congress, his administration had taken an affirmative position on the right of the executive branch to withhold information. Furthermore, in agreeing to cooperate with Congress, Washington established as a condition that legislators review in closed session any information that, if publicly disclosed, would bring harm to the national interest. The historian Raoul Berger correctly concluded that the St. Clair incident "teaches that Washington would not claim privilege to hide a shameful failure within his administration, a lesson that has been lost on several presidential administrations."[12]

On January 17, 1794, the U.S. Senate advanced a motion directing Secretary of State Edmund Randolph, "to lay before the Senate the correspondence which have been had between the Minister of the United States at the Republic of France [Morris] and said Republic, and between said Minister and the Office of Secretary of State."[13] The Senate later amended the motion to address the president instead of Minister Morris. Significantly, the amended version also "requested" rather than "directed" that such information be forwarded to Congress.[14]

Believing that disclosure of the correspondence would be inappropriate, Washington sought the advice of his cabinet as to how to handle the Senate's request. On January 28, 1794, three of Washington's cabinet members expressed their opinions.

General Knox is of the opinion, that no part of the correspondence should be sent to the Senate. Colonel Hamilton, that the correct mode of proceeding is to do what General Knox advises; but the principle is safe, by excepting such parts as the president may choose to withhold. Mr. Randolph, that all correspondence proper, from its nature, to be communicated to the Senate, should be sent; but that what the president thinks is improper, should not be sent.[15]

Attorney General William Bradford separately wrote that "it is the duty of the Executive to withhold such parts of the said correspondence as in the judgment of the Executive shall be deemed unsafe and improper to be disclosed." On February 16, 1794, Washington responded as follows to the Senate's request: "After an examination of [the correspondence], I directed copies and translations to be made; except in those particulars, in my judgment, for public considerations, ought not to be communicated. These copies and translations are now transmitted to the Senate; but the nature of them manifest the propriety of their being received as confidential."[16]

Washington allowed the Senate to examine some parts of the correspondence, subject to his approval. He believed that information damaging to the "public interest" could constitutionally be withheld from the Congress. The Senate never challenged the president's authority to withhold the information.[17]

In 1796, John Jay completed U.S. negotiations with Great Britain over issues unsettled from the American Revolution. Because many considered the settlement unfavorable to the United States, Congress took a keen interest in the negotiations.

Not only did the Senate debate ratification of the Jay Treaty, the House set out to conduct its own investigation. The House passed a resolution requesting from Washington information concerning his instructions to the U.S. minister to Britain regarding the treaty negotiations, "excepting such of the said papers as any existing negotiation may render improper to be disclosed."[18] That resolution raised the issue of the House's proper role in the treaty-making process. Washington refused to comply with the House request and explained:

> The nature of foreign negotiations requires caution, and their success must often depend on secrecy; and even when brought to a conclusion a full disclosure of all the measures, demands, or eventual concessions which may have been proposed or contemplated would be extremely impolitic; for this might have a pernicious influence on future negotiations, or produce immediate inconveniences, perhaps danger and mischief, in relation to other powers. The necessity of such caution and secrecy was one cogent reason for vesting the power of making treaties in the President, with the advice and consent of the Senate, the principle on which that body was formed confining it to a small number of members. To admit, then, a right in the House of Representatives to demand and to have as a matter of course all the papers respecting a negotiation with a foreign power would be to establish a dangerous precedent.... [T]he boundaries fixed by the Constitution between the different departments should be preserved, a just regard to the Constitution and to the duty of my office...forbids a compliance with your request.[19]

The House of Representatives debated Washington's refusal to disclose the documents. After a lengthy debate, the House took no substantive action other than passing two nonbinding resolutions. One resolution asserted that Congress need not stipulate any reason for requesting information from the Executive. The other proclaimed that the House has a legitimate role in considering the speed at which a treaty is being implemented.[20]

During that debate, our chief constitutional architect, then Representative James Madison, proclaimed on the House floor "that the Executive had a right, under a due responsibility, also, to withhold information, when of a nature that did not permit a disclosure of it at the time.... If the Executive conceived that, in relation to his own department, papers could not be safely communicated, he might, on that ground, refuse them, because he was the competent though responsible judge within his own department."[21] In response to a proposed resolution requesting information from the president, Madison introduced to the House language to except such information "so much as, in [the president's] judgment, it may not be consistent with the interest of the United States, at this time, to disclose."[22] The House ultimately voted to appropriate funding for the treaty without reviewing the disputed materials. The president's action helped establish the principle of executive branch secrecy in negotiations. It also firmly fixed the House's appropriate role in the treaty-making process.

Washington never included the Senate in the negotiation stage of the Jay Treaty. During the ratification stage, the Senate voted to keep the treaty secret, as Hamilton wrote, "because they thought it [the secrecy] the affair of the president to do as he thought fit."[23] The Senate minority opposed to ratification listed seven objections to the treaty. None cited Washington's decision not to seek Senate advice.[24]

There are important common threads to these early exercises of executive privilege. First, presidents do not possess an unlimited right to withhold information. Rather, Congress has the right of inquiry and may request the production of materials and testimony. Second, the president's constitutional authority to withhold information must necessarily be limited to matters of national importance (e.g., diplomatic negotiations, national security) or to protecting the privacy of internal deliberations when it is in the public interest to do so (or perhaps when disclosure may result in public embarrassment for no public gain). Third, the legislative power of inquiry, though substantial, is not absolute.

These common threads established the framework for the proper exercise of executive privilege by presidents. Executive privilege has come to mean that presidents may withhold information regarding such weighty matters as national security or internal White House deliberations over official governmental matters.

To be sure, as the Nixon and Clinton administrations so clearly reveal, not all presidents have acted properly in exercising this constitutional power. Nonetheless, few today reject the right of presidents on occasion to withhold information. Washington established irrefutable precedents for the exercise of executive privilege by his successors. Some used this power quite elaborately—none more so than President Dwight D. Eisenhower, who asserted executive privilege at least forty times. Others have claimed executive privilege sparingly—for example, there were four executive privilege controversies during Ronald Reagan's two terms and in each case the president backed away from his initial refusals to provide information to Congress.[25]

Because of the misuse of that power by President Richard Nixon—he unsuccessfully tried to use executive privilege as a shield to cover up presidential wrongdoing—executive privilege unfortunately developed a negative connotation. With the exception of Bill Clinton, presidents since the Watergate scandal have been reluctant to assert executive privilege for fear of being characterized as engaged in Nixonian efforts to conceal and deceive.

The Clinton presidency has brought about a reinvigoration of the debate over executive privilege. Unlike his immediate predecessors, Clinton has not been shy about asserting executive privilege. He has claimed that power on numerous occasions—none so controversial as his failed effort to use executive privilege in the Monica Lewinsky investigation.

How did Clinton's exercise of executive privilege in the Lewinsky investigation measure up to the traditional standards for applying that doctrine? There obviously was no national security justification to withholding information about presidential and staff discussions over how to handle that episode. Nonetheless, Clinton's White House counsel made the argument that by harming "the president's ability to 'influence' the public," the investigation undermined his ability to lead foreign policy and protect the national interest.[26] Judged against the standards established by Washington, this argument does not withstand scrutiny. The St. Clair incident, for example, was a huge embarrassment to the Washington administration, one that clearly harmed the president's public reputation. Yet the president believed that it was more important to be forthcoming and accept any public rebuke for a policy mistake than to conceal information to protect his reputation. Washington did not equate his personal political interests or his public reputation with the national interest.

CONCLUSION

It is hard to imagine the eventual shape of the presidency had George Washington not been the first occupant of the office. Although today Washington is not recognized among the great thinkers of the founding era, he left behind a large corpus of personal and public records. From some of his writings it is clear that he was well aware of the unique role that he played in establishing the presidency. He accepted that role reluctantly, in effect creating a long-standing precedent that presidential aspirants should not appear to eagerly seek the office but instead should hear the call to duty from the nation. Today, candidates for the office often follow in that tradition, but their feigned reluctance to serve hardly convinces anyone.

Washington acted carefully to establish a presidency firmly based on proper constitutional principles. The contrast between his approach to presidential secrecy and the modern exercise of executive privilege could not be more striking. Whereas Washington thought first and foremost about how to protect constitutional principles and the long-term well-being of the presidency, Nixon and Clinton could think only of their own political self-interests.

Not all of Washington's precedents lasted. But many important ones did, and the success of the office is due in large part to the prudent actions of the first president. The unfortunate reality is that Washington does not receive the respect and attention of contemporary presidential scholars and students who are wedded to a model of the office derived from idealized interpretations of the first "modern" president, Franklin Roosevelt. This state of affairs led scholars Sidney M. Milkis and Michael Nelson to lament that the academic community in presidency studies treats 1933 "as the year 1 A.D. of presidential history."[27] The largest selling and most influential presidency text in the history of the profession begins with the FDR years and makes only a single reference to George Washington.[28] Yet it is impossible to understand the nature of the office of the presidency—its powers and limits—without examining the nation's first president and the precedents he established. It is hoped that future generations of scholars will have a greater appreciation for the most important role that Washington played in establishing the presidency for all of his successors.

SIX

Foreign Policy and the First Commander in Chief

RYAN J. BARILLEAUX

One of the most unfortunate elements of the American character has been its ongoing attempt to escape history. On some occasions, this characteristic has been manifest simply as a studied indifference to history. More often, it has taken shape as a conviction that we Americans are exempt from the lessons of history. One thinks of Henry Ford's quintessentially American statement that "history is bunk."

Americans often assume that the present is so different from the past that there is little we can learn from such less-enlightened times. Why should anyone take instruction from dead white males such as George Washington? After all, he owned slaves and never shared his feelings with others. We may use the first president as an icon to mark mattress sales in February or lend his Christian name to a slick magazine of political journalism, but we avoid taking him seriously. But taking George Washington seriously is exactly what the nation needs to do. Almost half a century ago, Marcus Cunliffe argued that Americans misunderstood their first president because they saw only what he called the "Washington Monument."[1] Would that we still did that. Today, Washington is *persona non grata* in many history textbooks and he is treated as a forgettable relic of a less-enlightened past. Attempting to escape history, the nation forgets the legacy of the Father of his Country.

The Washington legacy is rich and diverse, but today perhaps its most important element may well be leadership in war and peace. George Washington supplied several important precedents on which recent presidents have based their power as commander in chief and chief diplomat, but it is clear that many—President Clinton in particular—have ignored the lessons that our first chief executive had to teach us.

In the sagacious words of Lighthorse Harry Lee, George Washington was "first in war, first in peace, and first in the hearts of his countrymen." As we shall see, successive presidents have relied upon his actions as the first to make war and strive for peace. What many of Washington's countrymen have tended to overlook is his wise counsel regarding how best to preserve peace and prepare for war. If today's officials and citizens had not tried to escape history, or if they had seen more than the iconic side of Washington, they might not have to experience yet another scramble to rebuild the nation's security structure because they undermanned and underfunded it.

FIRST IN WAR

When George Washington became president in 1789, he resumed the title that he had held during the War of American

Independence: commander in chief. As the commander of the Continental Army, Washington had been the servant of the Continental Congress. Would the new President, in his role as commander in chief, continue to be the agent of the legislature, or was this new presidential commandership something larger? And what of ending war? Would the power to end hostilities lay with the president or Congress? The answers came to depend on Washington's practice.

During the Constitutional Convention, the question of who had the responsibility to make war and peace was a matter hotly contested. For example, Pierce Butler suggested that the power to create war be vested with the president, which placed him in the minority.[2] James Madison believed that, in light of past abuses of the war power, the legislature should be the natural caretaker of the various instances of war and that if the executive was not involved there wouldn't be "much of a war."[3] But a motion to give Congress the power to declare peace itself was defeated by the Convention.[4] The Convention ultimately decided that Congress should have sole authority to declare war (an earlier draft of the document gave Congress the power to "make war") and approve treaties, but it made the president commander in chief of the armed forces and gave him important diplomatic powers as well.

As he assumed the presidency, George Washington was well placed to give actual shape to the war and peace powers of the new government. By his actions and decisions he established the precedents on which his successors would depend as they set about to preserve, protect, and defend the United States.

From the beginning of his tenure in office, George Washington made it clear that the president would be more than the military agent of Congress. As commander in chief, he bequeathed to his successors the legacy of executive leadership in military matters. This legacy has three main elements: active presidential control over the deployment of American military forces; selection and supervision of subordinate commanders, and leadership in recommending appropriate military policy to the legislature.

The President Shall Be Commander in Chief

Washington took an active role in directing the use of American forces. This ongoing control of forces clarified a point that would be vital to subsequent chief executives: the president would not only serve as commander in chief after a declaration of war—nor in more than a strictly ceremonial fashion—but would be supreme commander and take the initiative in defining American military policy. This engagement can be seen in the president's supervision of the American campaign against Indian tribes in the Northwest Territory and in his response to the Whiskey Rebellion.

First, the Washington administration confronted the problem of bringing security to western settlements by dealing with the Indian tribes on the American frontier. The First Congress placed responsibility for Indian affairs under the secretary of war—the various tribes would not be regarded as foreign nations or a domestic problem, but as a military and security concern. But President Washington did not leave westward military strategy and action to War Secretary Henry Knox alone. Rather, he took an active role in shaping and overseeing the policies that would bring the new American army into a five-year conflict with the Indians. He approved and monitored the plan of General Arthur St. Clair, governor of the Northwest Territory, to push back the Indians through skirmishing and ultimately through invasion. He stayed abreast of the progress of the conflict and the implementation of St. Clair's plan. And he ultimately replaced St. Clair with Anthony Wayne when he became convinced that the governor was not the commander to defeat the young nation's most immediate security threat.[5]

A second example of Washington's active control of America's military forces came in his response to the Whiskey Rebellion. When anti-tax resisters suppressed civil government in western Pennsylvania in 1794, the president responded carefully but decisively. With the bulk of his regular army engaged in General Wayne's campaign against the Indians in the Northwest, Washington exercised the authority granted him in Article II to call state militias into federal service. He eventually raised a force of fifteen thousand men, which he called, in a shrewd act of political labeling, "the Army of the Constitution."[6]

The Army of the Constitution was under the direct control of the president. He personally appointed its top three field officers, choosing governors for each of these posts to emphasize the principle of civilian leadership. He named Governor Henry Lee of Virginia as overall commander, but with the proviso that Lee would be in charge "if I do not go out myself."[7] Clearly, Washington was holding open the option to command in the field as well as from the rear. The second-in-command was Governor Thomas Mifflin of Pennsylvania, while the third-ranking post was given to Governor Richard Howell of New Jersey.

In October 1794, Washington arrived at Carlisle, Pennsylvania, to inspect the eastern wing of his Army of the Constitution and, finding the assembled troops far from being ready for a fight, set about issuing headquarters directives and orders aimed at whipping his troops into shape. Within a week, enough progress had been made toward military discipline that the president could proceed to Cumberland, where Henry Lee was already at work drilling the other wing in preparation for battle.[8]

Although he had retained the option of leading his troops into combat, Washington ultimately elected to send his army forward under Lee's command. By this point, in mid-October 1794, the Whiskey Rebellion had begun crumbling. With Lee in command, Washington was confident that the remaining military tasks would be handled effectively. The rebellion was soon over, and the commander in chief had set an important precedent regarding presidential control over military operations. He had demonstrated that the chief executive's authority was not just one of setting policy, but extended to conduct on the field of battle. A few decades later, during the Civil War, both Abraham Lincoln and Jefferson Davis would rely on Washington's precedent: each closely followed the conduct of military operations, and, on rare occasions, each would personally supervise troops in action. In 1862, each of the opposing American presidents acted as a military commander: Davis rallied disorganized Confederate forces at the first Battle of Bull Run; Lincoln directed an operation to seize Norfolk, Virginia, only to find that the city had been deserted by his enemy.

The President Shall Commission All the Officers

President Washington took a direct and specific interest in selecting and supervising his military commanders. As the Northwest Indian conflict and the Whiskey Rebellion illustrate, the president was attentive to the question of who would actually lead American forces.

When Arthur St. Clair demonstrated that he was not up to the job of dispatching the tribes in the Northwest Territory, Washington turned to Anthony Wayne. Washington's selection of General Wayne was somewhat controversial: the general had a reputation for erratic behavior and an explosive temper (he was "Mad" Anthony to his detractors). But the commander in chief had confidence in him and placed Wayne in command of the bulk of the nation's standing army, charged with the incomplete task of ending the Indian threat and opening the Northwest for more aggressive settlement by westward-moving Americans. In the end, Wayne vindicated the president's trust in him. His appointment also gave substance to presidential power over the assignment and dismissal of military commanders.

In the Whiskey Rebellion, the president further demonstrated the extent of his powers. He selected the senior commanders, combining in Governor Lee a man of military and political talent. He also held open the option that he might personally command the Army of the Constitution. Thus,

Washington made it clear that the commander in chief is not merely the symbolic leader of the nation's forces, as is the British monarch, but is supreme commander in fact.

The President Shall Take Such Measures as He Shall Judge Necessary and Expedient

Finally, as commander in chief and chief executive, President Washington also took the initiative in recommending to Congress legislation that would promote American security. What Washington wanted Congress to establish was a standing army that would be backed by a well-trained and federally controlled militia. This sort of defensive establishment would, he believed, provide the nation with a permanent professional force to maintain fortifications, provide ongoing defense, and serve as the nucleus of an enlarged citizen army that could be mobilized in emergencies. Over the course of his years in office, and even as he anticipated retirement, President Washington admonished Congress to give the nation the sort of defensive establishment that he judged "necessary and expedient."

In his First Annual Message to Congress, Washington enjoined the legislature to give attention to the need for a military establishment. In successive annual messages, defense remained an important theme. The president called for a national military academy, expenditures to maintain a sufficient standing army, and a review of military fortifications to determine whether enhancements were in order. Each of these messages included language hinting at—or openly advocating—the creation of an adequate military force. In his Sixth Annual Message (November 19, 1794), which contained a lengthy report on the resolution of the Whiskey Rebellion, the president used the opportunity to again remind Congress of the nation's defensive needs:

> The devising and establishing of a well regulated militia would be a genuine source of legislative honor and a perfect title to public gratitude. I therefore entertain a hope that the present session will not pass without carrying to its full energy the power of organizing, arming, and disciplining the militia, and thus providing, in the language of the Constitution, for calling them forth to execute the laws of the Union, suppress insurrections, and repel invasions.

Nor did his impending retirement discourage the president from recommending to Congress defensive legislation that he thought necessary. As always, however, he made such a proposal in general terms: "Taking care always to keep ourselves by suitable establishments on a respectable defensive posture...." While, in his Farewell Address, Washington noted that an overly large military establishment was unwise, he did not appear to worry that there was much danger that Congress would create too large a standing force. Since he had to repeat each year his admonition to Congress to provide "suitable establishments" for defense, he probably did not expect there to be much of a chance that the legislature would invest too much money in the military.

Future presidents relied on all of Washington's precedents as commander in chief. Abraham Lincoln labored unceasingly to find a general who would aggressively take on Confederate forces, and he often commented on military planning to his commanders; he even borrowed books from the Library of Congress to study the strategy and tactics of warfare. Franklin Roosevelt selected Dwight Eisenhower to be Supreme Commander in Europe, while Harry Truman reminded Douglas MacArthur of the president's constitutional role by dismissing the illustrious general. Lyndon Johnson selected bombing targets in Vietnam, while George Bush reached past more senior officers to appoint Colin Powell to the post of chairman of the Joint Chiefs of Staff. In this respect, American chief executives have all followed in the footsteps of the original president. Washington's conduct in the role of commander in chief established a foundation for assertive presidential military leadership that his successors and the nation would need. As we shall see, however, not all of Washington's successors would heed his advice on military preparedness.

FIRST IN PEACE

Although the Constitutional Convention gave far less attention to making peace than it did to making war, George Washington's presidency would demonstrate that the peace powers of the chief executive would be as important as its war powers. Indeed, the true Washington legacy in statecraft has been that the president can employ an array of instruments and actions—or inactions— in promoting overall national security goals. When the chief executive threatens to use force against an adversary, or concludes that restraint is the better course, then he is standing on the foundation laid by America's first president.

The president's powers to make peace flow from specific grants in Article II and some of the same ambiguous clauses in the

Constitution that give the chief executive expansive war powers. If Congress declares war and the commander in chief makes war, then who decides to avoid violent conflict or terminate military action? This question came to the fore in 1793, when President Washington faced the outbreak of war between Britain and France.

The Neutrality Proclamation

France looked to the United States to support its cause against colonial powers such as England, Austria, and Prussia. The United States had a defensive treaty with Paris, but the French government believed that the Americans would assist them. President Washington believed that the worst thing that could happen to his young Republic would be for it to be dragged into a European war for which it was unprepared. Therefore, he issued the Neutrality Proclamation, thus setting American policy by fiat and preempting any attempts to place the United States on a path toward military support of one side or the other.

While the Proclamation was a controversial, unilateral action by Washington, it was done not as a seizure of presidential power, but rather as a consistent effort by Washington to keep the fledgling United States out of the historical disputes of Europe. The Neutrality Proclamation came in response to Washington's rejection of the efforts by France's Citizen Genet to draw the United States into a war on the side of France against Great Britain.[9] Although public opinion favored the French, Washington's Proclamation received support in Congress, which enshrined its provisions in the Neutrality Act of 1794.

Although Congress approved of the Proclamation, there were

those within the Washington administration who believed the
president's actions were improper. Secretary of State Thomas
Jefferson argued that since "Congress had the sole authority to
declare war, the president lacked the authority to decide *unilaterally* that the nation would not fight a war."[10] As was often the case
in that first administration, Jefferson's argument was steadfastly
opposed by Secretary of the Treasury Alexander Hamilton.

The Pacificus-Helvidius Debate

Hamilton touched off a debate over executive power in a series of
essays that appeared under the *nom de plume* "Pacificus." To offset
Hamilton's argument, Jefferson asked his friend James Madison
to argue against the expansive nature of executive authority being
championed by Hamilton. Jefferson did not wish to argue the
case in public, although he was perfectly capable of doing so,
noting that to attack Hamilton publicly would not be proper for
a member of Washington's cabinet.

Hamilton's argument involved a broad interpretation of the
president's executive power and a broad interpretation of his capacity as chief executive. He argued that the president was given
expansive "inherent powers" that allowed him to be active in those
gray areas not addressed by the Constitution. While Congress was
given the power to declare war, the power to issue proclamations
that avoided war was clearly a presidential power, even if it "interfered with the free exercise of Congress's power to declare war."[11]
Hamilton thus asserted that in those areas in which the
Constitution is not specific or clear, the president has the authority
to develop very broad powers. In fact, he conceded that this partic-

ular power is probably a concurrent power, shared by the president and the Congress, and thus was an "unavoidable conflict."

Madison's response, written under the pseudonym of "Helvidius," was framed in the language of a strict constructionist. It was also quite straightforward: the president's power was to execute laws that were passed by Congress and signed by him. Madison argued: "All his acts, therefore, properly executive, must presuppose the existence of the laws to be executed."[12] This interpretation of presidential power is a very restrictive one that reduces the office of president to one of executing faithfully all "laws, treaties, and declarations" that pass congressional muster.

The Pacificus-Helvidius debate highlighted the ambiguities of presidential power. While Hamilton's arguments were never entirely accepted, they did provide future presidents with a framework through which to expand presidential power. Washington's conduct in office tacked closer to Hamilton's interpretation of the executive than to Madison's more limiting views.

The U.S. Supreme Court was also divided during this period on the question of the president's power to act in minimizing hostilities without a declaration of war from Congress, including in defending U.S. interests up to the point of war. In *Bas v. Tingy*,[13] the Court recognized that not all wars would be easy to identify. The Court then proceeded to make the distinction between "perfect war" and "imperfect" war. The case at hand involved the seizure of an American vessel and cargo that was "recaptured" from the French. While Congress had not declared war against France, the Court recognized that the initial seizure of the American vessel by France was a hostile act "amounting to war." The Court thus recognized the principle of "an undeclared war." And it was the president as commander in chief who was responsible for the successful negotiation of this undeclared war. This opinion is significant not so much because it is a statement in favor of broad presidential war powers, but because it appears to be a general acceptance by the Court and the Congress that the president is responsible for seeking an end to hostilities, declared or undeclared—in essence, to keeping the peace.

The Other Side of War

In the same cases in which President Washington demonstrated the breadth of his war powers—the Indian conflict and the Whiskey Rebellion—he also showed how the chief executive could act on the other side of war. In each case, Washington attempted to negotiate peace before he resorted to force. Before he authorized Governor St. Clair to launch offensive operations in the Northwest Territory, the president had St. Clair try to broker a peace with the tribes. Likewise, before he dispatched the Army of the Constitution into western Pennsylvania to confront the anti-tax rebels, the president named three commissioners to meet with the rebels in an effort to resolve the conflict without force. Acting on his own authority, Washington appointed Attorney General William Bradford, Senator James Ross of Pennsylvania, and Justice Jasper Yates of the Pennsylvania Supreme Court to offer amnesty to any whiskey rebels who agreed to give up their fight and accept the lawfulness of the hated whiskey tax.[14] It was only after his peaceful overtures failed that the president drew the sword of the United States.

Allied with the president's power to negotiate treaties, which he used to conclude agreements with Indian tribes and the Jay Treaty with Great Britain, Washington employed presidential peace powers to frame a foreign policy for the young American republic. Wielding both the olive branch and the sword, he established an institutional legacy of presidential autonomy and leadership in foreign and defense matters.

Washington's successors would stand on the first president's foundation in exercising power on both sides of war. While several chief executives, including James Polk, Harry Truman, John Kennedy, Ronald Reagan, and George Bush, would initiate military actions on their own, others exercised presidential autonomy to forestall or avoid armed conflict. Grover Cleveland resisted congressional pressure to begin a war with Spain, going so far as to declare that he would not send American troops into such a conflict even if Congress were to declare war against that nation. Likewise, William McKinley resisted calls for war with Spain even after the sinking of the *Maine*, and did not acquiesce to a fight until 1898. In 1956, President Eisenhower proclaimed that the United States would not support Britain, France, and Israel in their attempt to reverse Egypt's nationalization of the Suez Canal, thus in one move setting American policy and effectively halting the move to intervene against Egypt's plans. Of course, presidents have also suspended and terminated wars, as they did in Korea, Grenada, Panama, Cambodia, and successive bombing pauses in Vietnam. In the Persian Gulf War, President Bush unilaterally decided the day and the hour for the termination of offensive operations against the forces of Iraq.[15]

FIRST IN THE HEARTS OF HIS COUNTRYMEN?

Presidents have been eager to employ Washington's precedents in exercising power, but Americans have not always been eager to recall or to heed his advice to them. Even in his own time, Washington's calls for a credible defense establishment often went unheeded; in later decades, successive administrations and Congresses would often skimp on defense in the name of economy.

Sentiments on a Peace Establishment

George Washington's counsel to the nation on how best to preserve peace and prepare for war was consistent and often repeated. It was followed sporadically in his own time and occasionally in later times, but the United States would not be as constant in following the first president's advice as he was in giving it.

Washington's military recommendations to the government began even before he became president; indeed, they began even before there was a Constitution. On May 2, 1783, in response to a request from Alexander Hamilton, then a member of the Continental Congress, the commander in chief of the still operative Continental Army wrote out his recommendations for a defensive structure for the newly independent United States. His recommendations, which he entitled "Sentiments on a Peace Establishment,"[16] sketched the outlines of an approach to which he would remain true for the rest of his career.

Washington provided Congress with an analysis of the security situation of the United States. While shielded from Europe by the Atlantic Ocean, the United States still faced potential military threats from British forces in Canada, the Spanish in Florida,

Indians in the Northwest Territory, and a long coastline. He asserted that physical security was a high priority, but that a military establishment would also be necessary to protect commerce and trade and to help open the territories in the west. In short, Washington concluded that a permanent military structure was needed as badly in peacetime as in time of war.[17]

He recommended five broad measures to create his "Peace Establishment." First, the United States needed a standing army, a proposal that struck some republicans as inimical to their liberty. Washington acknowledged that too powerful an army might threaten republican liberties, but that liberty itself needed defending. This army would be responsible for establishing and maintaining fortifications on the frontiers of the United States. Second, he proposed a well-organized and uniformly disciplined militia in each state, to provide a second line of defense behind the standing army. Third, stocks of weapons and ammunition should be gathered and stored in convenient places, so they could be used in time of necessity. Fourth, one or more military academies ought to be established to train future leaders of the armed forces. Finally, the United States needed a navy and a coastal defense system.[18]

Washington would repeat some or all of these recommendations in his years as president. At times, he would be frustrated by the unwillingness of Congress to act on his advice, but he held fast to these ideas whether they were politically popular or not.

The Farewell Address

In the last year of his presidency, Washington gave his fellow citizens a parting statement that provided a summary of his views on the principles of wise public policy. Not surprisingly, his counsel gave extended attention to matters of America's relations with the outside world and its defense and security.

The principles that Washington recommended to the nation were consistent with those he had both preached and practiced during his two terms in office. He admonished the United States: "Observe good faith and justice toward all nations. Cultivate peace and harmony with all." He repeated and reemphasized the policy that he had declared to be the American position two years earlier, but framed it as a principle to guide policy makers rather than as an absolute rule of governance.

Within the same discussion where he urges a continuation of neutrality, President Washington also recognizes that there will be occasions when the United States will find itself temporarily in conflict with other nations, or acting in support of another nation; and he advises that participation in such alignments, for or against a state, ought to be temporary and undertaken according to a sense of the interests of the United States. Washington did not counsel absolute neutrality of the sort that Switzerland has practiced for so long; rather, his advice is that the nation ought to remain aloof from alignments, alliances, and conflicts that do not affect its real interests.

To that extent, the advice of the Farewell Address is reminiscent of the maxim of British foreign policy; that Britain has no permanent friends, only permanent interests. Eschewing a foreign policy of favoritism toward one nation or another, as Jefferson urged upon the president at the outset of the Anglo-French conflict that stimulated the Neutrality Proclamation,

Washington prescribed neutrality as the course most likely to serve the long-run interests of the United States.

Of course, he noted that even a policy of neutrality would not work without a concomitant commitment to national security. "Taking care always to keep ourselves by suitable establishments on a respectable defensive posture, we may safely trust to temporary alliances for extraordinary emergencies." Given Washington's consistent and oft-repeated views on what a "respectable defensive posture" ought to be, the message of the Farewell Address is one of seeking national security through deterrence and a foreign policy that avoids needlessly provoking other nations.

Washington's Forgotten Maxim

As for the legacy of George Washington's advice, Americans have frequently treated it as Hamlet said the Danes treated the custom of wassail: "More honor'd in the breach than in the observance" (*Hamlet*, act I, scene IV). The nation has experienced successive periods of economizing on defense, and then had to make up for it by a rapid rearmament in the face of actual or impending war. Perhaps the problem is that Americans have paid more attention to the monumental Washington than to the statesman who had real political and military experience.

President Theodore Roosevelt, a devoted student of Washington the statesman, held that there was much wisdom in his original predecessor's principles of statecraft: "Among Washington's maxims which he bequeathed to his countrymen were the two following: 'Observe good faith and justice toward all nations,' and 'To be prepared for war is the most effective means to promote peace.' These two principles taken together should form the basis of our whole foreign policy."[19] An advocate of national military preparedness who practiced peacemaking as well as warmaking during his career, Roosevelt proclaimed at several places in his writings and speeches the need to follow the counsel of George Washington.

Roosevelt insisted that Washington's preparedness maxim had obvious consequences for national policy. First, the nation needed a strong military force. This force would be composed of a standing army and a broad-based national militia. As Roosevelt put it in an essay on Washington and Lincoln, "One of Washington's earliest acts as President was to submit to Congress a plan for universal obligatory military training and service."[20] Second, the nation needed a strong navy. Third, the nation needed leaders who understood that just talking about peace was not an effective way to preserve peace.

Unfortunately, according to Roosevelt, Washington's principle that preparedness helps to prevent war has been his "forgotten maxim."[21] While serving as assistant secretary of the navy, in 1897, he told the Naval War College:

> We pay to this maxim lip loyalty we so often pay to Washington's words; but it has never sunk deep into our hearts. Indeed of late years many persons have refused it even the poor tribute of lip loyalty, and prate about the iniquity of war as if somehow that was a justification for refusing to take the steps which can alone in the long run prevent war or avert the dreadful disasters it brings in its train.[22]

Too often, he maintained, critics of military preparedness had undermined the real security of the nation by weakening national defense in the name of peace or economy. Roosevelt, like Washington before him, however, argued that the repeated lesson of history is that constant attentiveness to preparedness resulted in more economy and greater peace than the rapid rearmament that necessarily occurs when an underprepared nation faces the threat of war.

From the perspective of Roosevelt's time, we see that at the dawn of this century America continued to resist the counsel that Washington had given. Here, at the dawn of the twenty-first century, it is obvious that many policy makers continue to ignore the wisdom of Washington and Roosevelt. A good example is Bill Clinton, whose defense policies left the nation's military forces ill-prepared to protect American security and carry out the decisions of the government. In the spring of 1999, news reports revealed that the U. S. Air Force had almost exhausted its supply of cruise missiles, the long-range precision weapons that have been used so effectively in the Persian Gulf War and subsequent conflicts to spare soldiers' lives while attacking enemy targets. At the same time, the Defense Department also admitted that the U. S. Army and U. S. Navy faced serious manpower shortages, as well as inadequate supplies of ammunition and spare parts for weapons and vehicles. In addition, the Clinton administration worked diligently to thwart attempts to develop a ballistic missile defense for the United States (although it protested otherwise) and to make further cuts in the size and strength of the armed forces. The administration also jeopardized national security by allowing Chinese intelligence operatives to penetrate the government's advanced weapons research facilities.

REVIVING THE WASHINGTON LEGACY

Our age is one that has nearly forgotten George Washington. It is certainly the age that has come closest to forgetting his maxims of statecraft. The task for America in the twenty-first century must be to reclaim the Washington legacy.

Interestingly, Teddy Roosevelt made an observation about Washington and Lincoln and what made them great. Aside from particular actions, policies, or speeches, Roosevelt held that one core truth that made Washington great was that he "never spoke a word which he did not make good by an act, and always acted with serene, far-sighted wisdom and entire fearlessness...."[23] What made these great presidents so great was that they spoke their convictions and then had the courage to stand by those convictions. They did not pay "lip loyalty"—as Roosevelt called it— to certain virtues and then betray those virtues with contrary decisions or hidden vices. They did not proclaim one policy and then pursue another. They did not speak of peace and freedom, but undermine both by embarking on policies that left the nation ill-prepared to defend either.

By forgetting what Washington preached and practiced, our nation has lost its grip on the real legacy of George Washington. First, we turned him into an iconic figure, whose face adorned our currency and symbols of national unity. This enshrined the man as a national hero, but often drained the Washington legacy of any substance. Washington came to represent a vague sort of honesty and patriotism and little more. More recently, we have moved to a second phase in forgetting Washington's legacy: we have turned him into a comic figure. His visage is now plastered on advertisements for furniture and clothing sales or used to hawk the most trivial of consumer goods. Politically correct school curricula and textbooks have made him a minor—or even regrettable—figure in American history; Washington is presented as the militaristic, slaveholding, patrician landowner who was selected by the oligarchs of his day to protect their wealth and social order by lending his name and reputation to the new constitutional order that was implemented to forestall any attempts to create a democratic political order in early America.

This process of transformation has all but ensured that Washington will not be taken seriously and that his legacy will be lost. The road to recovery lies in confronting these developments directly. First, Americans need to be reintroduced to Washington the statesman. He was more than a successful general; he was a political leader who "never spoke a word he did not make good by an act." He was not a great communicator or expert at town meetings and photo opportunities, but he was a man who did his best to promote the public interest as he understood it. Second, Americans need to be introduced to Washington the political thinker. Few people today have read or heard a word that he wrote or spoke; he tends to be a silent figure in our history and political culture. But as those few of us who have paid attention know, Washington was a skillful and at times eloquent writer, whose addresses, messages, reports, and correspondence contain much wisdom.

In this review of Washington's legacy for war and peace, we have seen but a fragment of Washington's wisdom. He did not produce a systematic exposition of political philosophy, but the written record he left behind is a trove of observations and counsel from a life spent in action. His ideas and his example are accessible to any person who is interested in studying them and would provide grand counsel to our magistrates and our fellow citizens.

SEVEN

The Symbolic Dimensions of the First Presidency

GARY L. GREGG II

T he creation, manipulation, and recognition of symbols has
been central to human history and seems somehow essential
to the formation of human community. Coats of arms have helped
kin recognize each other as part of a unity transcending their families and themselves. Logos help consumers recognize a corporate
entity and carry meaning to those we come into contact with—
one might be accepted or not accepted in many subcommunities
based upon the corporate logos attached to our clothing or car.
Religious symbols of various sorts serve in every religion as
reminders of essential beliefs and connections to the transcendent. The human mind somehow seems to need the clarification,
compartmentalization, and simplification that symbolic representatives can provide. This is no less the case in politics as it is
in any other aspect of human life.

The institution of the monarchy and the person of the
monarch in a parliamentary democracy are symbolic entities representing the nation and the people. He or she "stands for" the

community as it exists in his or her own time and as it has existed previously. The institution and the person function as a symbolic "center" for a people and as a living embodiment of the nation. The Federal Farmer noted the importance of having such an individual standing as the symbolic representative for the internal cohesion and unity of any large group of people. "In every large collection of people," he said, "there must be a visible point serving as a common center in the government, toward which to draw their eyes and attachments."[1] The institution of the presidency and incumbent presidents serve this function in the American political system. As Attorney General Stanberry argued before the Supreme Court in the 1867 case of *Mississippi v. Johnson,* "He [the president] represents the majesty of the law and of the people as fully and as essentially, and with the same dignity, as does any absolute monarch or head of any independent government in the world."[2]

Whereas in many other modern nations the two roles of chief of government and chief of state are separated and distinct, such as in Great Britain where the queen provides symbolic representation and the prime minister provides executive power and legislative leadership, in the United States they are inescapably fused into one office. As designed, the president would be an executive, but his office would also be an office of ceremony and symbolism. It was this understanding that inspired men like John Adams and Alexander Hamilton to urge that the trappings of royalty be placed in the office. "Take away thrones and crowns from among men, and there will be an end of all dominion and justice," John Adams wrote.[3] The Senate, in fact, originally wished to refer to the president as "His Highness the President of the United States, and Protector of the Rights of the Same," but it eventually compromised with the House to settle on the simple but respectful "Mr. President."

Forrest McDonald has written that the presidency has been in decline since the moment George Washington left office. In no other aspect of the presidency is this more true than at the level of political symbolism and republican ceremony. It was Washington's features, his character, his reputation, his stature, and his mode of proceeding that infused the office and the Republic itself with the dignity and majesty they had not yet earned by age. He was tall and well-built. He moved with a grace and command garnered from dance lessons and practice, and considerable time on horseback. His movements, his very body, spoke volumes about the man and what was appropriate for his station, even when he spoke less eloquently or not at all. Jefferson claimed him to be "the best horseman of his age, and the most graceful figure that could be seen on horseback."[4] His dress was always proper and appropriate for his station. "His demeanor at all times composed and dignified. His movements and gestures graceful, his walk majestic...."[5] Benjamin Rush, who would later become somewhat of a critic, wrote that "if you do not know General Washington's person, perhaps you will be pleased to hear, that he has so much martial dignity in his deportment, that you would distinguish him to be a General and a Soldier, from among the thousand people: there is not a king in Europe but would look like a valet de chambre by his side."[6] Washington seemed to understand well that sight is the king of the senses.

Even before he would take an action as president, his physicality
and reputation stood him apart from nearly any other man of his
time.

PRESIDENTIAL PRECEDENT
AND SYMBOLIC POLITICS

It is in the nature of the office that virtually all presidents establish some degree of precedents that set a tone for their activity as
well as those of future magistrates. It is through the trial and
error of precedents that we learn and, thereby, can prosper. An
institution without it is like a being without memory, constantly
revisiting the most routine questions of propriety and utility and
never finally establishing the order necessary for growth.

Article II of the Constitution declares that "The executive
Power shall be vested in a President of the United States of
America." These few simple words and the ones that follow in
Article II establish only the most rudimentary outlines of the
office of the American presidency. As Ralph Ketcham has so aptly
put it, Washington was entrusted with an office where, "far from
everything being settled, virtually nothing was."[7] Was the office
to be simply one of execution? Was it to be a ceremonial office?
What was to be the officeholder's relationship to the rest of government? Was he a facilitator? A leader? A check, merely? What
would be the proper address and etiquette of the office? What
would all the various powers and roles mean in practice? For
instance, as commander in chief, would he be the actual military
commander of the army and the navy?

Where the Constitutional Convention had taken pains to

outline the powers and limits of the legislative branch, they had left the presidency to "the live touch of history"[8] and hence to the able hands of George Washington. The questions, the challenges, the opportunities, and the dangers were almost endless. At any time, improper precedent could have collapsed the office into irrelevancy or elevated it to nearly despotic heights of authority. Because he was the first president, and to the degree the office is still relatively the same one he held two centuries ago, no president can match Washington as a setter of precedent.

Washington was well cognizant of the importance of the situation that fortune had placed about him and the awesome responsibility that weighed upon his shoulders. In May 1789, he would write to James Madison, "As the first in everything, in our situation will serve to establish a Precedent, it is devoutly wished on my part, that these precedents may be fixed on true principles."[9] In striving to enact the nascent office upon "fixed and true principles," Washington set the necessary precedent for the executive to be a republican institution—something largely unprecedented in human history.

Most presidents contribute some precedents to the office, be they laudatory or signposts of warning to future office holders. Many of these are small and become routine to the degree that their origins and original meaning have been largely lost to all but the most specialized scholars or trivialists. But others are so important that the principal himself becomes a symbol, the embodiment, of the precedent set. This is the case with Washington. In doing the most unnatural of acts, ceding power peacefully, even with relief and reverent joy, he became the

symbol of republican restraint. In retiring to Mount Vernon after
his second term, he became the living symbol of the two-term
president, a cultural expectation so powerfully set that no president dared to challenge it for more than 130 years. In the end,
because of who he was, when he lived, and how he carried himself in and out of office, he largely became the face of the presidency itself. We celebrated his birthday; his portrait hung in
every classroom in the land; the story of his life and his words
were prominently found in textbooks for young people; his likeness was featured on coins and bills. He became an essential part
of our national self-understanding and the major figure of our
national lore.

LEVELS OF PRESIDENTIAL SYMBOLISM

All presidents serve as symbols in the American political system
and in our national culture. They may be personal symbols in the
way Eisenhower was considered to be a father figure. They serve
as cognitive aides helping citizens come to grips with the com-
plexities of modern government. As the only nationally elected
officials, they stand as symbolic representatives of the American
people—allowing for their transcendence from pluralism, diversity, and parochial concerns to a more truly national identity; a
"cosmion," to borrow Eric Voegelin's word. On the other hand,
presidents also tend to be symbols of faction, the embodiment of
their particular political party. They serve as shorthand guides to
our American history—"Jacksonian Democracy," "Camelot," and
"The Reagan-Bush Years"—and also serve as the one-man distil-
lation of the nation to foreign observers.[10]

As president, George Washington served as a powerful symbol in the nascent Republic. It is impossible, however, to separate Washington's career into neat and self-contained units to fit our analysis here. The symbolic dimensions of the Washington presidency were largely sewn during his earlier years as soldier, farmer, and political leader. Unlike a man who is made by the office he holds, Washington had long before built a reputation of historic importance both in North America and in Europe. He didn't need the office; the office needed him.

One could list dozens of ways in which the Washington presidency was symbolically important to the Republic and ways in which Washington himself has served as a powerfully edifying symbol through the ages. This essay will offer some reflections on five symbolically important aspects of Washington and his presidency. He was (1) a symbol of national unity, (2) a symbol of the rule of law and the constitutional order, (3) a symbol of virtue and morality, (4) a symbol of what it is to be "presidential," and (5) a symbol of America's religious self-understanding.

THE SYMBOL OF NATIONAL UNITY

Presidents tend to unite and presidents tend to divide, but the institution of the presidency is designed as an inherently unifying force in American politics. A singular office filled by a figure that is elected, at least de facto if not fully by design, by a national majority comprised of multiple member bodies elected from regional units that make up the federal government, the presidency is unique in its place in American public life. But, with the rise of political parties, the occupants of the office often are understood more as partisans than unifying symbols. They have been known as Federalists and Republicans, Democrats and Whigs. A powerfully unifying force that with time would come to be identified with the Federalist party, George Washington was no exception to this paradox of the presidency. But, at least until well into his tenure, Washington was the center pole around which the nation formed and grew.

The very force of Washington's hold on the imagination of the American people made him a vital symbol that could transcend boundaries of class, religion, and region. America was a young nation, her only ancient ties being rooted across two divides—the Atlantic Ocean and a violent War of Independence. Abstractions will not do in the place of life-giving tradition. Mass democratic politics cannot thrive without symbols that transcend the ballot box. The former colonies now uniting had neither ancient tradition nor adequate transcendent symbolism to unite a nation. Into this void stepped a victorious military officer of uncommon virtues and nearly unblemished reputation. In many ways, some too intricate to attempt to untangle, the existence of George Washington made the Constitution and the subsequent Union possible. As Forrest McDonald has summarized it,

> As a man idolized by the people—almost all the people, whatever their station in life—he could make it possible for them to indulge their habitual adulation of a monarch without reneging on their commitment to republicanism. As a symbol of the Union, he could stimulate, at least for a time, the emotional attachment to the Nation that normally requires centuries in the building.[11]

For a people without a long and ready history, Washington was, in the newly created office of president, the republican substitute for an American monarch. Even during the Revolution, Washington had come to be referred to as the Father of his Country. George III, "the Father of his People," had been replaced in the hearts of English North Americans by George Washington "the Father of his Country." The importance of such symbolism should not lightly be dismissed. Later, with victory over Great Britain, and his role in drafting and then securing the passage of the Constitution, his prestige was refreshed and solidified.

His experience of great frustration with strong and independent states during the Revolution made Washington more of a thoroughgoing nationalist than he had been previously.[12] The weaknesses of the Articles of Confederation only served to strengthen this conviction. His ideas, but what is more, his very existence as the trusted national presence and the embodiment of American republicanism, did much to make a stronger union possible.

Though it is seldom remembered and even less often remarked upon, a unified executive power such as the American presidency was not a foregone conclusion at the Constitutional Convention. Many of the states had weak executives or executive councils, and there was no separate executive force at all under the Articles of Confederation. Various alternative schemes to form the executive power of the new government were discussed by the delegates in Philadelphia. Some, such as North Carolina's Hugh Williamson and Virginia's George Mason, argued on behalf of a plural executive. Under such a scheme, the various members making up the executive would be drawn from the various regions of the Union as a way to insure a proper balance between the rival and competing sectional interests.[13] Any such attempt to weaken the executive force, both in terms of political power and in terms of unifying symbolism, would have spelled disaster for the project of union. To a significant degree it was George Washington and certain delegates, those who understood they were creating an office for which he would be the first occupant, that made the unified presidency possible. To the degree that such a center of power and symbolic importance was essential to a more unified and invigorated union, Washington's place as the beloved heir apparent made union itself possible.

From being at the Constitutional Convention, lending his name in the ratification battles, and taking up the most prominent position in the new government, Washington, the symbol of the Revolution, fused with the nascent constitutional order, lending it his precious reputation and infusing it with legitimacy. Washington risked his precious reputation in order to make the experiment itself possible. Would a lesser man have done the same?

In 1789, Washington's trip from Mount Vernon to New York was more than a utilitarian need to get to the capitol to take office. Rather, it allowed people all along the route to join together—Virginians, Pennsylvanians, New Yorkers—in a common national ceremony to celebrate the man, their new president, and the new political order that he was to represent. Six years before, Washington had taken a similar trip, though this one in the opposite direction and to resign his power rather than take it up. It had caused similar spontaneous celebrations in large and small towns from New Jersey to Annapolis, Maryland. No other American enjoyed a similar reservoir of popular adulation. And, it should be recalled, no other president has ever come close to the unanimous selection of the electoral college that took Washington again from his vineyards to public business. In many ways, he was a unifying force.

Once in office, his actions and stature were used to solidify the Union and continue to legitimate the constitutional order. After visiting New England in 1789, he made sure to pay his respects to the southern states two years later. In fact, within a few years he traveled to every state in the Union, symbolizing their participation in the larger constitutional order. Representing a people of Protestant origins and convictions, he reached across the divide of religious sentiment to Roman Catholics and Jews. In August 1790, for instance, he would write to the Hebrew Congregation in Newport of the nation's "enlarged and liberal policy" of toleration. "[T]he Government of the United States, which gives to bigotry no factions, to persecution no assistance, requires only that they who live under its protection should demean themselves as good citizens in giving it on all occasions their effectual support."[14] With such efforts, Washington took it upon himself to become the symbol of the new regime's placement of objective good conduct toward (and within) the community above religious sectarianism.

The increasing factionalization of politics that came with the split between Jeffersonians and Hamilton's Federalists troubled Washington tremendously. He could have been swept into the ideological currents many times, but he took pains to avoid such partisan strife as long as he could and made attempts to avoid opening faults when possible. During the Whiskey Rebellion in 1794, for instance, he insisted that the laws would be enforced and called the militia into service to ensure that they would. Then in 1795, the President extended mercy nearly to all the captured insurgents by issuing them a presidential pardon. Order was restored, but the rebels and their supporters were not permanently alienated from the national consensus, which would have been the bitter price of pure justice.

Institutionally, Washington similarly worked for unity and cooperation rather than confrontation and deadlock. He formed the officers of the executive branch into a cabinet that became a truly consultative body, with each official enjoying the privilege of a minister without portfolio, advising the president on any subject. Representing the various and growing factions of the new Republic, each would take part in discussions on all subjects. They would thereby have something invested in national policy. But Washington's quest for national unity and governmental harmony went further, as he attempted even to overcome the strict understandings of the separation of powers and checks and balances by bringing both the Court and the Senate into a consultative and cooperative relationship with the presidency.[15] Of course, as the authors of *The Federalist* might have predicted because of the institutional designs of the Constitution, these attempts did not bear fruit. What is important to note, however, is Washington's continuous care to hold the Union together through cooperation and common values. His reputation, his place, and his words made him the very embodiment of the new nation.

Notwithstanding this discussion of Washington's care for the unity of the nation and his embodiment of a stronger, more vital Union, one should not be led to take this too far. In his effort to strengthen the central government, he was symbolically creating neither a wholly consolidated nor a weak confederation. Rather, like his own properly balanced character, he was enacting a balanced constitutional system—a central government at once strong and vigorous in its sphere, yet controlled and limited. Washington was providing for the leadership the nation needed under prevailing circumstances. Confronting an unbalanced political system with a too-weak center, he had to use his powers and symbolic place to pull toward national unity in the same way that later presidents confronting an overly centralized and unbalanced system should employ their symbolic powers to support the forces of decentralization. Coming from a weak confederation of independent states, Washington understood the necessity of building stronger national ties to counterbalance the already strong loyalty of the people to their various states. It was what the times demanded of him. However, he was not a zealot of unified government wishing to rip the states up by the roots and replant them in an undifferentiated bed of peat. During the Revolution, he had fought against centralized control from London; and, if he would have lived during a time of overbearing central authority in America, he no doubt would have fought against it, too. Working for a government both energetic enough and properly controlled, he sought the proper balance.

In 1832, a debate took place on whether to move Washington's body from Mount Vernon, across the Potomac River, to Washington, D. C., where it would be enshrined in a national monument. The debate largely pitted northerners, who wanted to move the body, against southerners who did not. In the three decades since he left office, the nation had grown and prospered, and the central government had increased greatly in power. In the end, Washington's body stayed entombed at his farm. Even in death, he continued to symbolize the properly balanced union. During his life, he had worked to strengthen the federal government in a decentralized situation; however, by 1832, the situation had changed. The Union had been significantly strengthened and now it was time to balance the other way—toward the states and decentralization. The body of the military hero of the Revolution, the president of the Constitutional Convention, the first president, and the Father of his Country would continue to represent the virtues of home, community, and private life by lying in the hillside near the cultivated fields of his farm in the state of Virginia.

THE SYMBOL OF THE RULE OF
LAW AND THE CONSTITUTIONAL ORDER

George Washington was a monarchical symbol of republicanism. He acted with the dignity and understanding of a king, yet with the restraint required of officials in a representative form of government. The American people had just been through a failed attempt at national constitution making in the form of the Articles of Confederation and would not lightly embrace a new scheme for governing the Union. And yet the stakes were higher for the Constitution—the plan would more tightly bring semi-autonomous states into an alliance and forge a more powerful central government. Until the Constitution could prove itself and prove itself worthy of being loved, an alternative symbol of republican government would be necessary. George Washington played this role for the early American Republic.

Until the Constitution would prove worthy of standing alone at the center, Washington would serve as the unifying symbol of the Republic; but, he also would conduct himself in such as way as to come to embody the essence of republicanism and the rule of law—accountability, civilian control of the military, and self-restraint. As in most of his other roles as president, the seeds were sown long before he assumed the office. He was, after all, America's Cincinnatus—the military hero who renounced power to return to family and farm.

George Washington brought a legendary self-discipline and ability to resist the temptations of power to the presidency. One of his first acts as president-elect, in fact, was to refuse to act, out of a concern for observing propriety and proper constitutional procedures. Everyone knew in December 1788 that the presidential electors had met in their states, as required by the Constitution, and had unanimously cast their ballots for Washington to be the first president. Most men would have set out immediately to New York, which was the temporary capital, to set up government and to assume the presidency. Washington did not. He refused to leave Mount Vernon until after Congress had counted the votes, as required in the Constitution, and had notified him of his election. Congress being slow to obtain a quorum, Washington's inauguration was delayed two months beyond when it was to take place. Demonstrating further the power of the rule of law, without a care for his own lack of cash resources, he insisted that his pay be docked for those two months not in service.

Washington also came to the presidency having proven time and again his understanding of the importance of civilian control of the military and hence the rule of law and not of men. His record of resigning his power voluntarily has become legendary, as it was, historically speaking, of legendary importance. How many conquering generals, having suffered considerable physical and financial hardships, have laid down their swords before a legislative chamber and resigned themselves to the toil of their own vineyards? When he could have exercised power without authority, he did not; when he could have kept power beyond its use for the nation, he sheathed his sword. The Republic was more important than the man; the common good, the trump of private concern.

Although Washington's public resignation of power is well known, other important incidents are not. Shortly after independence had been declared, Admiral Richard Howe sent emissaries to Washington with hints of a peace offer. His sense of protocol was so strong that he refused them twice because they addressed him with an improper title. On their first attempt, Howe's letter was addressed to "George Washington, Esq." After it was refused, Howe added "&ca. &ca," hoping, it would seem, to appeal to Washington's vanity. He again refused, until they addressed him properly as "His Excellency, General Washington." In our age of informality, the nuanced importance of these various titles would be lost, but they were not on Washington. Only in the last form of his address, in referring to him as *General* Washington, was he understood in his proper role—as a military officer commissioned by the civilian authority of an independent nation. His power was constitutional, not personal. The Continental Congress endorsed his conduct and lauded his acting "with dignity becoming his station." It was a symbolic act, but it held great import.[16]

One could mention Washington's unfailing determination to hand over to civil authorities every single one of his men, both soldiers as well as officers, accused of violating the rights of citizens. Many of the charges had no merit, but Washington understood that setting the proper precedent for the rule of law was more important than his own command or that absolute justice be meted out. Like the occasional "dictators" of the Roman Republic, who were empowered during times of military emergency to save the republic, Washington was on several occasions entrusted with nearly dictatorial power by a civilian authority fleeing before the enemy force. In 1776 and again in 1777, Washington exercised his considerable powers to "direct all things relative...to the operations of the war"[17] with a republican restraint not always recognized in his Roman forebears and a fidelity to his ultimate role as a servant of the representatives of the people.

Coming to the presidency, his person was already invested with heavy symbolism representing the rule of law and republican restraint at using political and military power. Despite (perhaps because of) his dedication to a stronger central government, once in the presidency Washington acted with characteristic deportment and restraint. He denied his own power and that of the federal government on several occasions and demonstrated that even he, the Great Washington, the Father of his Country, was bound by the words and meaning of the people's higher law. The people, but also the government, would be ruled by law and not by the will of any one man.

In voluntarily leaving the presidency after two terms, George Washington reinforced and further solidified his reputation on this score and his symbolic importance to the American regime. At the inauguration of his successor, John Adams, Washington, the ex-president, elder statesman, hero of the Revolution, the man that was very much first in the hearts of his countrymen, very deliberately motioned the new vice president, Thomas Jefferson, to precede him off the dais. America was about constitutional procedures and not any cult of personality. From his early career to his fading days, George Washington, the greatest American of any age, was the living embodiment of the rule of law and invested the constitutional system with a reverence that lasts, in many quarters, into the present hour.

THE SYMBOL OF VIRTUE AND CONSTITUTIONAL MORALITY

Presidents are more than political representatives and holders of constitutional power. Their position at the center of the political system and life of the nation invests each of them with symbolic importance. The position of the office belies the modern construct of a wall between private character and public conduct. It has always been thus. To contemplate the importance of the symbolic dimensions of the presidency is to understand how futile and artificial it actually is to draw a hard line between private and public conduct. To argue that the private conduct of the president is not important, or that it is not a concern for the political system or the commonweal and its guardians, is to rob the presidency of its very essence and to leave in its place the shallow bureaucrat of the managerial age.

This is particularly so with the post-Watergate journalistic ethic of maximum exposure of the moral failures of public men. We now know that no private secrets are to be kept and all actions of the president must be done with the sobering realization that they will someday soon become public, with the potential of damaging the office and the country. This new situation makes the private conduct of officeholders that much more crucial and adds to the responsibility of public men to observe private virtues. That certain indiscretions may have been overlooked in previous years does not excuse them now. America has not yet learned this important lesson and neither have those who would excuse the sins of the hour by citing the indiscretions of yesterday.

To George Washington, no wall separating private and public conduct would have been contemplated. His public reputation was based, at least in part, on his reputation for honor and proper deportment in private. The private fed the public. Washington also knew from an early age that our public masks must be chosen well, for they have the power to mold our inner soul. Washington chose his public mask deliberately and well. The public fed the private.

Presidents represent the public morality, the public mind.

They are products of the political culture that speeds their ascension, but they also have the capacity to elevate or degrade that culture with their actions, their rhetoric, and their example. Is there any doubt that William Jefferson Clinton in some ways represented the logic of the spirit of the age or that he in so very many ways served to degrade the culture and undermine the constitutional morality that forms the foundations of the Republic? In important ways, George Washington was a symbol of the dominant political culture of his age. John Adams once remarked that Washington's virtues were America's and not vice versa. But Washington also well understood the awesome possibilities and responsibilities of popular leadership and undertook always to improve the better angels of our natures and to instruct our moral and political compasses. He symbolized the life of the good man and also set solid precedence for being the good citizen. Of course, as the written Constitution relies upon an unwritten constitution of the culture, clear and complete demarcations between the two would be fatuous.

Washington had an unparalleled reputation for virtue and worried about the public's own stock long before he became president. His conduct taught lessons as no philosopher's treatise could. Where so many of our contemporary public officials are obsessed with public opinion polls, he was ever concerned with his well-earned reputation. To understand how important a man's reputation was to him in the eighteenth century may border on the impossible for contemporary Americans. But to a man of Washington's era, few things were more important than a man's reputation and keeping it unsullied. Despite this, Washington repeatedly demonstrated an unparalleled willingness to self-sacrifice by placing his reputation on the line in the service of his country. Each time he was asked to serve his country, he fretted on the damage that could be done to his reputation, not to mention his finances and beloved Mount Vernon.

Nevertheless, Washington never shirked his duty for self-interest. In his actions and his words, he taught the nation how to act properly. In words that may ring hollow and self-absorbed to some modern ears, but that would thunder with gravity in the hearts of his countrymen, he would write to the United Baptist Churches in Virginia in May 1789 that his retirement from public life after the war was intended to be permanent. "But when the exigence of my country seemed to require me once more to engage in public affairs, an honest conviction of duty superseded my former resolution, and became my apology for deviating from the happy plan which I had adopted."[18]

He served out of duty, not out of ambition. In placing the needs of his young country above his own happiness, he taught his generation and those that would follow valuable lessons in community and service and selflessness. In his preference for the private sphere of family and farm, he reminds us of the truly valuable in life. In his reluctance, we see the classical lesson that politics is a burden whose embrace is not to be made too welcome—less still should it be seduced by fortunes raised and spent with the regularity of the flies of summer. One is struck by the thought that if we had the time to unpack fully this characteristic of reluctance to service combined with commitment to duty, there would be found innumerable levels upon which more contemporary political figures could be pilloried and in which the solution to many of our public ills might be found.

Even long after his reputation had soared and had been sorely tested, even after two terms of service in the nation's "first office" and a pledge never again to travel more than ten miles from Mount Vernon, Washington heeded President Adams's call to come out of retirement one last time to serve as the commander in chief of the army during the 1798 crisis with France. All he had built and worked for could have been lost in a single military blunder or misjudgment here at the twilight of his life. And still, he served.

Those who knew him remarked lavishly upon his character and demeanor. Abigail Adams remarked upon his properly balanced character, calling him "polite with dignity, affable without familiarity, distant without haughtiness, grave without austerity, modest, wise, and good."[19] Benjamin Latrobe would remark that there is "something uncommonly commanding and majestic in his walk, his address, his figure, and his countenance."[20] He influenced those around him as an exemplar of manly virtue.

But, even more so, the public accounts of his private character served to influence thousands whose understanding of propriety would be strengthened in the retelling of Washington's virtue, who would strive to emulate their hero, and who would name their children after a man they wished would serve as the premier example to the young. A newspaper in Pennsylvania in 1777 would write, "If there are spots in his character, they are like the spots in the sun, only discernible by the magnifying powers of a telescope. Had he lived in the days of idolatry, he would have been worshipped as a god."[21] Soon after his death, a printed cotton kerchief was produced and sold with a representation of his deathbed and a description of Washington as having died "like a Christian and a Hero, calm and collected, without a groan and without a sigh." It also listed his virtues as "Self command and Self denial, moderate in Prosperity, undaunted amid Danger, unbroken by adversity...unperverted by great and general applause."[22] His private conduct was such that he was able to serve as the symbol and embodiment of virtue for those who walked with him and those who would come to know him only in the translation of newspapers, music, poetry, and histories.

Washington was careful to use his words to encourage right conduct and moral duty as goods to be sought in themselves, but also for their good public results as well. The private and the public dimensions of life were intimately interrelated. In his First Inaugural Address, he hoped that "the foundations of our national policy will be laid in the pure and immutable principles of private morality."[23] After witnessing Washington's delivery of the Inaugural Address, Fisher Ames, the new Speaker of the House, would record that "[i]t seems to me an allegory in which virtue was personified, and addressing those whom she would make her votaries. Her power over the heart was never greater."[24] According to his famous Farewell Address, "'Tis substantially true, that virtue or morality is a necessary spring of popular government." He would also claim that

> Of all the dispositions and habits which lead to political prosperity,
> Religion and morality are indispensable supports. In vain would that

man claim the tribute of Patriotism, who should labour to subvert these great Pillars of human happiness, these firmest props of the duties of Men and citizens. The mere Politician, equally with the pious man ought to respect and to cherish them. A volume could not trace all their connections with private and public felicity.[25]

In so many ways Washington may have been our nation's greatest early teacher of virtue and morality, and their consummate relationship to public concerns. Perhaps in no other way are his lessons more important to contemporary America.

THE SYMBOL OF BEING PRESIDENTIAL

George Washington was the first president in more than chronology. He set the standard for executive leadership in a republic that would last in the public mind for decades. Indeed, he showed in practice the very possibility of circumscribed and popular executive leadership to an age when some believed it possible in theory but just as many or more found it a dangerous and profoundly unrepublican innovation. We now take what Washington proved for granted, but in our age of hyperpopular politics, where the least common denominator so often rules, it is sage Washington to whom we ought to return to ensure the continued success of our experiment in having presidents in our Republic.

The Articles of Confederation had no central executive authority, and the make-up of state-level executives varied widely. Coming into the Constitutional Convention, it was far from sure there would be a chief magistrate of the Republic under any reforms; and after the convention did its work during that hot summer in Philadelphia, no one could really be sure what the delegates had created. Had they created a largely symbolic office as a "head of state"? Had they created the fetus of monarchy, as one leading Anti-Federalist would put it? Had they created a weak office that would docilely enforce the will of the legislature? No one really knew the answers to these questions, and to some degree, that is because there were no answers to give. The truth is they had created an office of potential only, the barest outline of which had been constructed. Into this void stepped Washington and those he trusted for advice and counsel, and in a very real way, they enacted the office and thereby made it real.

There is a considerable amount of theater and acting in leadership. Many people mocked Ronald Reagan for being an "actor," but the truth is there is much relating leadership to acting. Washington was an avid theater-goer and even had his men put on plays during the Revolution. He knew how to act a part, and he would learn how to act as president at the same time that he would virtually create the role. He molded much of what became our expectations for acting "presidential." Some of those expectations are with us still, many are lost, but all are worthy of our attention and reconsideration.

At its core, being "presidential" requires an uncommon degree of dignity and grace that commands the respect of the public and the elite. Washington's well-controlled public deportment was unsurpassed. Our era, where political figures openly and unashamedly display their inner emotions, where they discuss such intimate details as their choice of undergarments, where there is almost no item of life that is beyond public display, would strike Washington dumb. Indeed, among his first orders of business was the need to establish a proper etiquette for presidential activities and relationships and to guide those with whom he would interact.

Shortly after assuming office, Washington was daily besieged by visitors who wished an audience with the president. Professing an inability to attend to the public business under the pressure of men arriving from the time he awoke until he sat down to his evening meal, Washington had to find a way to accommodate the public's right to have access to their president, but also maintain a more formal distance from the whim of any individual or group that would make a demand on his time. He had to reconcile the dignity of office with republican rights and republican jealousies. To that end, he developed the practice of setting aside the hour of three to four on Tuesday afternoons, during which anyone who wished could be received by the president. These would not be informal sessions of pals, but neither would they be audiences with royalty based upon a European model. Washington refused, for instance, the pomp of being dramatically announced into the room. Instead, he would be posted at the door in formal dress, including his dress sword, where he could greet his visitors with a mutual salute. In this mode of operating, he had created, in his own words, a "just medium between much state and too great familiarity."[26] This, it strikes me, is one of the great challenges of presidential leadership, of creating a healthy balance between formality and dignity, on the one hand, and popular familiarity, on the other. The egalitarianism inherent in democratic politics always pulls toward familiarity (even in Washington's day these regular appearances reminded Senator William Maclay of "an Eastern lama"[27]), but the objective needs of republican governance depend upon a more formal and removed approach.

Washington would also entertain guests at dinner parties often held after the end of the weekly receptions. Long before the Reagans would come under such fire for spending what was taken to be an exorbitant figure on new table settings they felt would best represent the dignity of the White House, Gouverneur Morris went shopping for the Washingtons in Paris and bought twelve porcelain allegories of the arts and sciences, with a centerpiece depicting Apollo instructing the shepherds. Morris wrote to Washington that his purchases were "of a noble Simplicty." He added, "I think it of very great importance to fix the taste of our Country properly.... It is therefore my Wish that every Thing about you should be substantially good and majestically plain...."[28] Republican and dignified.

The dignity of the office had to be established and would not be readily acceded to by all. During the winter of his first year as president, for instance, Washington traveled to Massachusetts where he expressed an interest in dining with the governor, John Hancock. He understood that Hancock would make the first courtesy call. Hancock would call upon the president and then they would repair to the governor's residence to dine. When Hancock declined to visit the president, citing ill health, Washington abruptly canceled the engagement, assuming the governor was attempting to make the president pay the first courtesy call and thereby making a point about his superior position as a governor of a sovereign state within the Union. Washington fired off the following note to Governor Hancock: "The President of the United States presents his best respects to the Governor, and has the honor to inform him that he shall be at home 'till 2 O'clock. The President of the United States need not express the pleasure it will give him to see the Governor; but at the same time, he most earnestly begs that the Governor will not hazard his health on the occasion."[29] Hancock was put in his place and came to call upon the president later that day.

Modern presidents have a large array of staff and servants, limousines and chauffeurs, personal planes and helicopters, and a mansion that dwarfs George Washington's rented quarters. Modern presidents are surrounded constantly by palace guards. They live in opulence and splendor unknown to Washington, and yet they seem so small by his majestic strides. Our presidents cannot be Washington, but they can be presidential. He is the symbol of proper presidential conduct and should be the lodestone by which the contenders of our age set their compass. Only then will we return a dignity to the office and a balance to our politics.

THE SYMBOL OF AMERICA'S RELIGIOUS SELF-UNDERSTANDING

According to Eric Voegelin, societies erect symbols as part of their effort of "self-interpretation." Such symbols are essential to all human societies because they enable members to "experience it as more than an accident or a convenience; they experience it as of their human essence." According to Voegelin, these symbols also express the experience "that man is fully man by virtue of his

participation in a whole which transcends his particular existence."[30] Washington functioned in a related role as president. I
have already offered some reflections on his symbolic representation of the nation as a whole, but an additional element that
cannot be forgotten is the importance of religion to Americans of
the Founding generation and their understanding of the place of
America within a larger divine order.

Washington was a profoundly religious man and it is clear
that he understood faith both as a believer of conviction, but also
as a student of his fellow man. In his general orders to his troops
in July 1775, he would write that as general he "requires and
expects, of all Officers, and Soldiers, not engaged on actual duty,
a punctual attendance on divine Service, to implore the blessings
of heaven upon the means used for our safety and defence."[31] In
his famous Farewell Address of 1796, a public letter which is still
read each year in the United States Senate, Washington wrote to
the people, "Of all the dispositions and habits which lead to
political prosperity, Religion and morality are indispensable supports." And he went further to add,

> And let us with caution indulge the supposition, that morality can be
> maintained without religion. Whatever may be conceded to the
> influence of refined education on minds of peculiar structure, reason
> and experience both forbid us to expect that National morality can
> prevail in exclusion of religious principle.[32]

Religion, then, is not a private matter, merely, but something at
the very core of public happiness and the success of republican

government. He would urge tolerance of various sects and denominations within the nation. He would write to Catholics and Jews assuring them of their place within the overwhelmingly Protestant national community, and he even attended a Catholic service during the Constitutional Convention. He also did not object to laws requiring Christians to support their churches, as long as they allowed for exemptions for Jews, Muslims, and others.[33] His support of religious freedom did not break down into a rampant relativism, nor did it erect any type of "wall" between church and state. Rather, Washington understood America as a Christian nation which depended greatly upon its faith and which took part in a larger order that transcended it.

In Washington's worldview, Providence played a very large role. His writings, both public and private, are full of references to the need to pray for God's intervention in affairs, and of affirmations of God's role in American life and America's related role in God's plan. In a letter to Benjamin Lincoln in 1788, he would write of America's special place and how regrettable it would be if the nation departed "from the road which Providence has pointed us to, so plainly." "The great Governor of the Universe," he went on, "has led us too long and too far on the road to happiness and glory, to forsake us in the midst of it."[34] In a missive to Jonathan Trumbull just a month later, he wrote that one could "with a kind of grateful and pious exultation, trace the finger of Providence through those dark and mysterious events" related to the drafting and ratification of the Constitution; and he offered, "That the same good Providence may still continue to protect us and prevent us from dashing the cup of national felicity just at is

has been lifted to our lips, is the earnest prayer of, My Dear Sir,
your faithful friend, &c."[35]

Perhaps most famously and importantly, his Thanksgiving
Proclamation of October 3, 1789, called upon the nation to unite
in giving thanks to God for all the many blessings of which they
had been the beneficiary in the war and in establishing the new
government for their safety and happiness. By such a public and
official pronouncement, Washington was clearly placing the
American people within a transcendent order and teaching them
that they were beholden to the beneficence of the governor of that
order for any success they might find. Note as well the other very
important result of Washington's use of the rhetoric of
Providence. By so clearly crediting a higher being for the good
things that have happened to the former English colonies,
Washington was also effectively deflecting credit from himself
and thereby helping to prepare the nation for the day when the
Republic would have to stand without him. It was also, let us not
forget, Washington himself that added "so help me God" to the
end of the presidential oath of office—an addition that has lasted
into the current hour.

The religious iconography and symbolism that was built up
around Washington was really quite extraordinary. After his
death, painters created renderings of his apotheosis with him
rising from the grave with arms stretched like Christ's during the
crucifixion, ascending into Heaven lifted by the wings of angels,
and being crowned by a member of the Heavenly host after his
arrival. A later painting would even have Washington in Heaven
crowning an ascending Lincoln after the assassination. It has also

been said that Native Americans even have had lore of Washington being admitted to Indian Heaven, where he resides in a great mansion and greets Indians as they arrive.[36]

In so many ways Washington served the nation by symbolizing and manipulating symbols that represented the American people's connection to a larger transcendent order upon which they depended. Not completely unlike the English monarch who serves as head of the Church of England, presidents since Washington have served in their various ways and degrees as symbolic representatives of the nonestablished, but until very recently largely taken for granted, American religious order.

CONCLUSION

The presidency is at the very heart of the American experience. The office has not always had the power we see today or the trappings of the court which have surrounded recent occupants, but it has always been central to the political imaginations of the American people. The presidency outlined in the Constitution held this potential, but Washington made it a reality. Since his time, we have come to love our presidents and to hate them. Holding Washington's office, they have alternately inspired us and repulsed us because we recognize them as great symbolic carriers of meaning for our culture and our politics. As the most admired man of his age, a man idolized by the great majority of the people, Washington established this powerful aspect of the office more than 200 years ago, and it is with us still.

Washington realized that men are moved by silences as much or more than by words or reason. The exemplar fires the imagination and inspires men to greatness in a way that tracts of philosophy never will. The proper character acting in a manner appropriate to republican government can motivate men to proper action and the duties of citizenship. His public words were meant to further teach constitutional morality. They were meant to instruct in the proper demeanor and understanding of ordered liberty and republicanism. Rather than to further finely argued political theories, his rhetoric was meant to pluck the stings of the hearts of his countrymen—both the living and the yet unborn. In these ways, he was more useful to the establishment and flourishing of republican government under the Constitution than were the more intellectually sophisticated Hamilton, Madison, Jefferson, and Adams.

To later generations of people and magistrates he became the symbol of the office and of proper leadership. He should be still. Unfortunately, however, he was eventually eclipsed in the popular imagination and in the scholarly accounts of the office by a new symbol, a symbol of energy, frenetic activity, quickness to act, and, most of all, "power." Woodrow Wilson set the intellectual underpinnings, and Franklin Delano Roosevelt became the symbol of the modern presidency, with its focus on overcoming constitutional limits, quick action, policy agendas, social programs, and energetic public policy leadership. Where our presidents once lived "in the shadow of Washington," they now have come to live "in the shadow of FDR." Though it has seldom, if ever, been remarked upon, we have paid a high price for this transformation from one type of symbol to another—a transformation that in many ways has culminated in the presidency of

William Jefferson Clinton. In our current hour especially, but always, Americans would do well to remind themselves of George Washington and how he enacted the office of president and in so doing set a worthy example for republican governance.

EIGHT

Washington's Farewell Address and the Form of the American Regime

VIRGINIA L. ARBERY

For faithful adherents of America's Founding, it is relatively easy—and indeed, good sport—to point to the progressive historians, the courts, and the law schools as the major destroyers of national *pietas*. Many obvious influences such as these have undermined pride in what was once a stirring belief: that the Constitution binds us together in one *form,* as Americans.

Yet this belief, necessary as it is to national unity of purpose, has never been achieved without effort. Even in 1787 or a decade later, the people's attachment to union under the new Philadelphia Constitution was neither natural nor automatic. Both Publius in *The Federalist* and Alexis de Tocqueville in *Democracy in America* argue that the states hold the people's affection more immediately than the national government. Republican cohesion on such a large scale has always depended upon the habit, achieved through the experience of a well-administered national government, of perceiving the Union's good as the common good.[1] From the beginning, presidential rhetoric has played a crucial role in securing piety toward the Constitution and the Union it ensures, the realized *form* from which we seem to be increasingly disaffected.

Patriotism toward the *idea* of a large extended republic was first of all an achievement of the imagination. A relatively obscure, almost hidden passage, in Tocqueville's discussion of the Union's permanence suggests the initial role the imagination played in assuring the prospect of lasting adhesion to the Federalists' ratified plan: "And the Union which at first was the child of their imagination, is now a part of their [the confederated states'] habits."[2] By implication, the Founders' task was to open up the imaginations of the citizens so that their souls in fact would submit to the form, to the regime. The habits of the people would reflect their regime's ends, institutions, and subsequent laws only to the extent that their imaginations had seized the form of rule.

George Washington projected the Union's permanence as one with that of the Constitution itself.[3] His image of the fledgling nation mirrored her form of rule. I shall argue that the Farewell Address (1796) enforced in the American imagination the principles of union articulated in *The Federalist.* Citizen habits were still in formation in this first stage of the Republic. Jefferson's First Inaugural Address (1801), on the other hand, shows a deliberate shift away from the Founders' effort to form the imagination of Americans by contemplating constitutional form, a shift reflecting pre-Publian habits of self-rule more localized and rights-centered.

Critics of the Publian model of 1787 who look at these two

presidential addresses—and, *a fortiori,* at all presidential speeches—in each case might ask the following questions: How does each president understand his constitutional object? How is his own ambition reflected in achieving it? Are both his understanding and his ambition in keeping with the Publian teaching on the executive?

To answer these questions in light of the two addresses is to begin to discern not only how its earliest officeholders imagined the office of presidency but also how the chief executives' perceptions aimed to shape citizen virtue. The Washingtonian model reflects the Publian teaching, arousing attachment to the form of union as it fulfills the duties of presidential office. In short, Washington's address aims to encourage the formation of habits necessary for citizen virtue. Contemplating his effort leads us to inquire whether the sources of patriotism are undermined when the chief executive's own imaginative grasp of the regime is awry. The alternative presidential rhetoric, typified by Thomas Jefferson, might be said to be non-paradigmatic precisely because, in its tendency to court changing proponents for individual liberties or partisan interests, it fails to instruct citizens in the formal unity that binds them together. Aristotle says that in political oratory, the speaker must first prove his ethical strength. Despite Washington's enormous popularity, it was common knowledge that the first outgoing president had been reluctant even to assume public office. Profound respect for him, as well as the newness of the office, made it difficult for Congress itself to decide the simple matter of how to address the already lionized general. Common usage resulted in his being called "Mr.

President," although he himself is said to have favored "His Mightiness, the President of the United States."[4] Whatever the truth of his preference, Washington's final address as the nation's first president can in no way be construed as memorializing his own "mightiness"; rather, it emphasizes his deep sense of "the weight of years" upon him.[5] In his self-perceived decline, he claims that he would delay retiring from public office if he thought his absence detrimental to his country; his patriotic duty would outweigh his personal interest.

At the beginning, in the part of the address familiarly addressed to friends and fellow citizens, he thus establishes his character by a deft downplaying of his grand stature as the man who defeated the best armies of Europe. He was "not unconscious" of his inferiority from the beginning. The experience of office holding has not changed his inclination for a private life, but he shows confidence that both the internal and external "state" of the citizens is strong enough now for him to pursue his own inclination without sacrificing "the sentiment of duty."

In this guarded yet favorable view of the infant nation's stability and safety, he indirectly disposes his readers to focus on his forthcoming instructions and admonitions. He thus achieves another key component of Aristotle's political rhetoric—putting the "audience" in the right frame of mind. In bowing out of politics, he is acting with prudence, with virtue, and with good will ("solicitude for your welfare which cannot end but with my life")—three aspects of character which satisfy Aristotle's ethical proof of the speaker. Moreover, in establishing the right grounds for his remarks to his fellow citizens, he suggests there may be "dangers" that he must offer to their "contemplation." To heed these yet unnamed dangers is to ensure the "permanency of your felicity as a people." In composing warnings through the vehicle of presidential self-effacement, he enhances the belief in them as "disinterested," prompted by "no personal motives." Washington's disclaimer echoes Publius, who, at the end of *Federalist* 1, exhorts his readers to look at what he says, not at his motives.

Washington's tacit claim is that his first constitutional object is to serve the citizens' central piety, the love for liberty. As president, his commitment to liberty reflects the people's commitment to liberty: "[N]o recommendation of mine is necessary to fortify or confirm the attachment." But soon into the address the public's patriotism appears to be not as firm as his own; like his closest advisor, Alexander Hamilton, had said, Washington must "produce the event" of the Union. (It was, Hamilton said, quoting Demosthenes, the duty of the statesman to "march at the head of affairs" and "produce the event.") The Union is the event still under production. In the phrase "*now* dear to you," repeated in the phrase "sacred ties which *now* link together the various parts," Washington reminds Patriots of how short the time has been since true Union was crafted. (Emphasis added.) Washington's rhetoric aims to ensure that Americans not regress from this well-earned moment.

He focuses Americans on the solid image of the Union as the "main pillar in the edifice of your real independence." His parting presidential rhetoric must correct for those who undermine in the "minds" of citizens the equation of liberty and union. In the same paragraph, he suggests the remedy for countervailing influences from both inside and outside the country: "[Y]ou should cherish a cordial, habitual, and immoveable attachment to it; accustoming yourselves to think and speak of it as of the palladium of your political safety and prosperity...." By exhorting lovers of liberty to habituate their thought and speech to attachment to union, Washington fathers the image in the liberty-loving citizens of union and liberty being married in principle.

At this point in the speech, the constitutional object of the president might be said to be educational. He inculcates the correct image of liberty. Washington achieves this object by indoctrinating citizens in the constitutional form which informs the "minds" of citizens. Noticeably, he avoids addressing the fears of citizens for their rights (Jefferson's concern).

In the next paragraph Washington makes a distinction between natural bonds—old habits of self-rule—and habits of mind chosen through reflection, or, as he puts it, "solemn contemplation." In much the same way as in *Federalist* 2, Washington's "speech" acknowledges preregime factors (religion, manners, habits, and political principles embodied in the state constitutions) that bind Americans together. These elements are necessary but not sufficient for union. They do not in themselves make for constitutionalism. He exhorts: "[Your] country [whether one is born here or not] has a right to concentrate your affections." Although "local discriminations" may attach Americans to aspects of societal life, they do not impose the binding political imperative that union under the Constitution does. Thus, rather than affirming government's protection of rights, the first president asserts the "right" of the country's union to claim central allegiance, patriotism, and citizen virtue. In other words, Washington understands patriotism as a duty that governors have a right to insist on. The constitutional object of his office and his personal ambition will be served, then, to the extent that he can literally formalize the wedding of private interest to constitutional allegiance. The first aspect of danger arises from those who place local interest (or minority personal rights) over "the permanent and aggregate interests of the community" (*cf. Federalist* 10). The potential for the violence of majority faction is still keen enough after ratification to warrant Washington's warning and his reassertion of Publian constitutional morality. In the next nine paragraphs, Washington persuasively reenvisions the contrary view of why the states joined the new Union. North, South, East, and West are depicted as having entered the new Union not so much for their private interests as for the good of the whole. Indeed if the states would adopt this perspective, their more local or sectional interests would be better served. He assumes that most Americans are not clamoring, discontented sectionalists, but that—echoing *Federalist* 1 and 6— "designing men... excite a belief that there is a real difference of local interests and views." He suggests a link between these designing men and those reluctant to supersede altogether the Articles of Confederation. The bad habit of looking backward to that time is not unlike looking back to a bad marriage—"Your former intimate union" was not efficacious, a poor manager of your "common concerns." True happiness is derived from the "true offspring of your own choice," one sprung from reason, not passion, a choice "uninfluenced and unawed," a mature political marriage.

The clear resonance of the opening question in *Federalist* 1 apparently is still being echoed. Can "reflection and choice" prevail over "accident and force" in the body politic? The answer is yes if citizens remain cool in their thought, like Washington himself. Washington urges a recommitment to a reasonable union achieved in the "mild season of peace" (*Federalist* 11), unlike the Articles, which were conceived through and during the passion of the Revolution.

Driving home his point on sectionalism's inadequacies, Washington invites his fellow citizens to view themselves now as Americans who, out of their love for the truth of liberty, have replaced their maiden names (Virginians, South Carolinians, New Yorkers, etc.) with that of "American." Get rid of, he urges, "any appellation derived from local discriminations." As when the bride gives herself to the groom, her new naming with his surname is of no little symbolic importance. The new Constitution is "sacredly obligatory upon all." The name American thus refers to citizens who share even more than the same "habits of the heart," Tocqueville's phrase for the whole intellectual and moral state. In the unifying name of "American," Washington identifies citizenship with constitutionalism. The very law of the land, which, since ratification, has stood above *ethos* or feeling, has now become formative of and central to *ethnos* or national character. To be an American thus means to be a lover of union as defined by the ratified Philadelphia Constitution.

Washington's next admonition judiciously upholds the

Publian conception of presidential office, identifying it with "energy," "efficient management," and "as much vigor as is consistent with the perfect security of liberty" (cf. *Federalist* 37, 67, 70). With a "feeble" executive, the "preservation of your Government and the permanency of your present happy state" are endangered. He upholds the executive against "the spirit of innovation." The Anti-Federalists of less than a decade ago (reconstituted under the new democratic-republicans of Jefferson's leadership) are now imagined as innovators rather than as former malcontents. "Reverence for the laws" (cf. *Federalist* 49) necessitates that "time" and, again, "habit" fix the true character of government. The citizens of the states are not unlike newlyweds who, in marrying, have not given up their own families but who have entered into a contract that takes precedent over all other associations. They have entered *peacefully* into what Machiavelli calls "new modes and orders."

At this point in his address, Washington employs the word "solemn" again. We feel the full weight of his stature and of the great respect he enjoyed behind its use. "The baneful effects of the spirit of party generally," i.e., beyond local or state interests, are heralded in the most candid and dispassionate way. Three reasons are given to avoid this tendency sown in human nature. The argument is supplemental to *Federalist* 10: parties distract public councils, agitate the community, and leave the door open to foreign influence and corruption. Two relevant details outside the speech might be noted with some profit here. When Washington asked Hamilton and Jefferson for their opinions of the Bank Bill, he specifically asked them to avoid discussing whether they thought it desirable or not; he wanted to know whether each man thought it would be constitutional. And in 1799—the last year of his life—when he had been out of office for two years—and was urged for his country's sake to be a candidate for president, he refused, explaining that "principle, not men, is now, and will be the object of contention." Party, he thought, removed men from standing on their duty, which in his case was one with the preservation of constitutional forms. Character is duty. Using the fire imagery from *Federalist* 10, Washington teaches that "party" ("a fire not to be quenched...") is a natural tendency that lovers of the Union should "mitigate" and "assuage."

His thought turns from sectionalism, party, and faction to a reiteration of the Publian understanding of the separation of powers. He affirms the teaching of *Federalist* 51 that "ambition must be made to counteract ambition." Governors must stay within their "respective constitutional spheres." "To preserve them must be as necessary as to institute them." The preservation of "reciprocal checks" depends in large measure upon the proper inculcation of the right "habits of thinking." No little part of his rhetorical legacy is his insistence that citizens develop a habitually orthodox, i.e., Publian, way of viewing the branches of the national government, lest tyranny itself result.

Washington's vision of Constitutional Union culminates in the promotion of educational institutions, for "Of all the dispositions and habits, which lead to political prosperity, religion and morality are indispensable supports." They are the "foundation of the fabric" of free government. The development of "institutions for the general diffusion of knowledge" is of "primary importance." In the example of oath taking in court, he underscores that justice depends upon piety. His argument further links the "cherishing" of public credit with the formation of a virtuous people. His insistence that good policy cannot be achieved without citizens being both moral and religious balances the Publian warning in No. 10 that neither can be relied upon as adequate controls to men's vices. Washington looks to Providence to bolster the claim that America will be a "great nation" known worldwide for her "magnanimity" and "exalted justice and benevolence." His projected image for America might seem chimerical: a non-Machiavellian modern nation which for the first time will join national interest to objective virtue.

Is this Washington's personal standard grafted on the Publian model, or is it the bona fide Publian image of America in the world? I believe the answer is the latter. In *Federalist* 11, Publius concludes that America must "teach our assuming brother [Europe] moderation." After having linked national virtue with religious strength, Washington here begins his famous discussion of the second danger to the nation after that of parties. "A passionate attachment of one nation for another produces a variety of evils." Washington bases his argument on foreign affairs on the premise that there can be no "real common interest" among nations, only partial interests. Why? Because the source of common interest cannot be extraconstitutional. Just as the natural bonds of the country are not truly solid and safe, neither are international ties of any description politically cohesive. Those who claim otherwise, whether citizens or not, are deluders. His words grow stronger as he moves toward the famous line,

"Our true policy [is] to steer clear of permanent alliances." Those who persuade to the contrary are "base," "foolish," complying with "ambition," "corruption," or "infatuation." No doubt the strength of the opprobrium owes to the fledgling nation's need to consolidate itself sufficiently to withstand European ambitions. He particularly casts aspersions on "lovers" of the people: "Real patriots..." he says, "are liable to become suspected and odious" while accomplices to favored nations "usurp the applause and confidence of the people, to surrender their interests."

In holding that commercial interests should be the sole basis for temporary alliances, Washington's teaching refines the Publian perspective on the advantages of becoming a commercial republic, best articulated in *Federalist* 12. Indeed, if we are following closely Washington's meaning, an important distinction is being made between commercial and political interests. America's common *internal* interest is not identifiable with merely her collective commercial interests. The fulfillment of commercial aims is only one facet of union under the Preamble's "more perfect union." America's political interest is her national interest, and, outside of the nation's borders, no attempt to legally embody America's self-contained political reality can succeed. Where there is only opportunistic arrangement there is no constitutional order, no binding regime, and no ordering view of the political good.

At the end of the address, Washington, in acknowledging his fallible judgments and the limitation of mortality, bows to the still higher teaching that there is no genuine regime that does not recognize the immortality of the soul. His final words instruct all subsequent generations that each man's political actions be judged by the sense of duty that governed his choices. Such a gauge serves to moderate each soul in the same way that the new Republic should control its lust for power, for empire. With a clear conscience, the first holder of the highest office in the land submits his performance to God himself: "Though in reviewing the incidents of my administration, I am unconscious of intentional error, I am nevertheless too sensible of my defects not to think it probable that I may have committed many errors. Whatever they may be, I fervently beseech the Almighty to avert or mitigate the evils to which they may tend." His reliance is ultimately not on the voters or his fellow citizens but on the Almighty. A transcendent power is the final arbiter over all human mistakes; it alone, above constitutional provisions, can remedy unintended political evils.

As outgoing president, Washington thus caters to neither public approval nor disapproval but asserts his length of service comported with a wearying "upright zeal," making him eager for the "mansions of rest." "I shall also carry with me," writes Washington, "the hope that my country will never cease to view them [my defects] with indulgence; and that after forty-five years of my life dedicated to its service, with an upright zeal, the faults of incompetent abilities will be consigned to oblivion, as myself must soon be to the mansions of rest...."

Washington's view of the constitutional orthodoxy he espouses suggests that an energetic presidency is free of slavish desires to please the majority, one's allies, or one's fellow partisans. Like the Constitution itself, Washington's personal ambition is served best in serving the "permanent and aggregate good" (*cf. Federalist* 10). His duty is to urge citizens to base their own patriotism on the same deference to the American Union. By habituating their minds and speech to conform to the Constitution, citizens will truly be Americans, not just part of a happy majority or disaffected minority on any given issue. Such an habituation will indeed make possible the "magnanimity" of spirit so antithetical to partisanship and so conducive to lasting community.

The presidency of Thomas Jefferson poses an early test of the durability of the American Founding. Can the nation avoid turning to the lure of a demagogue? Washington, following Hamilton's structural insights into the presidential office, had been a nearly perfect embodiment of the Federalists' conception of that singularly held office. After Washington's symbolic last words, Jefferson's first words strike, at the very least, a regressive, pre-Publian tone.

Jefferson's First Inaugural Address begins by doing what Washington, throughout his Farewell Address, is loathe to do: he indirectly thanks the citizens for their votes.[6] His overture confirms the Publian charge that lovers of the people are more to be feared than those who insist on strong, stable, and energetic government: "A rising nation...traversing all the seas with the rich productions of their industry, engaged in commerce with nations who feel power and forget right, advancing rapidly to destinies beyond the reach of mortal eye—when I contemplate these transcendent objects...I shrink from the contemplation...." The soaring ascent (rather than a gradual one as in Washington's Farewell

Address) to transcendent truths elevates the office of the presidency above the Constitution rather than acknowledging it as derivative of and subject to it.

The establishment of his character seems as significant as his assertion of the magnitude of the office he has just assumed. Protestations of his own humility aside, Jefferson's tone is different from Washington's simple concern that he made some mistakes in doing his job. Jefferson's ethical proof, like Washington's, is tied to the emotional proof—the establishment of the citizens' right frame of mind toward his own view of the office he assumes. Rather than liberty or the Union, he asserts that the highest good is the dogma of the sovereignty of the people. By identifying their sovereignty with the legislative function, he ostensibly downplays his own executive role, which is merely to "steer" the vessel "with safety."

The effects of party about which his predecessor warned have been baneful indeed, "agitating" the community so much so that Jefferson, himself a cause of this agitation, must now speak in terms of the need for the sentiment for unity rather than for a recommitment to the principles of union (to the form) itself. The phrase "arrange ourselves under the will of the law" suggests a composite of groups divided to such an extent that they must be placed in relation to each other before they can be united under constitutional rule. The view that the Constitution is the formal order which definitionally informs the common interest shifts to the view that individual wills make constitution, hearkening to an Anti-Federalist emphasis.

Jefferson's own imaginative framework, and that within

which he views the Constitution, elevates will over cool reflection. It is Publian to emphasize that the will of the majority "to be rightful" "must be reasonable"; however, Jefferson's departure point is will. Jefferson's "sacred principle" is clearly different from Washington's "sacredly obligatory" commitment to the ratified Constitution as such. It is useful to remember that Washington's aversion to running in the election of 1796 was based on his conviction that men should run on their character, assuming that all worthy men are formed by the Constitution's architectonic edifice, not by their separate principles. The office of the presidency is thus viewed as one that keeps wills attached to unity. The Jeffersonian emphasis requires a higher rhetoric, less restrained speech, and more self-assertion rather than self-effacement in the Publian mode. The personality of the president thus acts as the cohesive force, rather than the Constitution itself.

Again, Jefferson's appeals to unity are not based on the priority of Constitutional Union but on the hope of party members' abilities to reimagine themselves as alike only in their partisanship: "We are all Republicans—we are all Federalists." Even his assertion of the strength of the nascent government relies more on the passions accompanying partisanship than on Americans' reverence for the law.

In speaking of natural bonds, Jefferson fails to drop the point of party membership; each can pursue "his own federal and republican principles." He avers that "our courage" (patriotism) and "confidence" subsist in them. The executive's energy, then, is derivative of this supra-constitutional vitality. Jefferson's listing of the essential principles of liberty presumes that the Constitution itself needs clarification to show its conformity to Jefferson's extra-constitutional framework. The list is stacked with the terms of that seminal American document, the Declaration of Independence, with its principle of equality as centerpiece. States' rights figure in as intrinsic to the preservation of republicanism, a bulwark indeed. The principles of the Revolution are elevated to the status of a "bright constellation" that wisdom and blood have attained. The rhetoric continues to ascend in a list, including equal and exact justice to all men, absolute acquiescence in the decision of the majority, the supremacy of the civil over the military authority, encouragement of agriculture (and of commerce as its handmaid), freedom of religion, freedom of the press, freedom of person under the protection of the habeas corpus clause, and trial by juries impartially selected. And like the Nicene Creed, the list itself becomes the "creed of our political faith."

The Jeffersonian failure to include the notion of habit, understood as habituation to constitutionalism by all patriotic Americans, distances him from Washingtonian, Publian sobriety and moderation. The Union, the "child of [the Founders'] imagination," is removed from view and replaced by the impetus of self-submission to union only because and to the extent that it conforms with one's own will and not because it is seen as the essence of one's patriotic duty, the political good.

Jefferson's charge to his fellow citizens to become politically religious is followed by his praise of Washington, a gesture he must make to appear consistent with the constitutional enterprise on its original terms. He is concerned that history judge him well, whereas Washington would like his mistakes to be forgotten and the form he served to be remembered by those he leaves behind with his catechetics of constitutional rhetoric. But, interestingly, to invoke Washington restrains Jefferson's own rhetoric and resets his executive sights in line with the constitutionalism from which his speech veered. He asks for the confidence that "will give firmness and effect to the legal administration of your affairs." Despite this statement of purpose, characterized by Publian sobriety, Jefferson generally conceives of his service as popular in focus rather than primarily constitutional. Washington, we saw, states his task differently; in fulfilling his constitutional object he states the case for liberty being necessarily tied to Constitutional union. He produces the event. Jefferson's rhetoric changes the identification of executive energy with constitutional permanence (the Publian model) almost imperceptibly. He equates presidential ambition with the maintenance of rights antecedent to the model.

Washington would not approve of this shift. He would be put to no little unrest in his mansion if he knew how much further the shift, from Andrew Jackson to Woodrow Wilson to William Jefferson Clinton, has undermined the Publian model.

NINE

Making Citizens: George Washington and the American Character

MATTHEW SPALDING

When the Continental Congress appointed George Washington to be commander in chief of all continental forces in 1775 they did so because he had military experience and was from Virginia, to be sure, but most of all because he displayed the qualities of character—courage, integrity, loyalty, and dedication—that were needed to build and lead a republican army. "The moderation and virtue of a single character," Thomas Jefferson said of Washington, "probably prevented this Revolution from being closed, as most others have been, by a subversion of that liberty it was intended to establish."[1] The vast powers of the presidency, as one delegate to the Constitutional Convention of 1787 noted, would not have been made as great "had not many of the members cast their eyes towards General Washington as president; and shaped their ideas of the powers to be given to a president, by their opinions of his virtue."[2] Here's how Lighthorse Henry Lee eulogized the man that he concluded was "[f]irst in war, first in peace, and first in the hearts of his countrymen":

...second to none in humble and enduring scenes of private life. Pious,
just, humane, temperate, and sincere; uniform, dignified, and commanding; his example was as edifying to all around him as were the
effects of that example lasting.... Correct throughout, vice shuddered
in his presence and virtue always felt his fostering hand. The purity
of his private character gave effulgence to his public virtues.[3]

Today it is almost a cliché to speak of Washington's character. We
are more likely to hear appeals to his honesty from people selling
cars than from people judging men. Matters of virtue and vice are
usually relegated to the province of personal integrity and private
conscience, and the notion that individuals can and should be
held up to standards of behavior outside of themselves is roundly
criticized by many as "imposing one's values" on others. We are
especially reluctant to apply the terms used to describe
Washington to our politics: holding leaders to higher standards
of moral conduct and personal integrity is seen more often than
not as partisanship, signifying narrow interests rather than noble
ideals.

Not so for George Washington or the American Founders
generally. Character, as Washington understood it—and so thoroughly came to epitomize—was not merely the unhypocritical
application of his own personal value choices. Quite the contrary,
Washington's view was that rules of character—what he called
"the pure and immutable principles of private morality"—
applied to all men and all nations, at all times. And character had
implications for politics. Republican government, far from being
unconcerned about questions of virtue and character, was under-

stood to require *self*-government. Just as the individual government of the self requires rules and good habits of behavior, so popular self-government requires laws and good habits of citizenship. Washington set out to create a nation of both.

THE FORMATION OF CHARACTER

Washington's concern for character is evident from the very beginning. One of his earliest writings was an adolescent copybook record of one hundred and ten rules labeled *Rules of Civility and Decent Behaviour in Company and Conversation.* Drawn from an early etiquette book, these social maxims teach lessons of good manners concerning everything from how to treat one's superiors ("In speaking to men of Quality do not lean nor look them full in the face") and moderate one's own behavior ("Let your recreations be manful not sinful") to more significant expressions of civility as "keep alive in your breast that little spark of celestial fire called conscience."[4] Simple rules of decent conduct, he always held, formed the backbone of good character.

In his later letters Washington constantly warns young correspondents of "the necessity of paying due attention to the moral virtues" and avoiding the "scenes of vice and dissipation" often presented to youth.[5] Because an early and proper education in both manners and morals would form the leading traits of one's life, he constantly urges the development of good habits and the unremitting practice of moral virtue. "To point out the importance of circumspection in your conduct," advised the corespondent, "it may be proper to observe that a good moral character is the first essential of man, and that the habits contracted at your age are generally indelible, and your conduct here may stamp your character through life." "It is therefore highly important that you should endeavor not only to be *learned* but *virtuous*."[6]

Washington's view of education was primarily practical. It cannot be said that he was either unaware or unappreciative of more speculative knowledge and the scholarly life, for he wrote: "From the high ground of mathematical and philosophical demonstration, we are insensibly led to far nobler speculations and sublimer meditations."[7] Nevertheless, his conception was foremost that of a solid and ethical general education. Washington believed that the first object of learning is to acquire as much knowledge as one can, thereby establishing habits of earnestness, industry, and seriousness. And whereas the beginnings of education depend upon it, the end product of education was never unattached in Washington's mind from moral character. The "advantages of a finished education" are both a "highly cultivated mind, and a proper sense of your duties to God and man."[8]

Washington's own life is a good example of this advice, as he was constantly striving to control his own passions and habituate qualities of good character. As a young man he displayed high ambitions and a desire for military glory; in accepting one early military command, he noted that he would have to give up "what at present constitutes the chief part of my happiness; i.e., the esteem and notice the country has been pleased to honour me with."[9] But for Washington what ultimately mattered was that his reputation be deserved: self-respect preceded public respect, and self-respect required good intentions and virtuous behavior.

"I hope I shall always possess firmness and virtue enough to maintain (what I consider the most enviable of all titles) the character of an honest man," he once told Alexander Hamilton, "as well as prove (what I desire to be considered in reality) that I am."[10] The best way to establish a good reputation is to be, in fact, a good man.

The connection between education and morality is central to his first message to Congress in 1790. Washington calls for the general promotion of knowledge—"the surest basis of public happiness"—because it reminds those in power that the ends of government are found in "the enlightened confidence of the people." More importantly, it teaches citizens to know and defend the rights the government was formed to protect, to distinguish between oppression and lawful authority, and "to discriminate the spirit of liberty from that of licentiousness—cherishing the first, avoiding the last."[11]

It comes as no surprise that Washington believed that the first and most important step toward independence, prosperity, and happiness was the acquisition of good character. What is forgotten is that he held this to be true regardless of whether one is speaking of an individual, a people, or a nation. "[T]he first transactions of a nation, like those of an individual upon his first entrance into life, make the deepest impression," Washington wrote at the time of the ratification of the Constitution, "and are to form the leading traits in its character."[12] Politics, then, was naturally concerned with character formation and character-forming habits and institutions.

Over the course of his lifetime—as revolutionary, military

leader, and chief executive—Washington's great project, and thus the cornerstone of his statesmanship, was the formation of an independent, national American character. He sought to establish the nation—to found a new order of the ages—in the hearts and minds of the people by personifying, defining, and encouraging what he believed ought to be the leading habits and dispositions of this character. By doing so, Washington became more than hero, general, and president; he truly became the Father of his Country.

THE LESSONS OF WAR

During the American Revolution, General Washington fully expected his soldiers—one group traditionally thought exempt from moral standards—to follow rules of behavior and conduct. He insisted that they, as Patriots deserving their freedom and independence, display the character of republicans. In fact, his political and military leadership turned on the sense of character and common purpose he imparted and encouraged in the Continental Army as a way of building the diverse forces under his command into a unified and committed fighting force. As the first means of advancing the larger project of making seemingly disparate groups into one nation, Washington made the army not just an instrument of war but also a mechanism for demonstrating and transmitting a national character.

Early in his tenure as commander in chief, Washington observed that the men of the Continental Army were brave and good, "who with pleasure it is observed, are addicted to fewer Vices than are commonly found in Armies."[13] In his private correspondence, however, he reflected deep misgivings about relying on patriotism, bravery, and virtue alone to build an army. Once the patriotic passions of the moment had settled down, Washington noted, most soldiers were motivated by their self-interest. In order to act as a unit, it was necessary for that narrow interest to be directed, if not transcended, by a common interest compatible with the principles and ends of the Revolution. Thus the first element of Washington's wartime policy stemmed from a general reform of the existing army and centered on encouraging discipline and the basic civility needed to build camaraderie and teach the greater good of their common cause. "If we would pursue a right System of policy," Washington believed, "there should be none of these distinctions. We should all be considered, Congress, Army, etc. as one people, embarked in one Cause, in one interest; acting on the same principle and to the same End."[14]

Over the first six months of the war, Washington reorganized the existing forces under his command with the intent of creating a disciplined army. "Men accustomed to unbounded freedom, and no controul," Washington averred, "cannot brook the Restraint which is indispensably necessary to the good order and Government of an Army; without which, licentiousness, and every kind of disorder triumphantly reign."[15] His initial orders laid out the rules by which he "expected and required" his army to act: all geographic distinctions were to be laid aside "so that one and the same Spirit may animate the whole"; exact discipline and due subordination, the failure of which leads to "shameful disappointment and disgrace," were to be observed; there would be a "due observance" of the rules that forbade profane cursing, swearing, and drunkenness; all officers and soldiers not on duty were to attend divine services "to implore the blessings of heaven upon the means used for our safety and defense"; and officers were to pay attention to the neatness and cleanliness of the soldiers.[16] His hope was that "every officer and man, will endeavor so to live, and act, as becomes a Christian Soldier defending the dearest Rights and Liberties of his country."[17]

In his orders to the reorganized Continental Army in 1776, Washington hoped that "a laudable Spirit of emulation, will now take place, and pervade the whole of it; without such a Spirit, few Officers have ever arrived to any degree of Reputation, nor did any Army ever become formidable."[18] The character that he wished to have emulated and encouraged—the reputation for which the army was to be known—was high indeed. "Our own Country's Honor," Washington wrote in his General Orders of July 2, 1776, "all call upon us for a vigorous and manly exertion, and if we now shamefully fail, we shall become infamous to the whole world. Let us therefore rely upon the goodness of the Cause, and the aid of the supreme Being, in whose hands Victory is, to animate and encourage us to great and noble Actions."[19]

Washington's officer corps played a unique role in this character-building effort. In addition to ensuring the discipline of the army, the officers had the important job of being role models for their soldiers: "Enjoin this upon the Officers, and let them inculcate, and press home to the Soldiery, the Necessity of Order and Harmony among them, who are embark'd in one common Cause, and mutually contending for all that Freemen hold dear." This would serve to raise the tone and character of recruits who

Washington knew were often influenced by concerns of narrow self-interest by substituting for self-interest an enlarged sense of the common good. "Discourage vice in every shape," Washington told one of his officers, "and impress upon the mind of every man, from the first to the lowest, the importance of the cause, and what it is they are contending for." Thus Washington sought men of good character—those motivated by the gentlemanly virtues—as officers in his army.[20]

At the end of the war, in his Farewell Orders to the armies of the United States in November 1783, Washington posited that the victory in the Revolutionary War was "little short of a standing miracle." Few besides Washington could have imagined from the beginning that "the most violent local prejudices would cease so soon, and that Men who came from different parts of the Continent, strongly disposed, by the habits of education, to despise and quarrel with each other, would instantly become one patriotic band of Brothers." With the end of the war, Washington expected all of his officers and soldiers to become loyal and productive citizens and play a role in establishing the new nation. His "last injunction to every Officer and Soldier" was that they—now "his worthy fellow Citizens"—support the principles of the federal government and an increase of the powers of the Union. More importantly, he hoped that his troops would "carry with them into civil society the most conciliating dispositions; and that they should prove themselves not less virtuous and useful as *Citizens*, than they have been persevering and victorious as *Soldiers*."[21] By bringing their good habits and dispositions to the new nation—that is, those habits compatible with republican government—Washington's soldiers would now be models of citizenship for the rest of their countrymen.

CRISIS IN CHARACTER

After the American Revolution, Washington believed that the whole nation needed a transformation of its conduct and that a complete revision of the American system of government was the "only constitutional mode" to remedy the defects of the Articles of Confederation. By the time of the Constitutional Convention, he was of the opinion that the new constitutional structure must provide adequate powers and energy for the federal government, allow for the secrecy and dispatch characteristic of good administration, and give the government the confidence and ability to exercise national powers and pursue national policies.[22] While the Constitution was the great vehicle for these structural changes, the transformation that Washington sought required more than the reform of America's financial or legal structure.

The real problem under the regime of the Articles of Confederation and the dominance of the state governments, in Washington's opinion, was that jealous and petty politics invited and encouraged a jealous and petty spirit in the people. By nourishing petty politics, speculation, and special interests, and in general aiding narrow political passions, bad government generated licentious appetites and corrupted morals. For the common man, Washington feared that indolence, drunkenness, and licentiousness would replace the republican virtues of industriousness, sobriety, and private virtue. He believed that the narrow, local prejudices that dominated the Confederation had to be replaced by a sense of interest in and patriotism for a common, national good. The key was the creation of a national character: "This is the time of their political probation," he proclaimed of the American citizenry at the end of the war, for "this is the moment when the eyes of the World are turned upon them; this is the moment to establish or ruin their national Character forever; this is the favorable moment to give such a *tone* to our Federal Government, as will enable it to answer the *ends* of its institution...."[23]

Washington strongly supported the government proposed by the Constitutional Convention, noting that it took advantage of improvements in the science of politics by proposing more checks and barriers against tyranny than any government "hitherto instituted among mortals." But he did not believe that new institutional arrangements, however necessary and good, were sufficient in and of themselves to define and maintain a national character. A good constitution, no matter how well constructed, did not remove the need for good citizens and sound morals:

> I would not be understood...to speak of consequences which may be produced, in the revolution of ages, by corruption of morals, profligacy of manners, and listlessness of the preservation of the natural and unalienable rights of mankind; nor of the successful usurpations that may be established at such a juncture, upon the ruins of liberty, however providently guarded and secured, as these are contingencies against which no human prudence can effectually provide.[24]

This leaves us with a difficult question: If prudent constitution making is effectually incapable of providing against the corruption of morals, the profligacy of manners, and the listlessness of the preservation of natural and unalienable rights—yet all of these things are necessary for self-government—what can be done to make the American experiment possible?

Virtue and Happiness

When Washington became president, his primary responsibility was to fulfill the constitutional responsibilities and obligations of the office. Nevertheless, he saw the presidency as an opportunity to establish and further define the character of the nation, raising the moral tone of the government and the citizenry. By encouraging the virtues appropriate for republican government, Washington could further his goal of evincing the goodwill of his countrymen and founding a people in the fullest sense. In order to make the proper impression on the nation, then, it was important for Washington to begin the government by encouraging the proper characteristics and habits.

In the draft of his first inaugural address, Washington warns yet again that the republican form of government depends upon certain characteristics above and beyond its constitutional arrangements. These arrangements depend on virtue and character not only in the people in general but also—perhaps more so— in individual leaders. Washington writes:

> Should, hereafter, those who are entrusted with the management of this government, incited by the lust of power and prompted by the Supineness or venality of their Constituents, overleap the known barriers of this Constitution and violate the unalienable rights of human-

ity: it will only serve to shew, that no compact among men (however provident in its construction and sacred in its ratification) can be pronounced everlasting and inviolable, and if I may express myself, that no Wall of words, that no mound of parchment can be so formed as to stand against the sweeping torrent of boundless ambition on the one side, aided by the sapping current of corrupted morals on the other.[25]

That a concern for the proper character of both the rulers and the ruled was the first theme of his presidency is seen in the inaugural address that Washington did deliver to Congress on April 30, 1789. Rather than laying out an agenda for his administration, Washington paid homage to "that Almighty Being who rules over the universe; who presides in the councils of nations; and whose providential aid can supply every human defect." Then, although it was within his duties to recommend measures to Congress for consideration, he did no more than point the new representatives toward the objects defined in "the great constitutional charter" and instead spoke of "the talents, the rectitude, and the patriotism, which adorn the characters selected to devise and adopt" those measures. It is here and not in the institutional arrangements or measures themselves that Washington saw the "surest pledges" of wise policy. The prevalence of these virtues would ensure that neither local prejudices nor party animosities would misdirect the efforts of the representatives and guarantee that "the foundation of our national policy will be laid in the pure and immutable principles of private morality."

Washington was moved to "dwell on this prospect" for much deeper and profound reasons:

[T]here is no truth more thoroughly established than that there exists in the economy and course of nature, an indissoluble union between virtue and happiness; between duty and advantage, between the genuine maxims of an honest and magnanimous policy, and the solid rewards of public prosperity and felicity: since we ought to be no less persuaded that the propitious smiles of Heaven can never be expected on a nation that disregards the external rules of order and right, which Heaven itself has ordained: and since the preservation of the sacred fire of liberty, and the destiny of the republican model of government, are justly considered as deeply, perhaps as finally, staked on the experiment entrusted to the hands of the American people.[26]

The connection between private morality and public policy is not made for merely utilitarian purposes—far from it. For Washington, there is "no truth" more thoroughly established in the economy and course of nature than the "indissoluble union" between virtue and happiness. The "external rules of order and right"—"the eternal line that separates right from wrong" in the draft—suggests that morality and policy are informed by principles that are inflexible, permanent, and teleological, thus applying to both private and public life.[27] This formulation implies that some degree of virtue according to the external rules of order and right—as in the pure and immutable principles of private morality—is both necessary and good for the preservation of liberty and the destiny of republican government, a destiny placed in the hands of the American people.

The modern idea of liberty as the emancipation of the passions simply had no place in Washington's conception of things.

While there are practical differences between them, there is no radical break. Today's demarcation separating private and public morality does not exist. Moral character—understood as the ability to restrain the passions and maintain good habits—is necessary for the preservation of government based on reflection and choice, and hence the safety and happiness of the American people. Thus it can be said that *self*-government, i.e., the governing of one's own passions, necessarily precedes *free* government.

ADVICE AND SENTIMENTS

Washington's most famous advice concerning the nation's future is to be found in his Farewell Address of 1796. Written as he was retiring from the presidency, it presents the policies that Washington thought to be most conducive to the long-term safety and happiness of the American people. Washington hoped his advice would have a moderating effect on the body politic, controlling the current of political passions and thereby preventing the American regime from following the path that had "hitherto marked the Destiny of Nations."[28]

In the Farewell, Washington warns of "the baneful effects of the Spirit of Party," a spirit inseparable from "our nature" and rooted in the "strongest passions" of the human mind; a similar argument is found in *Federalist* 10. There James Madison argues that there are two unacceptable ways to remove the causes of faction—either by "destroying the liberty which is essential to its existence" or by "giving to every citizen the same opinions, the same passions, and the same interests." Madison concludes that relief was to be found in controlling its effects by extending the sphere of government so as to include a variety of parties and interests.[29] Washington, while generally agreeing with Madison, is interested in controlling, or at least moderating, the causes of party spirit and faction. An effort ought to be made to mitigate and assuage them, Washington argues, not by law or coercion but by "the force of public opinion."

Washington's solution is not to increase the diversity of interests so much as to shape a common opinion that will transcend the petty and self-interested differences that divide men. This demands the cultivation of the proper habits and dispositions on the part of the people, habits and dispositions that will moderate the natural passions that, among other things, encourage party animosities. The common opinion will be shaped by strengthening important common characteristics: public justice, religion and morality, education, and national independence.

The most important opinion is a common understanding of the rights and responsibilities of constitutional government and, indeed, of the Constitution itself. Thus a large element of Washington's solution is in the promotion of education in general and republican education in particular. Throughout his writings, it is clear that the consent that is necessary for just government must be informed. The "best means of forming a manly, virtuous and happy people, will be found in the right education of youth," he noted in 1784. "Without this foundation, every other means, in my opinion, must fail." Education and knowledge were to be encouraged for "qualifying the rising generation for patrons of good government, virtue, and happiness."[30]

"Promote, then, as an object of primary importance, institutions for the general diffusion of knowledge," he wrote in the Farewell Address. "In proportion as the structure of a government gives force to public opinion, it is essential that public opinion should be enlightened." By "enlightened" Washington means not only the basic parameters of liberal education but also knowledge of the rights of man and the obligations of citizenship. He supported the creation of a national university in which the arts, sciences, and belles lettres would be taught, providing the liberal education "necessary to qualify our citizens for the exigencies of public, as well as private life."[31] Here is how Washington described this project in his Eighth Annual Message:

> Amongst the motives to such as Institution, the assimilation of the principles, opinions and manners of our Country men, by the common education of a portion of our Youth from every quarter, well deserves attention. The more homogeneous our Citizens can be made in these particulars, the greater will be our prospect of permanent Union; and a primary object of such a National Institution should be, the education of our Youth in the science of Government. In a Republic, what species of knowledge can be equally important? And what duty, more pressing on its Legislature, than to patronize a plan for communicating it to those, who are to be the future guardians of the liberties of the Country?[32]

Washington believed that good opinions in the people and good government have a complementary effect on politics. Obeying just government and the rule of law would shape the people's opinions—and morals. On the one hand, he writes in the

Farewell Address, the "habits of thinking" in a free people would
"inspire caution" in their representatives and thereby confine
them to their constitutional responsibilities and prevent a spirit
of encroachment in government: "A just estimate of that love of
power, and proneness to abuse it, which predominates in the
human heart is sufficient to satisfy us of the truth of this position." On the other hand, the people would learn from the lawmaking process to curb their own passions for immediate
political change and abide by the legitimate legal process. This
causes the people to be moderate and circumspect.

Indeed, it is Washington's position that the new
Constitution actually encourages moderation and good habits of
government. First, the separation of powers and the system of
checks and balances thwart governmental despotism and promote
responsibility in public representatives. A responsible government, in turn, bolsters responsible people. Second, the legitimate
constitutional-amendment process allows democratic reform at
the same time that it elevates the document above the popular
passions of the moment, thereby encouraging deliberation and
patience in the people.

The most famous argument of the Farewell Address concerns
the moderation of private passion through the encouragement of
private morality. "Of all the disposition and habits which lead to
political prosperity, Religion and morality are indispensable supports," Washington writes. Religion and morality are the props
of duty, the indispensable supports of the dispositions and habits
that lead to political prosperity, and the great pillars of human
happiness. They aid good government by teaching men their

moral obligations and creating the conditions for decent politics. While there might be particular cases where morality does not depend on religion, Washington argues that this is not the case for the morality of the nation. Religion is needed to give weight to morality: "And let us with caution indulge the supposition, that morality can be maintained without religion."

Lastly, Washington recommends that the United States "observe good faith and justice towds. all Nations." Both religion and morality as well as good policy enjoin this conduct. As there is a connection between private morality and public happiness in a people, so there is a connection between the virtue and happiness of a nation. As there are proper dispositions and habits of people, so too with nations. Primary among these is the independent character promoted and fostered by an independent and self-determined foreign policy. The main reason, in addition to cultivating friendly relations with other nations, was not so much to directly influence world affairs as to present a model of good government and character to the rest of the world: "It will be worthy of a free, enlightened, and at no distant period, a great Nation, to give to mankind the magnanimous and too novel example of a People always guided by an exalted justice and benevolence." Such conduct toward other nations would serve further to elevate and distinguish the national character. "The experiment," Washington wrote, "is recommended by every sentiment which ennobles human Nature."

THE POLITICS OF PRUDENCE

George Washington believed as firmly in individual freedom, in the pursuit of economic well-being, and in the material fruits of modern science, as any of the other Founders. His view of the American Revolution was based on a conception not only of conventional rights to be found guaranteed in charters and constitutions, but also of higher rights grounded in nature, coming as it did at "an Epocha when the rights of mankind were better understood and more clearly defined, than at any former period."[33] But he was no starry-eyed idealist; he fully recognized the interested and passionate character of individuals and politics. "We must take the passions of Man as Nature has given them, and those principles as a guide which are generally the rule of Action," Washington wrote in 1778.[34] The interesting and decisive question for Washington was this: Liberty, progress, and rights to do what?

Far from abandoning virtue, Washington's understanding of natural rights requires the moralization of politics. While the separation of church and state disentangled the doctrines of theology from political authority—a policy Washington strongly maintained—that does not free men (or politics) from "the external rules of order and right, which Heaven itself has ordained." Washington saw the ground of civil and religious liberty in the doctrine of equal rights, but always maintained that the legitimate exercise of those rights must nevertheless remain in accord with the larger moral order that gave rise to those rights in the first place. Whatever else religious liberty meant, it allowed (just as Washington summoned) morality and the moral teachings of religion to actively shape the nation's character and influence public opinion.

The Farewell Address reminds us that the American character will always depend fundamentally on the proper dispositions and habits of the people. Public virtue cannot be expected in a climate of private vice, nor will individual morality flourish in the absence of a sense of civic responsibility. To be sure, the precise relationship between the two has always been difficult to establish. Washington and the Founders believed that there must be a significant degree of public separation between religion and freedom of conscience, and politics. Moreover, they believed that this separation, properly constituted, actually strengthened both private morality and public virtue. But although the private and public spheres are practically separated in American republicanism, they remain indissolubly linked in "the economy and course of nature."

The link between private morality and wise public policy is described by the classic virtue of prudence, the practical reasoning by which principles are applied to concrete reality. Prudence is the ability to exercise sound judgment in practical matters, giving to political reasoning its particular character and distinguishing it from abstract or speculative thought. The catch is that it presupposes, indeed requires, the presence of moral character: it is the intellectual virtue of deliberating well on the proper means to the ends set by moral virtue. As prudence or practical wisdom is the preeminent skill needed for political leadership, the measure of the prudent man is first and foremost moral character.

It is no coincidence or slight, then, that Washington is praised first and foremost for his good character, for character is the substance of prudence and the preeminent virtue of the statesman. "More solid than brilliant, *judgment*, rather than *genius*, constituted the most prominent feature of his character," John Marshall says in his biography of Washington.[35] Perhaps the best portrait of Washington left by a close associate was that written by his erstwhile critic Thomas Jefferson. "His mind was great and powerful, without being of the very first order" and his mind was "not so acute as that of Newton, Bacon or Locke," Jefferson writes, but he was "in every sense of the words, a wise, a good, and a great man." What was it that made Washington great? Jefferson concludes:

> Perhaps the strongest feature in his character was *prudence*, never acting until every circumstance, every consideration, was maturely weighed; refraining if he saw a doubt, but when once decided, going through with his purpose, whatever obstacles opposed. His integrity was pure, his justice the most inflexible I have ever known, no motives of interest or consanguinity, of friendship or hatred, being able to bias his decision.... On the whole, his *character* was, in its mass, perfect, in nothing bad, in few points indifferent.[36]

During his lifetime Washington embodied the American character. His virtues and actions made him the indispensable man, the catalyst without whom the political reaction of the American Revolution would not have successfully taken place. He demonstrated the possibility of, and the relationship between, public and private character; he proved that a nation of rights and equality is neither incompatible with nor indifferent to good character and great men. Daniel Webster observed in 1834:

> To him who denies or doubts whether our fervid liberty can be com-
> bined with law, with order, with the security of property, with the
> pursuits and advancement of happiness; to him who denies that our
> forms of government are capable of producing *exaltation of soul*, and
> the *passion of true glory*; to him who denies that we have contributed
> any thing to the stock of great lessons and great examples; to all these
> I reply by pointing to Washington.[37]

But even George Washington's character and deeds, while they qualify him as one of the greatest figures in American history, do not fully capture the sense in which he was a *founder*.

Washington's career aimed at creating not just an independent country but a national character that was at once distinctly American and republican. In order to realize the improvements in political science and perpetuate the modern republican institutions of the early Republic, he relied on the old methods of moral virtue and character formation. By personifying and elaborating the traits of good character in both private and public life, he sought to moderate the passions of citizens and ennoble the deeds of statesmen. To the extent that his words and his model placed an emphasis on these two qualities—moderation and nobility—Washington should be judged not according to modern political science but, rather, the classical principles of statesmanship and political life.

Although it cannot be said that Washington gave America her laws, he did give America her character. This difficult and challenging task—forming the moral character of a people—places Washington in the highest ranks of statesmen. This is why

Washington—and not Madison, Jefferson, or Hamilton—is remembered as the Father of his Country.

TEN

"Our Illustrious Washington": The American Imaging of George Washington

MARK THISTLETHWAITE

E ver since Charles Willson Peale executed the first life portrait of George Washington in 1772 (fig. 1), Washington's image has been continuously woven into the fabric of American culture. Washington has been portrayed in amazingly diverse and seemingly limitless ways, not only in paintings, prints, and sculptures, but also on coins, currency, stamps, and chinaware, as well as in advertisements and other objects of popular culture. Though styles, formats, and intentions have varied tremendously, Washington imagery has been for more than 225 years a vital visual touchstone for America. Like the Declaration of Independence and the Constitution, George Washington's image has generated and endured a variety of interpretations, uses, and abuses, yet all the while has remained firmly embedded in the American imagination and at the core of our national identity. How and why have Americans imaged "our illustrious Washington"?[1]

The easy answer is that Americans have continually returned to depict George Washington simply because he is the Great

American Hero. The abundance and diversity of Washington's representations demand, however, a more expansive response.[2] But that same abundance and diversity also argue against the possibility of a thorough account and assessment of Washington imagery in the limited space available here. This essay aims, then, to approach answering the questions of "how and why" by discussing specific visual representations that illuminate the general nature of Washington imagery, focusing on three types of representations: the Iconic Washington, the Heroic Washington, and the Familial Washington. Although a blurring of boundaries does occur, these categories are nevertheless helpful in making sense of the wealth of Washington imagery. All three types appeared during Washington's lifetime, and they still shape the portrayal of the Father of our Country. Despite this continuity, twentieth-century images of Washington often differ significantly from those produced in the eighteenth and nineteenth centuries. The essay will conclude with a consideration of those salient differences.

THE ICONIC WASHINGTON
In 1793, Gilbert Stuart returned to the United States, after studying and practicing art in Britain for eighteen years. He came back specifically to enhance his reputation by portraying George Washington. Stuart was not alone in his pursuit, for already dozens of portrayals of Washington had been executed in oil paints, pastels, and a variety of printmaking techniques. Individual artists often replicated their own work. For instance, Charles Willson Peale produced at least nineteen variations of his

portrait *Washington at Princeton* (fig. 2). The original, life-sized painting was commissioned in 1779 by the Supreme Executive Council of Pennsylvania for the purposes of honoring Washington, providing an image of virtue, and, in essence, personifying the country. Washington had become, and would continue to be, so completely identified with the nation that virtually every portrait of him could be understood as both a likeness of the man and an image of America itself. It is no exaggeration to claim that representations of Washington assumed the quality of religious icons.

Traditionally, an icon is a likeness that functions as a sacred object of veneration because it embodies the character and transmits the values of the religious person depicted. The image of George Washington, whom citizens have regarded as godlike, the American Moses, and "the Patron-Saint of our soil,"[3] became America's civil icon.[4] This reverent attitude toward the image of George Washington was observed in the early nineteenth century by Pavel Svinin, a Russian diplomatic officer: "Washington's portrait is the finest and sometimes the sole decoration of American homes.... It is noteworthy that every American considers it his sacred duty to have a likeness of Washington in his home, just as we have images of God's saints."[5] The necessity of this American icon was asserted by an 1836 writer: "No cottage should be without his likeness, no mansion without his picture, no legislative hall without his statue, that rich and poor, the highest statesman and the humblest citizen, may have him always before their eyes, and copy, each according to his station, the public and private virtues of Washington."[6] In 1852, when Americans were reading of Uncle Tom's cabin having a portrait of Washington adorning the wall above its fireplace, Ralph Waldo Emerson could not "keep [his] eye off" the image of Washington he had recently hung in his dining room.[7] Paintings from the nineteenth century, including John Lewis Krimmel's *Quilting Frolic* (1813) and Francis Edmonds's *Taking the Census* (1854), confirm the presence of Washington's image in American interiors. Twentieth-century painters have also perpetuated this Iconic Washington. Tom Wesselmann's *Still Life #31* (1963) shows a television set, not the hearth, as the center of the home, but his inclusion of Washington's portrait on the wall affirms the Americanness of this modern interior. Wesselmann followed the lead of many of his nineteenth-century predecessors by taking as his icon Gilbert Stuart's Athenaeum portrait.

The Rhode Island–born artist executed three types of Washington life portraits, known as the "Vaughan," the "Athenaeum," and the "Lansdowne." The first to be completed, in 1795, was the Vaughan, which shows the right side of Washington's face. This type was named for John Vaughan of Philadelphia, who had commissioned one portrait for himself and another to be sent to his father in England. Stuart was to produce about a dozen replicas of this portrait. The following year, the artist painted both the Athenaeum and Lansdowne portraits. The precise order in which these two were produced is debated, though Washington sat for Stuart for both, and the head of each (showing the left side of the face) is the same. The full-length Lansdowne portrait is so-named because it was presented by Mrs. William Bingham, who commissioned it, to the Marquis of

Lansdowne, a British supporter of the American cause during the Revolutionary War. The Athenaeum portrait (fig. 3), which quickly became, and remains, the best known portrait of Washington, was one of a pair of compositions commissioned by Martha Washington (the other being her own likeness).

Known as the "Mount Vernon" portraits during Stuart's lifetime, the current designation became attached after 1831, when the Boston Athenaeum purchased the works. Both portraits of the Washingtons are unfinished, apparently on purpose. Stuart, who had a difficult time "pinning" Washington's likeness (earlier, he apparently rubbed out the original Vaughan painting in frustration) realized that he had rendered a remarkable image of Washington and that it could serve as a model for numerous replicas that he might sell. And sell them he did; Stuart produced more than sixty copies, or what he called his "hundred dollar bills" (their going rate). In a wonderful instance of life following art, this metaphoric association of the portrait with currency became real, when the image began appearing on the one-dollar bill in 1869. However, long before being reproduced on money, the Athenaeum portrait had become ingrained in the American imagination.

The iconic status of the Athenaeum portrait had taken root in American culture by the 1820s, despite the scores of Washington portraits by other artists that existed and competed for the public's attention. For instance, Rembrandt Peale, son of Charles Willson Peale, declared his "Porthole" Washington portrait (1824) a more authentic likeness. In spite of artistic competition, Stuart's portrait emerged as the dominant representation of Washington. Popular evidence of this is found, for example, in John Neal's 1823 novel, *Randolph*, where a character asserts: "[t]hough a better likeness of him [Washington] were shown to us, we would reject it; for, the only idea that we now have of George Washington, is associated with Stuart's Washington."[8] Neal perceived that the iconic power of the Athenaeum portrait meant that Stuart's creation necessarily transcended mere likeness: "If George Washington should appear on earth, just as he sat to Stuart, I am sure that he would be treated as an imposter [sic], when compared to Stuart's likeness of him, unless he produced his credentials."[9] As an icon, the painting had "become" Washington.

This iconic sense of the Athenaeum portrait has remained powerful in the twentieth century. Writer Cynthia Ozick recalled the portrait as informing her school days in the Bronx during the 1930s, with Washington and "his little cloud corner presiding over all, not as a falsifying icon but as civic inspiration...representing, above all, a sense of stability, or call it security."[10] The reproduction Ozick saw over the classroom blackboard was likely one of the million prints distributed across the nation in 1932, as part of the bicentennial celebration of Washington's birth. Although it was not the official Washington image selected by the United States Bicentennial Commission (that honor belonged to a sculpture bust by Jean-Antoine Houdon), Americans preferred the Stuart portrait and the commission acceded to popular preference.[11] The ambitious national placement of the Athenaeum portrait in the 1930s emphatically reinforced the picture's status as a civic icon that served to model and inculcate moral behavior, as well as to convey fundamental values and ideals identified with Washington, such as courage, duty, and commitment to freedom. The ongoing belief in the portrait's iconic power was reconfirmed in 1999, when a New Jersey–based organization, Portraits of Patriots, set out to distribute reproductions of the Stuart painting to its state's schools. Americans still regard (though more ambivalently than in earlier days) the Athenaeum portrait as an icon. But what are its special qualities that have made it such a civic icon for Americans for over two centuries?

The Athenaeum portrait, in spite of its unfinished state, succeeds in projecting Washington's commanding physical presence and "his moral strength of character."[12] As a portraitist wonderfully skilled in rendering flesh, Stuart was able to conjure up an image of convincing vitality through his lively brushwork. By directing Washington's eyes at the viewer, the artist establishes an active relationship between the viewer and the sitter: we contemplate Washington as he, it seems, contemplates us. Stuart allows nothing to interfere with or distract from Washington's "peerless presence."[13] The artist forgoes props or background elements so that the viewer may focus on Washington alone and ponder the character as conveyed through his head. Such contemplation was particularly germane to eighteenth-century and nineteenth-century Americans, who embraced the notion that physical attributes of the head revealed an individual's character. By not finishing the body, Stuart could call even more attention to the edifying qualities of Washington.

Though his reason for not finishing the work was driven by economic consideration (claiming it was incomplete, he could keep it in order to make saleable copies from it), the unfinished quality enhances the image's aura and does seem to set him among the clouds. Being incomplete, the painting suggests that an artist can offer, at best, only a partial record of Washington's greatness and accomplishments. Also, its unfinished state allows us to read the composition in three ways as a metaphor for process. First, the partially completed representation of George Washington can be interpreted as portraying Washington's legacy as an ongoing process, one never truly finished. Second, the empty areas of canvas provoke and challenge viewers to "fill in the blanks," which further activates their process of responding to, and involving themselves in, the composition. For instance, Martin Scorsese, the movie director, recalled prints of the Athenaeum portraits hanging on his family's living room wall, along with images of saints and religious scenes: "To me, the unpainted canvas represented clouds and the president and his wife were heavenly figures."[14] Third, the canvas's bare areas, seemingly waiting for the artist to finish, connote Stuart's role as the active agent in the portrait process. That a portrait results from the interaction of at least two people—the sitter and the artist—was recalled by an 1853 author, who, in writing of the Athenaeum picture, observed that "the noble head, and that hand that traced the lineaments, have long ago crumbled to dust; but the genius of both is enshrined on canvass."[15] The writer's choice of "enshrined" is telling and reinforces the similarities of Stuart's painting to religious icons.

A painting from 1858 by Carl H. Schmolze further enhances Stuart's work as an icon. *Washington Sitting for His Portrait to*

Gilbert Stuart (fig. 4) shows the artist in his Germantown studio with Washington and the president's family and friends. The prominence of Martha Washington in the left foreground reminds us of the too-often overlooked fact that it was she who had commissioned this most famous work. In Schmolze's painting, the Athenaeum portrait is barely sketched out on the canvas. Washington, who sits on a dais in the center of the composition, looks nobly aloof, almost as though he were a statue, and, indeed, the military officer (perhaps Henry Knox) who gazes at Washington, seems to be intently scrutinizing an object, not a person. Schmolze does capture the feeling of equanimity that Washington was eventually able to bring to the frequent portrait sittings he had to endure. In 1785, Washington wrote to Francis Hopkinson that he could now sit before painters "like patience on a Monument whilst they are delineating the lines of my face."[16] In rendering the Athenaeum portrait in-process, the German-born Schmolze adopted not the grand manner associated with history painting, but an anecdotal approach in keeping with European and American art of the period. Nevertheless, this less elevated style did not diminish the painting's significant content: mid-nineteenth-century America had its own history of art and artists, who had played (and, presumably, will continue to play) important roles in fixing and perpetuating images of national identity.

Schmolze's composition also expressed current concerns, for in 1858, interest in rendering scenes from American history was particularly strong, as were opinions on whether Congress should commission foreign artists or native ones to carry out such work.

Where Schmolze stood in this debate is not known. In selecting
the scene that he did, he may have intended not only to show his
respect for the accomplishments of American art, but also his
own ability as a foreign-born artist to render a national subject.
Whatever his intentions, Schmolze's picture centers on the creation of the portrait that would become a national icon.

An obvious indication of its iconic status is how often the
Athenaeum portrait has been appropriated by artists, illustrators,
and graphic designers who desire or need to present an immediately recognizable George Washington. The image has appeared
seemingly everywhere and in all manner of forms. For instance,
pop artist Roy Lichtenstein derived his painting *George
Washington* (1962) from a woodcut version of the Stuart portrait
he discovered in a Hungarian newspaper. Sometimes the
Athenauem image is quoted directly; other times changes are
made. Frequently it appears reversed, as seen on the one-dollar
bill. The book jacket designed by Stark Design for Richard
Brookhiser's 1996 *Founding Father: Rediscovering George Washington*
features both a color reproduction of the Athenaeum Washington
and a muted gray-green version of the dollar bill. Of all its many
and diverse quotations, surely the most remarkable occurs in
Grant Wood's *Parson Weems' Fable* of 1939.

In Grant Wood's composition (fig. 5), Mason Locke Weems
draws back a curtain to reveal the story of George Washington
and the cherry tree, which first appeared in the fifth edition
(1806) of Weems's extraordinarily popular *Life of Washington*.
Weems, a bookseller and the self-styled rector of the fictitious
Mount Vernon Parish, wholly invented this episode about truth

telling. Grant Wood, concerned that debunking historians had drained American history of its colorful and useful fables, aimed to resurrect the nation's mythic heritage. He chose to produce this painting specifically at the moment when the world was on the verge of a second world war, because "in our present unsettled times, when democracy is threatened on all sides, the preservation of our folklore is more important than is generally realized."[17]

Wood cleverly constructed a composition that embraces the artifice of Weems's story by using an immaculate landscape, exaggerated perspective, theatrical obviousness of pointing hands, and cherries hanging from the tree like the curtain's tassels. Wood "steals" the motif of the parson holding back the curtain from Charles Willson Peale's *The Artist in His Museum* (1822). Peale reveals what he called his "world in miniature," while Weems entices us to enter a world of his own design. Most artificial of all, of course, is the Athenaeum head atop the body of the boy.

Wrestling with the problem of how to make the six-year-old George immediately identifiable, Wood hit upon the brilliant and audacious solution of transplanting the iconic Athenaeum head to the figure of the child. As bizarre as this is, it makes historical sense on at least two counts. In rendering the man-child, Wood conveys an essential lesson of Weems's story: in the child appears the man. The cherry tree fable reinforced the belief that the noble character of the mature Washington was evident in childhood. The other historical perception Wood played upon is the difficulty of envisioning Washington as a child. The authority of portraits such as Stuart's have become so embedded in our imagination that it is hard to imagine a convincing likeness of a young Washington. This is not to say that artists have not produced images of Washington's boyhood, for they have. To do so, however, they must grapple with the omnipresent Iconic Washington and try to banish it from the viewer's mind. The likelihood of achieving this was vividly commented upon by Nathaniel Hawthorne in 1853: "Did anyone ever see Washington nude! It is inconceivable. He had no nakedness, but, I imagine, was born with his clothes on, and his hair powdered, and made a stately bow on his first appearance in the world."[18] Grant Wood likewise perceived the difficulty of thinking of Washington as a child and, perhaps even taking a cue from Hawthorne, realized that in order to render the child absolutely recognizable as Washington, only the iconic Athenaeum image would serve his purpose.

THE HEROIC WASHINGTON

Charles Willson Peale's *George Washington at Princeton* (1779), which the Supreme Executive Council of Pennsylvania had commissioned for iconic purposes, is the first truly heroic depiction of Washington, in terms of its dimensions (nearly eight feet high) and subject matter (Washington as military victor). Surprisingly, however, Peale represents the general in a notably casual attitude, similar to Thomas Jefferson's description of Washington as "easy, noble, and erect."[19] Shunning the more formal European manner of rendering a military hero, Peale portrays Washington with body relaxed, one hand at his hip holding his hat, and the other hand resting on a cannon. Captured battle flags lie at his feet.

Washington exudes a relaxed confidence, which offered reassurance to Americans in their revolutionary cause. Washington's attitude, as much as his likeness and the picture's subject, accounted for the popularity of Peale's work. The casual heroism of the Peale painting is carried on in a slightly more formal fashion by the French sculptor Jean-Antoine Houdon, who received the commission to carve a life-sized marble image for the Virginia State Capitol in Richmond (fig. 6).

Houdon traveled to Mount Vernon in 1785 to study Washington, make sketches, and create a life mask. Following the dictates of contemporary European neoclassicism, Houdon intended to show the hero in a toga. Washington, however, considered such garb inappropriate, and Houdon agreed to portray him in his uniform. Nevertheless, Houdon did incorporate classicistic elements into his work. Washington's left hand rests upon a fasces, the Roman emblem of authority. Though in uniform, Washington has hung his sword from the fasces and supports himself with a walking stick. He stands, then, as the retired officer. Behind him is a plow, referring not only Washington's love of agriculture, but also to the ancient story of Cincinnatus, the Roman general who willingly gave up power to return to his farm. In Houdon's hands, Washington is represented as the heroic citizen-soldier, the American Cincinnatus. The balance between realistic detail and heroic attitude that infuses the Peale painting also characterizes the Houdon sculpture and has contributed to the appeal of his work. The synthesis of realism and idealism characterizes much earlier American art. When an artist miscalculated the combination of the two, the reception of the resulting work could be highly unfavorable, as Horatio Greenough discovered in 1841.

As the first commission awarded by the federal government to an American sculptor, Greenough's monumental marble *George Washington* (fig. 7) assumed major importance and aroused wide public attention. Unfortunately, Americans were not pleased with his efforts, finding the sculpture ridiculously heroic. Satirically dubbed George "Jupiter" Washington, Greenough's eleven-foot-high work presents a godlike, enthroned Washington. Basing his image on Houdon's life mask and a reconstruction of the ancient Greek sculptor Phidias's colossal statue of Zeus, Greenough shows a togaed and sandaled Washington offering his sword and gesturing triumphantly. Most Americans had difficulty taking the work seriously; one referred to it as a "warrior-like *Venus of the Bath*" with Washington "preparing his ablutions...in the act of consigning his sword to the care of the attendant until he shall come out of the bath."[20] Soon after being installed in its intended site in the United States Capitol Rotunda, the work was removed. Since the debacle of Greenough's work, most sculptors have looked to the Houdon image for inspiration and have wedded realistic details to an idealistic attitude in order to convey successfully the Heroic Washington.

Without a doubt the most successful heroic image of Washington is Emanuel Leutze's immense painting, *Washington Crossing the Delaware* (fig. 8). Like Stuart's Athenaeum portrait, Leutze's grand composition has been appropriated and manipulated countless times. Reproductions of the picture have hung in classrooms, illustrated scholarly and popular books, occurred in advertisements, and served political cartoonists. These and every other use of and reference to the picture evince and reinforce its visual potency, its immense celebrity, and its thorough assimilation into the American imagination.

The huge oil painting, measuring over twelve by twenty-one feet and which now hangs in New York City's Metropolitan Museum of Art, was created in Dusseldorf, Germany, and is the larger second version of the subject executed by the German-American artist. The first version, finished in 1850, had been severely damaged in a fire in Leutze's studio. The work we know today was unveiled to the American public in October 1851, in New York City. Enthusiastic critical and popular acclaim greeted the display of the painting—the *New York Evening Mirror* deemed it "the grandest, most majestic, and most effective painting ever executed in America."[21] The picture immediately became *the* image of the Delaware crossing, supplanting all earlier depictions of the event, while also becoming the paradigm to which all later representations were compared.

Before Leutze, virtually no artists had shown Washington in a boat. The general was depicted either mounted or standing on the river's west bank. Leutze's composition changed the point of view not only by resituating the leader, but also by emphasizing Washington's heroics. Contemporaries responded excitedly to Leutze's innovative approach, saying that the composition "with the majestic figure of Washington in this new and expressive attitude, presents an ensemble for the canvas, as new and striking as it is picturesque."[22] Another writer, echoing the sentiments of many Americans, declared: "Washington has never been presented in a more heroic or noble aspect."[23]

Leutze created an image of greater drama, more convincing realism, and grander scale than had been produced previously. The artist skillfully tied the tension of navigating the boat through the ice-choked river to the inspiring stability and steadfast leadership of General Washington, who seems to be impelling the Revolution forward through sheer willpower. In the words of another mid-nineteenth-century journalist, "You feel embued [sic] with its [the painting's] spirit, animated by its impulse, and flushed with its excitement."[24]

Washington Crossing the Delaware made its entry into American culture at an auspicious time. The year the painting was unveiled in New York City, 1851, marked the seventy-fifth anniversary of both the Declaration of Independence and the crossing of the Delaware River, an event considered by many to be the turning point in the American Revolution. In addition, by this date George Washington was firmly established as the great American hero, who "like Moses...led his countrymen through the dreary wilderness of the Revolution and when the journey terminated he planted them upon the promised land of Freedom and Independence."[25] In 1851, as the divisiveness of sectionalism increased, Americans turned with renewed interest to Washington for inspiration. At the same time, one author wrote, "Those convulsions which threaten the permanence of our Union, only render more and more dear the name of the Father of the American Republic."[26] Leutze's painting, which he probably hoped would be installed in the Rotunda of the United States Capitol, was clearly the right painting at the right time.

Washington Crossing the Delaware's popular appeal has

remained unabated, though critics began writing about the work negatively in the 1860s. As painting in the second half of the century moved toward a modernist aesthetic, art writers found Leutze's work old-fashioned in its realistic style and hyperpatriotic narrative. But those very qualities have continued to make the work a favorite of the public, who regard it, like the Athenaeum portrait, as a national icon and as the primary example of the Heroic Washington.

THE FAMILIAL WASHINGTON

Complementing, even contradicting, the image of Washington as icon and as hero are representations of a humanized Washington. Such depictions typically show Washington at Mount Vernon working his land and with his family. In theses images the *pater patriae* gives way to the *pater familias*.

The earliest such composition in this third mode is Edward Savage's *The Washington Family* of 1786–96 (fig. 9). Around a table sit Washington, his wife, and his two adopted grandchildren, Nelly and George Washington Parke Custis. A slave, likely William Lee, who attended the general during the Revolutionary War, stands behind them. On one side of the table, Nelly and Mrs. Washington hold open a map of Washington, D. C. On the other side sits Washington, with his arm casually draped over the shoulder of the boy. Washington's sword rests on the table. Young Custis places his right hand, in which he holds a compass, on a globe. More than just an image of Washington as a family man, the painting speaks to the future of America, represented by the children, the map of the new city, and the globe. The work of

the sword has given way to the work of the compass in the settling of a new nation.[27]

Despite this early picture by Savage, images of the Familial
Washington did not begin proliferating until the 1840s. By this
time, Americans had developed a sense of the past that allowed
for the humanizing of heroes. In addition, increased emphasis on
the family and childrearing, and the myth of Jacksonian democracy, encouraged a more familiarized view of the past. Genre
painting, which depicts ordinary people engaged in daily activities, had established itself as an important mode of art. History
painting, which traditionally portrayed great men and great
events in order to inculcate moral and patriotic lessons, was
affected by genre painting and began to include more anecdotal
episodes. This did not mean, however, a lessening of a didactic
agenda, for, as Reverend Henry F. Harrington opined in 1849,
"the lovers of Washington could gain from every event of his life,
whether little or great, only fresh evidences of his exalted purity,
his ennobling sense of right, his disinterested self-sacrifice."[28]
Images of the Familial Washington resulted in no loss of inspiring qualities and, in fact, could enhance those traits by making
them more accessible. In other words, "Washington on his farm
at Mount Vernon, performing his duties as a virtuous and useful
citizen, is not less worthy of contemplation than Washington
leading his country to independence, and showing her how to
enjoy it afterwards. The former example is indeed more extensively useful, because it comes home to the business and bosoms
of ordinary men, and is within the reach of their imitation."[29]

The influence of such mid-nineteenth-century thinking on

the art of the time is evident in the work of Junius Brutus Stearns. This New York artist was the only painter of the period who attempted to paint a cycle of images chronicling George Washington's life and career. As conceived in 1848, Stearns's series was to depict Washington as a soldier in the French and Indian War, his marriage to Martha Custis, his role as the Mount Vernon farmer, and his death. A fifth painting, showing him as a statesman, was completed a few years after the others; but, unlike the other four, it was not engraved. Tellingly, three of the four works forming Stearns's original conception present the Familial Washington.

In *The Marriage of Washington to Martha Custis* (1849), *Washington as a Farmer at Mount Vernon* (1851), and *Washington on His Deathbed* (1851), Washington is set among family and friends. The marriage scene visualizes what Americans had been reading about in novels and journals for years: Washington in love. Stearns captures the elegant, aristocratic flavor associated with colonial Virginia, which many of his contemporaries nostalgically viewed as "that ancient period."[30] This attitude provided a counterpoint to the more aggressive nationalistic spirit imbuing manifest destiny, the war with Mexico, and California gold rush fever.

The United States still had an agriculturally based economy when Stearns rendered his *Washington as a Farmer at Mount Vernon* in 1851 (fig. 10), and this painting can be understood as apotheosizing the American agrarian ideal, with Washington as the nation's First Farmer and America's Cincinnatus. Such connotations were readily understood by Americans, having grown up hearing and reading Parson Weems's *Life of Washington*:

He [Washington] abhors war; but, if war be necessary, to this end he
bravely encounters it. His ruling passion must be obeyed. He beats
his ploughshare into a sword, and exchanges the peace and pleasure
of his fame for the din and dangers of the camp. Having won the great
prize for which he contended, he returns to the plough. His military
habits are laid by with same ease as he would throw off an old coat....
The useful citizen is the high character he wishes to act—his sword
turned into a ploughshare is his favourite instrument, and his beloved
farm his stage.[31]

By focusing on Washington-the-farmer, Stearns reinforced the
American paradigm of the patriotic citizen-farmer, at a time
when the country was becoming increasingly industrialized,
urbanized, and sectionalized.[32]

In *Washington on His Deathbed*, the great man is rendered as
he expires among family and friends. Stearns includes
Washington's adopted grandchildren in the scene, although this
is historically inaccurate. By showing them and by moving
Martha Washington from the foot of the bed (where she was
recorded to have been) to Washington's side, the artist is able to
frame the *pater familias* with loved ones. Stearns's painting differs
significantly from the spate of mourning images and apotheoses
that had appeared immediately after Washington's death in
1799. Rendered in a more realistic and less emotional manner
than those earlier allegorical portrayals, Stearns represents a calm
Washington resigned to his fate. This depiction accorded well
with the mid-century's belief that Washington had died a triumphant death, that is, a death distinguished by Christian resig-

nation. Appropriately, when the painting appeared as a lithograph in 1853, it bore the title *Life of George Washington. The Christian.*

The Familial Washington was to become the most popular type of later Washington imagery. Depictions of George Washington produced after the centennial celebration and well into the 1920s were greatly affected by the Colonial Revival and typically featured elegantly costumed figures in charming, rococo-like compositions. Artists such as Jennie Brownscombe, John Ward Dunsmore, Henry A. Ogden, and, especially, Jean Leon Gerome Ferris rendered such subjects as *The Marriage of Nellie Custis at Mount Vernon: Washington's Last Birthday*, *Washington's Farewell to his Mother*, *Washington's Silver Wedding Anniversary*, and *Mount Vernon and Peace*. Often published as illustrations for books, magazines, greeting cards, and calendars, these popular works differed from Stearns's work in being decidedly more nostalgic and often appearing to emphasize style over substance. The earlier body of art created by Stearns and contemporaries was among the last images to reflect an almost unquestioned national belief that Washington, whether rendered familially, heroically, or iconically, was truly America's *exemplum virtutis*. This is not to say that later images did not strive to express this ideal but to suggest that subsequent imagery, except perhaps for that produced during the bicentennial celebration of his birth in 1932, could not unequivocally embrace the elevated conception of Washington embodied in earlier works of art. The reasons for this are too varied, complex, and numerous to discuss here, but two significant ones can be described briefly: the change in the nature of art and the increased commercialization of Washington's image.

The changing nature of Washington imagery occurred simultaneously with the declining stature of history painting (with which depictions of Washington are inherently linked) and the advent of modernist art. From the Renaissance to the mid-nineteenth century, the production of history painting was regarded as the highest aim of the serious artist. As a narrative and didactic form, history painting drew upon subjects from history, religion, mythology, and literature to show human beings engaged in significant actions. Scenes of Washington's life and career, and even his likeness, qualify as history paintings. Traditionally, an elevated subject and grand style were hallmarks of history painting. But in the nineteenth century, realism, with its emphasis on contemporary subjects and a more naturalistic style, challenged and ultimately defeated history painting's dominance. Although modernist art is most often associated with abstraction, it began as a movement concerned with realism. By the time abstract art did appear in the early twentieth century, modernism had already established its own hegemony—the tradition and shock of the new—and history painting was deemed an outmoded form of art.

Artists, such as the Colonial Revivalist painters and the later Regionalists, who persisted in producing history paintings, were considered nonmodernist, at best, and antimodernist, at worst. Any modernist attempting a historical composition, including images of Washington, leavened the work with humor or parody. Ironically, one way to shock the avant-garde was to render the past, as Larry Rivers did in 1953. Striving to assert his artistic independence from the reigning abstract expressionist movement, Rivers took as his subject Washington crossing the Delaware (fig. 11). He was, however, ultimately less concerned with depicting the historical event than in generating a composition that provocatively referenced Leutze's iconic painting. Rivers realized that for most people "Washington crossing the Delaware" meant the painting. To his art world contemporaries, Leutze's theatrically heroic, narrative composition could hardly have been more opposed to the abstract expressionist aesthetic. Further, the 1851 painting had been so often reproduced in popular forms that it had come to be reviled by modernists as the most hackneyed of all American images. Rivers understood this and knew that executing a work titled *Washington Crossing the Delaware* would ignite an artistic firestorm, which it did. Both his intention and his audience's hostile reaction were far removed from the world of earlier pictures of George Washington.

As modernist art was transformed by pop art in the 1960s and post-modernism after it, an increase in images of Washington occurred. Inclusivity and pluralism have come to characterize art (as with society in general) and have allowed the incorporation of historical and narrative elements. However, with history and narration regarded as social constructs, and "truth" as relative, artists have continued to imbue Washington imagery with irony and parody. For instance, Val Hunnicutt's *Washington Contemplates Crossing the Delaware* (fig. 12) parodies Leutze's painting by showing a paint-by-number landscape the artist found, to which she affixed a cheap statuette of Washington and a repro-

duction of *Washington Crossing the Delaware*. Looking beyond the
heroics of the event, the artist highlights the thought that
Washington put into his daring strategy. However, she humor-
ously subverts this by having the boat sail off without its commander. Additionally, in presenting the hero as a figurine,
Hunnicutt both reinforces the Iconic Washington and deflates his
monumental character. The plastic effigy and the reproduction of
the Leutze painting serve to remind us of the manufactured and
mass-produced nature of Washington's image. While the production of Washington kitsch has been a growth industry since
his death in 1799,[33] the link between such imagery and objects to
consumerism and capitalism is particularly strong at the end of
the twentieth century.

Since the 1970s, representations of George Washington have
increasingly quoted or been derived from the form of his image
on the one-dollar bill, a motif immediately recognizable by its
oval cartouche. The appearance of this "capitalistic" Washington
has certainly been fueled by, but not at all not limited to, the
innumerable advertisements for sales of all sorts that are published every Presidents' Day. Reflecting the times, Washington
has become an icon of capitalism. A fascinating synthesis of this
capitalistic representation with the iconic, heroic, and familial
ones is found in a 1997 painting by Steve Kaufman (fig. 13). His
large oil on canvas features Charles Willson Peale's Heroic
Washington immersed in a wildly colored dollar bill, with its
iconic Athenaeum portrait. In keeping with the late-twentieth-
century predilection for social familiarity, the Familial
Washington is evoked through the painting's title, *George*.[34]

Another striking variation on the capitalistic Washington, although not based on the dollar bill, is Komar & Melamid's *Washington as Victor*. In 1994, the two Russian-born artists Vitaly Komar and Alexander Melamid announced a five-year plan to celebrate "America's Greatest Revolutionary Hero," George Washington.[35] Declaring that "revolutionaries never die!" they called on "everyone who believes that the revolutionary legacy of the Founding Fathers is threatened with extinction to create work devoted to this patriotic theme."[36] The two artists themselves paid homage to Washington by staging an opera and executing a dozen paintings in a style they have dubbed American Social Realism. In *Washington as Victor* (fig. 14), the Revolutionary War general holds in his right hand the head of Adolf Hitler, while in his left is that of Joseph Stalin. Washington and what he represents—in particular, capitalistic democracy—is portrayed as triumphing over the competing ideologies of fascism and communism. However parodic and ironic Komar and Melamid's art may be (rendering the Great American Hero in a style associated with Soviet communism, for instance), it nevertheless does resonate with the nationalistic spirit woven into earlier Washington imagery. American democracy, personified by George Washington, continues to triumph.

While Komar and Melamid's mock-serious art exemplifies their belief that "Washington Lives!"[37] his image more likely lives not in oil paintings, but in advertisements, on mouse pads, and on refrigerator magnets. In late-twentieth-century America, where consumerism and celebrity run rampant, it is not surprising that the Father of our Country is most frequently represented to promote the sales of a variety of goods and services. While it is easy to lament such commercializing as debasing and abusing his image, it is important to realize that, though the objects bearing his image are new and their wide distribution and accessibility far greater than ever before, the phenomenon itself is not. From early on, Washington has been subjected to and, more importantly, survived all manner of portrayal and usage, from the inspirational to the trivial. Each era images Washington in light of its particular needs, expectations, and desires. Because of this his image is truly as diverse, pluralistic, and in flux as the nation he helped found. At the same time, his image, however rendered, has provided a form of historical and visual stability—a grounding, as it were—for a nation that has always been consciously moving toward the future.[38] That his representation, in whatever form, not only has persisted, but also proliferates, testifies to its enduring significance to our national identity, memory, and ideals. As a visual touchstone for Americans, "our illustrious Washington" is profoundly and ultimately an image of ourselves.

FIGURE 1 Charles Willson Peale, *George Washington in the Uniform of a British Colonial Colonel,* 1772, Washington-Lee-Custis Collection, Washington and Lee University, Lexington, Virginia.

FIGURE 10 Junius Brutus Stearns, *Washington as a Farmer at Mount Vernon*, 1851, Virginia Museum of Fine Arts, Richmond. Gift of Edgar William and Bernice Chrysler Garbisch. Photo: Wen Hwa Ts'ao. © Virginia Museum of Fine Arts.

FIGURE 11 Larry Rivers, *Washington Crossing the Delaware*, 1953, The Museum of Modern Art, New York. Given anonymously. Photograph © 1999 The Museum of Modern Art, New York.

FIGURE 1 Charles Willson Peale, *George Washington in the Uniform of a British Colonial Colonel*, 1772, Washington-Lee-Custis Collection, Washington and Lee University, Lexington, Virginia.

FIGURE 2 Charles Willson Peale, *George Washington at Princeton,* 1779, The Pennsylvania Academy of the Fine Arts, Philadelphia, gift of Maria McKean Allen and Phoebe Warren Downes through the bequest of their mother, Elizabeth Wharton McKean.

FIGURE 3 Gilbert
Stuart, *George Washington*
(Athenaeum Portrait),
1796, William Francis
Warden Fund, John H.
and Ernestine A. Payne
Fund, Commonwealth
Cultural Preservation
Trust. Jointly owned by
the Museum of Fine Arts,
Boston, and the National
Portrait Gallery,
Smithsonian Institution,
Washington, D. C.

FIGURE 4 Carl H.
Schmolze, *George
Washington Sitting for His
Portrait to Gilbert Stuart*,
1858, The Pennsylvania
Academy of the Fine Arts,
Philadelphia, Gift of Mrs.
John Frederick Lewis (The
John Frederick Lewis
Memorial Collection).

FIGURE 5 Grant Wood, *Parson Weems' Fable*, 1939, Amon Carter Museum, Fort Worth, Texas.

FIGURE 6 Jean-Antoine Houdon, *George Washington*, 1786-1796, State Capitol, Richmond, Virginia. Photo: The Library of Virginia.

FIGURE 7 Horatio Greenough, *George Washington*, 1832- 1841, National Museum of American Art, Smithsonian Institution, Transfer from the US Capitol.

FIGURE 8 Emanuel Leutze, *Washington Crossing the Delaware*, 1851, The Metropolitan Museum of Art, New York, Gift of John Stewart Kennedy, 1897 (97.34).

FIGURE 9 Edward Savage, *The Washington Family*, 1789-1796, National Gallery of Art, Washington, D.C., Andrew W. Mellon Collection.

FIGURE 10 Junius Brutus Stearns, *Washington as a Farmer at Mount Vernon*, 1851, Virginia Museum of Fine Arts, Richmond. Gift of Edgar William and Bernice Chrysler Garbisch. Photo: Wen Hwa Ts'ao. © Virginia Museum of Fine Arts.

FIGURE 11 Larry Rivers, *Washington Crossing the Delaware*, 1953, The Museum of Modern Art, New York. Given anonymously. Photograph © 1999 The Museum of Modern Art, New York.

FIGURE 12 Val Hunnicutt, *Washington Contemplates Crossing the Delaware*, 1997, Private collection.

FIGURE 13 Steve Kaufman, *George*, 1997, The Hotel George, Washington, D.C.

FIGURE 14 Komar & Melamid, *Washington as Victor*, 1997, Private collection.

ELEVEN

George Washington and the Religious Impulse

John G. West, Jr.

"Of all the dispositions and habits which lead to political prosperity," wrote George Washington, "[r]eligion and morality are indispensable supports."[1] These words are perhaps George Washington's best known statement concerning religion, and since their publication in 1796, they have been invoked time and again by defenders of religion in American public life.

During the nineteenth century, evangelical Christians active in politics regularly cited Washington's words against critics who claimed that religion had no place in the public square. In 1803, when evangelist Lyman Beecher called on churches to form voluntary associations to promote morality in public life, he cited neither the Bible nor another minister as the irrefutable authority on the subject. He instead invoked this passage from Washington. Beecher's underlying implication was clear: If Washington recognized that "a national morality" could not "prevail in exclusion of religious principles,"[2] surely no other American would dare brand this idea un-American. Similarly, when the inhabitants of Castleton, Vermont, petitioned Congress about the need for respecting the sabbath in 1830, they too relied on Washington as their authority, supplying a lengthy paraphrase of the Farewell Address. "Religion & morality are indispensible supports of political prosperity, & of all free governments," they wrote Congress. "No patriot will ever attempt 'to subvert these great pillars of human happiness; these firmest props of the duties of man.' The religious man & the politician ought to protect & cherish them alike."[3] A century and a half later, twentieth-century religious believers took similar inspiration from Washington's words when attacked for wrongly injecting God into politics.

Paradoxically, while Washington has become well known for his lucid defense of faith in public life, there has been considerable controversy over the years about the precise nature of his own religious convictions. As early as the 1830s, there were debates about whether George Washington was a Christian. In the pages of the *New York Free Inquirer*, Robert Dale Owen claimed Washington was a Deist,[4] and in lecture halls Frances Wright boldly asserted that "Washington was not a Christian...he believed not in the priest's God, nor in the divine authority of the priest's book."[5] Defenders of Washington's piety responded in 1836 with *The Religious Opinions and Character of Washington*, a 414-page tome by E. C. M'Guire that depicted the general as devoted to constant prayer, the frequent taking of Communion, and the diligent observance of the Christian sabbath.[6] An intervening century did nothing to dampen the enthusiasm for inquiries into Washington's religion. In 1919, William Johnson published a defense of Washington's orthodoxy titled *George Washington the Christian*; and in 1959 historian Paul Boller sought to lay to rest such accounts with his *George Washington and Religion*.[7]

By the 1980s, political theorist Walter Berns was including Washington among the clear enemies of traditional Christianity. Lumping Washington together with James Madison and Thomas Jefferson, Berns claimed that all three "were opposed to revealed religion and understood it to be incompatible with an attachment to 'Nature's God.'"[8] These men supported the separation of church and state "not primarily because they wanted to accommodate the varieties of religious beliefs," but because they supported the idea of natural rights, an idea clearly "incompatible with Christian doctrine...."[9] A few defenders of Washington's piety remained, largely among evangelical Christians. If Washington "were...living today," insisted Baptist minister Tim LaHaye in 1987, "he would freely identify with the Bible-believing branch of evangelical Christianity that is having such a positive influence on our nation."[10] Historically speaking, LaHaye's statement was not as presumptuous as it might first appear. After Washington's death in 1799, all sorts of religious groups in America, from Catholics to Unitarians, sought to claim the Father of the Country as their very own.[11]

RELIGION IN WASHINGTON'S PRIVATE LIFE

So what was Washington's personal religious life in reality? Was he an opponent of revealed religion, a conventional Episcopalian, an evangelical Christian, or something in between? Whatever he was in his private life, it is clear that he was no Deist. That is, he did not believe in a God who created the world and then left it to run itself. No one who reads either the public or private writings of Washington can seriously doubt that he devoutly believed in a personal God who controls human events through his continuing care. The doctrine of God's Providence, in fact, suffuses almost everything Washington wrote.

Washington was especially convinced that America's success in the Revolutionary War bore testimony to a God who actively rules the affairs of men. When writing his farewell orders to his soldiers at the end of the war, Washington reminded them: "The disadvantageous circumstances...under which the war was undertaken can never be forgotten. The singular interpositions of Providence in our feeble condition were such, as could scarcely escape the attention of the most unobserving."[12] In Washington's First Inaugural Address, his first official act as president, he likewise paid homage to the

> Almighty Being who rules over the universe; who presides in the councils of nations; and whose providential aid can supply every human defect.... No people can be bound to acknowledge and adore the invisible hand which conducts the affairs of men, more than the people of the United States. Every step by which they have advanced to the character of an independent nation seems to have been distinguished by some token of providential agency.[13]

Washington's unshakeable belief in God's sovereignty instilled in him a profound sense of humility and submission to God's will. Even Washington's public supplications to God are striking for their lack of presumption. Instead of calling on God to bless the nation with material blessings, Washington characteristically asked only that God "grant...such a degree of temporal prosperity as he alone knows to be best."[14] The same humility can be found in his personal correspondence. Responding to a report that his crops were failing because of drought, Washington wrote his manager at Mount Vernon with apparent calmness: "At disappointments and losses which are the effects of Providential acts, I never repine; because I am sure the alwise disposer of events knows better than we do, what is best for us, or what we deserve."[15] Similarly, upon learning that a friend had just lost three children, Washington gently advised him:

> From the friendship I have always borne you, and from the interest I have ever taken in whatever related to your prosperity and happiness, I participated in the sorrows which I know you must have felt for your late and heavy losses. But [it] is not for man to scan the wisdom of Providence. The best he can do, is to submit to its decrees.[16]

Washington clearly believed in a God who actively rules every part of the universe and who merits our worship and obedience. Washington also accepted the immortality of the soul and a transcendent moral law. What remains unclear is how much Washington believed in addition. What, for example, did he believe about Christ? The evidence on the subject is partial, contradictory, and in the end, unsatisfactory.

On the one hand, Washington was a regular member of a traditional Protestant denomination, the Episcopal Church of

Virginia; and he served faithfully in that church in the lay offices of vestryman and churchwarden, offices that would have required him to take an oath of loyalty to the doctrinal confession of the church.[17] Regarding Christ, Washington encouraged the Delaware tribe in 1779 to "learn our ways of life, and above all, the religion of Jesus Christ"; and in his Circular to the States in 1783, he referred to Christ as "the Divine Author of our blessed religion."[18]

On the other hand, there is substantial evidence that Washington refused the sacrament of Communion from the time of the Revolution until his death, and his references to Christ in his speech to the Delaware and in his Circular to the States are arguably his only specifically Christian doctrinal statements.[19] Usually Washington appeared to regard differences in theology as irrelevant, commenting at one point: "Being no bigot myself to any mode of worship, I am disposed to indulge the professors of Christianity in the church, that road to Heaven, which to them shall seem the most direct plainest easiest and least liable to exception."[20]

In the end, one cannot be dogmatic about the details of Washington's personal piety. He was a faithful member of his chosen church, and he certainly believed in a personal God who is sovereign over human affairs. Further than that, we cannot say with certainty.

RELIGION IN WASHINGTON'S PUBLIC LIFE

One does not need to untangle the subtleties of Washington's personal piety, however, in order to understand his view of the vibrant role religion plays in society. Whatever the ambiguities of his private theology, Washington's political theology was far from ambiguous. It incorporated three great propositions, propositions that helped form an American consensus on religion in public life that lasted for much of our nation's history. First, Washington believed that religion served as the necessary defender of morality in civic life. Second, he maintained that the moral law defended by religion was the same moral law that can be known by reason. Third, he saw religious liberty as a natural right of all human beings.

The Moral Function of Religion in Public Life

Washington was one of the clearest proponents of what James Hutson has called the "founding generation's syllogism"[21] concerning religion and public life: Morality is necessary for republican government; religion is necessary for morality; therefore, religion is necessary for republican government.

The first prong of this syllogism—the importance of morality for republican government—comes through repeatedly in Washington's public utterances. In his First Inaugural Address, Washington declared that "the propitious smiles of Heaven can never be expected on a nation that disregards the external rules of order and right, which Heaven itself has ordained," and praises the talents and virtue of those selected to serve in the First Congress because their "honorable qualifications" guaranteed that "the foundations of our national policy will be laid in the pure and immutable principles of private morality."[22] Washington again noted the importance of civic virtue in his

First Annual Message to Congress by urging the diffusion of knowledge so that citizens would be able "to discriminate the spirit of liberty from that of licentiousness—cherishing the first, avoiding the last."[23] Washington's clearest articulation of the need for morality—and religion—in public life came in the famous passage in his Farewell Address cited previously. In that address, Washington made clear that he believed it was "substantially true, that virtue or morality is a necessary spring of popular government. The rule indeed extends with more or less force to every species of free Government."[24]

The most salient fact about Washington's emphasis on the need for virtue in American public life was not that his view was so unique, but that it was so commonplace. Washington did not claim that he was saying anything radically new by claiming that morality was tied to politics. Rather, he thought he was articulating the common sense of the subject as accepted by the Founding generation. This point may seem odd to those schooled to believe that the Founders thought selfishness was the prime mover in politics. According to many modern scholars, the Founders thought they set up a government that was a machine that would run itself. By separating the powers of government among different branches, they created a system where "ambition must be made to counteract ambition," and government officials in one branch would find it in their interest to resist encroachments by officials of another branch.[25] In the words of George Will, it was "almost as though the Founders thought they had devised a system so clever that it would work well even if no one had good motives—even if there was no public-spiritedness."[26]

This claim is sheer nonsense. Washington and his generation knew perfectly well that citizens had to be self-controlled and honorable for free government to work. In the words of Benjamin Franklin, "Only a virtuous people are capable of freedom. As nations become corrupt and vicious, they have more need of masters."[27] The less control the people exerted over themselves, the more control the government would have to impose from on high. Countless clergymen of the period sounded the same theme. Congregationalist minister Nathanael Emmons, for example, argued that "nothing but the rod or arbitrary power is sufficient to restrain and govern a people, who have lost their virtue, and sunk into vice and corruption. Such a people are neither fit to enjoy, nor able to assert and maintain their liberties. They must be slaves."[28]

Washington accepted this view, but he also went further. It is one thing to claim that virtue is necessary for republican government. It is another thing to claim that *religion* is necessary for the creation of that virtue. While the majority of the Founding generation clearly believed that social morality was inextricably tied to religion, a small but influential group of rationalists—Benjamin Franklin and Thomas Jefferson, to name two—sometimes spoke as if secular education was at least a partial substitute for the moral function traditionally served by religion. By the time of the 1790s, this claim was being made in a much more virulent form across the ocean by the fanatical leaders of the French Revolution. Washington decided to make his own view of the matter explicit in his Farewell Address.

There Washington characterized the idea "that morality can

be maintained without religion" as a mere "supposition," indicating his sympathy with those who believed that morality was indissolubly linked to religion. Nevertheless, Washington met the rationalists half way: He argued that even if one concedes that education alone can instill morality, it can do so only in "minds of peculiar structure," for "reason and experience both forbid us to expect that National morality can prevail in exclusion of religious principle."[29] In other words, even if the morality of the ruling class may not be dependent upon religion, morality among the general citizenry is. Hence religion remains a *political* necessity if not an intellectual one.

Though often treated as a proof text, the passage on religion and morality in Washington's Farewell Address was far from empty rhetoric on Washington's part. It was a summary of how he had lived his public life. Indeed, the full meaning of this passage of the Farewell Address can only be understood in light of Washington's actions as a statesman. Throughout his public career he actively promoted piety as essential to temporal political prosperity.

As a general during the Revolution, he issued frequent orders encouraging his soldiers to attend worship services and to cease taking God's name in vain. On July 4, 1775, he wrote that he "requires and expects, of all Officers, and Soldiers, not engaged on actual duty, a punctual attendance on divine Service, to implore the blessings of heaven upon the means used for our safety and defence."[30] And on July 9, 1776, he directed commanding officers to see that all inferior officers and soldiers pay [the chaplains]...suitable respect and attend carefully upon religious services. The blessing and protection of Heaven are at all times necessary but especially so in times of public distress and danger—The General hopes and trusts, that every officer and man, will endeavor so to live, and act, as becomes a Christian Soldier defending the dearest Rights and Liberties of his country.[31]

In August 1776, Washington excused troops from fatigue duty on Sundays "[t]hat the Troops may have an opportunity of attending public worship, as well as take some rest after the great fatigue they have gone through...."[32] In the same order, Washington issued a rebuke of swearing, a reprimand he repeated with increasing fervor in the years that followed. On July 29, 1779, he finally wrote the following order, which is tinged by more than a little frustration:

Many and pointed orders have been issued against that unmeaning and abominable custom of *Swearing*, not withstanding which, with much regret the General observes that it prevails, *if possible*, more than ever; His feelings are continually wounded by the Oaths and Imprecations of the soldiers whenever he is in hearing of them.

The Name of That Being, from whose bountiful goodness we are permitted to exist and enjoy the comforts of life is incessantly imprecated and profaned in a manner as wanton as it is shocking. For the sake therefore of religion, decency and order the General hopes and trusts that officers of every rank will use their influence and authority to check a vice, which is as unprofitable as it is wicked and shameful.[33]

Washington also declared days of thanksgiving for the army after major victories;[34] and after the war concluded, he applauded a minister's proposal that Congress present a Bible to every soldier in the Continental Army, though he noted that the proposal came too late to put into effect, because most of the soldiers had already been discharged.[35]

Returning to private life in Virginia, Washington embraced Patrick Henry's Assessment Bill that would have taxed citizens to support Christian ministers of their choice. After it became clear that the assessment was attracting a great deal of opposition, however, Washington wished the measure a swift death because he thought enacting it over the wishes of a "respectable minority" would be "impolitic."[36]

As president, Washington continued to advocate a public role for religion, issuing two national thanksgiving proclamations, the first after the adoption of the Constitution at the recommendation of Congress, and the second in 1795 after Jay's Treaty had been negotiated with England and the Whiskey Rebellion had been successfully put down.[37]

Washington apparently saw no difficulty in incorporating religious duties such as Sabbath observance and reverence toward the name of God into civic morality. In the latter case, profanity against God was forbidden by "decency and order" as well as by revelation.[38] This view was undoubtedly in part a product of Washington's gentlemanly code of civility; but it was also a manifestation of his all-encompassing belief in Providence. Washington stressed time and again that the nation's prosperity depended upon God's Providence, which implied that impiety would make us the objects of God's wrath rather than the recipients of his mercy.[39]

THE EXISTENCE OF A TRANSCENDENT MORAL LAW

Although Washington believed that religion was the preeminent defender of morality in society, he did not think that the morality religion defended was something peculiar to itself. Unlike many in modern culture who dismiss the traditional morality taught by religion as somehow subjective, Washington maintained that the moral precepts propagated by religion were the same ones that could also be known by reason. In short, Washington believed in a natural moral order that could be known by reason as well as revelation. This belief in what might be called "natural law" was something Washington shared with almost all of the Founding generation. According to the Founders, when it came to morality, reason and religion spoke with one voice. One finds this idea restated in countless ways in the letters and documents of the founding era. Time and again when the Founders argued on behalf of some proposition, they pointed out that it was supported by both reason and revelation. Thus, John Adams appealed to "revelation, and...reason too,"[40] "the bible and common sense,"[41] "human nature and the Christian religion,"[42] and "God and Nature."[43] John Jay cited "experience and revelation."[44] James Madison invoked "reason and the principles of the [Christian] religion."[45] Hamilton noted that the moral doctrines of Hobbes are "absurd" [i.e., against reason] as well as "impious" [i.e., against revelation].[46] Even Thomas Jefferson in later years saw fit to appeal to the "obligation of the moral precepts of Jesus"[47] as coincident with the morality of conscience and reason.[48]

George Washington's writings express the same convention, appealing to the authority of "religion and morality,"[49] "Reason, Religion, and Philosophy,"[50] "religion, decency, and order,"[51] and "Prudence, Policy, and a true Christian Spirit."[52] In his Farewell Address, he claimed that the public benefits of religion should be recognized by "the mere politician, equally with the pious man."[53] Washington's clearest articulation of the claim that reason and revelation support the same moral code came in his First Inaugural Address, where he argued that God created the universe in such a way as to connect human behavior with natural rewards and punishments:

> There is no truth more thoroughly established, than that there exists in the economy and course of nature, an indissoluble union between virtue and happiness; between duty and advantage; between the genuine maxims of an honest and magnanimous policy, and the solid rewards of public prosperity and felicity: since we ought to be no less persuaded that the propitious smiles of Heaven can never be expected on a nation that disregards the external rules of order and right, which Heaven itself has ordained.[54]

It is important to emphasize that this belief in a natural moral order was shared by Christians and non-Christians alike among the Founding generation. Evangelicals like John Jay (first Chief Justice of the Supreme Court), no less than champions of the Enlightenment such as Thomas Jefferson, agreed that basic moral principles could be known by reason and conscience. Accordingly, the Reverend John Witherspoon, James Madison's old teacher at Princeton, began his first lecture on moral philosophy by stating that the subject "is an inquiry into the nature and grounds of moral obligation by reason, as distinct from revelation."[55] Witherspoon went on to tell his students that using reason to apprehend morality was not a threat to revelation, for "[i]f the Scripture is true, the discoveries of reason cannot be contrary to it; and therefore, it has nothing to fear from that quarter."[56] This acceptance of a natural moral order was not an invention of the Enlightenment; it had deep roots in the Christian natural law tradition articulated by a long line of Christian thinkers, including Augustine, Aquinas, Hooker, Calvin, and Luther.[57]

Washington recognized that reason and revelation might occasionally be seen to differ on certain questions of public morality and justice. But unlike some other Founders, he almost never probed the areas of potential disagreement, though he certainly knew that such disagreements were possible, as in the case of Quakers who refused to take up arms in defense of their country.[58] Washington's unwillingness to concentrate on the disagreements between reason and revelation is understandable. He was a statesman, and his preeminent concern was not speculation but practice. His purpose was to lay the solid foundations on which a republic could be built, and exploration of the tensions between reason and revelation would have detracted from this purpose.

RELIGIOUS LIBERTY AS A NATURAL RIGHT

Washington's solid support for religion's civic role was balanced by an equally firm defense of religious liberty, which he believed was a natural right possessed by all human beings. Curiously, some have suggested that Washington's support for religious freedom shows that he was opposed to traditional Christianity. Walter Berns, for one, claims that the support of religious freedom by Washington and other Founders indicated their hostility to revealed religion, because, according to Berns, religious liberty "derives from a non-religious source" that is "incompatible with Christian doctrine."[59] While there were influential Enlightenment theorists hostile to traditional Christianity who advocated religious liberty, Berns completely misses the American context of the concept. Within the American tradition, nearly all of the defenders of religious liberty were devout Christians, from Roger Williams, William Penn, and Cecilius Calvert in colonial America to Baptist Isaac Backus during the Founding.[60] Indeed, grassroots support during the Founding for ending government subsidies to churches came primarily from within evangelical sects like Baptists, Methodists, and Presbyterians.[61] These groups thought that tax support of churches corrupted true religion rather than promoted it. It is interesting to note that some of Washington's most passionate statements in favor of religious liberty were written to members of churches who were concerned that the new federal government might use its power to favor one church over another.

To the United Bapist Churches in Virginia, for example, Washington promised that if there were any threat of the federal government violating the rights of conscience, "no one would be more zealous than myself to establish effectual barriers against the

horrors of spiritual tyranny, and every species of religious persecution."[62] He likewise assured Roman Catholics that "as mankind
become more liberal they will be more apt to allow that all those
who conduct themselves as worthy members of the community are
equally entitled to the protection of civil government."[63]

It was through these letters to America's churches that
Washington made his most important contribution to the securing of religious freedom under the new Constitution. As the
nation's first president, Washington was keenly aware that his
acts set precedents for all future federal officials. Therefore, he
approached all of his official actions and utterances with great
care. By writing to members of various churches as equal citizens,
Washington helped to secure for each church the protection of
the natural rights proclaimed by the American Revolution.

Perhaps most precedent-setting of all were his letters to
Jewish synagogues, the most beautiful of which is likely his letter
to the Hebrew Congregation in Newport, Rhode Island.
Washington wrote to them:

> It is now no more that toleration is spoken of as if it were by the
> indulgence of one class of people that another enjoyed the exercise of
> their inherent natural rights, for, happily, the government of the
> United States, which gives to bigotry no sanction, to persecution no
> assistance, requires only that they who live under its protection shall
> demean themselves as good citizens in giving it on all occasions their
> effectual support.[64]

Washington ended his letter with a benediction and a prayer, part of which read, "May the children of the stock of Abraham who dwell in this land continue to merit and enjoy the good will of other inhabitants, while everyone shall sit in safety under his own vine and fig tree, and there shall be none to make him afraid." As Harry Jaffa points out, Washington through these words helped ensure that Jews would be

> full citizens for the first time, not merely in American history, but since the end of their own polity in the ancient world, more than two thousand years before.... From no one else could such a statement about Jews have carried the authority it did carry, when it came from Washington. No one could repudiate these words, once they had come from Washington, without making himself contemptible.[65]

Though Washington was a consistent defender of the rights of conscience, he did not think that the doctrine was unlimited. In his letters to various churches, Washington made a point of stressing the need for church members to obey the government and to fulfill all their obligations as citizens.[66] Indeed, he seemed to make religious liberty for a sect contingent on the good citizenship of its members. To the Quakers he wrote in 1789: "While men perform their social duties faithfully, they do all that society or the state can with propriety demand or expect; and remain responsible only to their Maker for the religion, or modes, of faith which they may prefer or profess."[67] The unstated, but implied, corollary is that when men do not perform their social duties faithfully because of religious objections, they must answer to the government as well as to God.

Of course, this is precisely what worried the Quakers, who were pacifists. They did not want to be persecuted for their refusal to fight during wartime; yet the very connection Washington drew between religious liberty and a religion's usefulness to the state seemed to invite persecution of religious adherents who could not in good conscience agree with state policy.

But Washington sought to circumvent this conclusion with a caveat. After observing that Quakers are "exemplary and useful citizens" except for "their declining to share with others the burthen of the common defense," he added: "I assure you very explicitly, that in my opinion the conscientious scruples of all men should be treated with great delicacy and tenderness; and it is my wish and desire, that the laws may always be as extensively accommodated to them, as a due regard to the protection and essential interests of the nation may justify and permit."[68] Ever the gentleman, Washington assures the Quakers that even they merit protection from the government whenever possible, for religious objections to general laws ought to be accommodated as long as they do not contradict "a due regard to the protection and essential interests of the nation...." In this passage one finds a distant anticipation of the "compelling state interest" test employed by the Supreme Court until recently in religious liberty cases.[69]

Washington appears to have applied this same sort of reasoning to the Virginia Assessment Bill. In a letter defending his initial support for the bill, Washington argued that non-Christians need not be penalized by its provisions because they could "declare themselves Jews, Mahometans or otherwise, and thereby obtain proper relief."[70] Here again Washington acknowledged the need for religious exemptions to a generally applicable law. Thus, Washington prized religious freedom even above the uniform application of the laws, as long as the "essential interests" of the nation did not dictate otherwise.

Washington's deep understanding of the role of religion in republican government has much to teach those interested in the interaction between faith and public life in contemporary America. In a time when public morality is discounted and religion's moral voice often goes unheeded, Washington's defense of the dynamic moral function of religion in civic life needs to be heard by both politicians and religious believers. In a time when many deny that reason and revelation teach the same moral truths, Washington's defense of the natural moral order shows religious believers how they can defend morality without raising the charge that they are merely trying to impose their particular religious dogmas on everyone else. Finally, in a period when expansive government is making it ever more difficult for traditional religious groups to maintain their identity, Washington's defense of religious liberty reminds us of the importance of safeguarding the rights of conscience against unnecessary intrusions by the government. In the realm of religion and civic life, as in other areas, Washington remains an indispensable man for our culture today.

TWELVE

Eulogy on Washington: "First in the Hearts of his Countrymen"

JOHN MARSHALL

Delivered December 26, 1799 by Representative Richard Henry Lee

In obedience to your will, I rise your humble organ, with the hope of executing a part of the system of public mourning which you have been pleased to adopt, commemorative of the death of the most illustrious and most beloved personage this country has ever produced; and which, while it transmits to posterity your sense of the awful event, faintly represents your knowledge of the consummate excellence you so cordially honor.

Desperate, indeed, is any attempt on earth to meet correspondently this dispensation of heaven; for, while with pious resignation we submit to the will of an all-gracious Providence, we can never cease lamenting, in our finite view of omnipotent wisdom, the heart-rending privation for which our nation weeps. When the civilized world shakes to its centre; when every moment gives birth to strange and momentous changes; when our peaceful quarter of the globe, exempt as it happily has been from any share in the slaughter of the human race, may yet be compelled to abandon her pacific policy, and to risk the doleful casualties of war; what limit is there to the extent of our loss? None within the reach of my words to express; none which your feelings will not disavow.

The founder of our federate republic—our bulwark in war, our guide in peace, is no more! O that this were but questionable! Hope, the comforter of the wretched, would pour into our agonizing hearts its balmy dew. But, alas! there is no hope for us; our Washington is removed forever! Possessing the stoutest frame, and purest mind, he had passed nearly to his sixty-eighth year, in the enjoyment of high health, when, habituated by his care of us to neglect himself, a slight cold, disregarded, became inconvenient on Friday, oppressive on Saturday, and, defying every medical interposition, before the morning of Sunday, put an end to the best of men. An end did I say?—his fame survives! bounded only by the limits of the earth, and by the extent of the human mind. He survives in our hearts, in the growing knowledge of our children, in the affection of the good throughout the world: and when our monuments shall be done away; when nations now existing shall be no more; when even our young and far-spreading empire shall have perished, still will our Washington's glory unfaded shine, and die not, until love of virtue cease on earth, or earth itself sinks into chaos.

How, my fellow-citizens, shall I single to your grateful hearts his pre-eminent worth? Where shall I begin in opening to your view a character throughout sublime? Shall I speak of his warlike achievements, all springing from obedience to his country's will—all directed to his country's good?

Will you go with me to the banks of the Monongahela, to see

your youthful Washington, supporting, in the dismal hour of Indian victory, the ill-fated Braddock, and saving, by his judgment and by his valor, the remains of a defeated army, pressed by the conquering savage foe; or, when oppressed America, nobly resolving to risk her all in defence of her violated rights, he was elevated by the unanimous voice of Congress to the command of her armies? Will you follow him to the high grounds of Boston, where, to an undisciplined, courageous, and virtuous yeomanry, his presence gave the stability of system, and infused the invincibility of love of country; or shall I carry you to the painful scenes of Long Island, York Island, and New Jersey, when, combating superior and gallant armies, aided by powerful fleets, and led by chiefs high in the roll of fame, he stood, the bulwark of our safety, undismayed by disaster, unchanged by change of fortune? Or will you view him in the precarious fields of Trenton, where deep gloom, unnerving every arm, reigned triumphant through our thinned, worn-down, unaided ranks; himself unmoved? Dreadful was the night. It was about this time of winter, the storm raged, the Delaware rolling furiously with floating ice, forbade the approach of man. Washington, self-collected, viewed the tremendous scene; his country called; unappalled by surrounding dangers, he passed to the hostile shore; he fought; he conquered. The morning sun cheered the American world. Our country rose on the event; and her dauntless chief, pursuing his blow, completed, in the lawns of Princeton, what his vast soul had conceived on the shores of Delaware.

Thence to the strong grounds of Morristown, he led his small but gallant band; and through an eventful winter, by the high efforts of his genius, whose matchless force was measurable only by the growth of difficulties, he held in check formidable hostile legions, conducted by a chief experienced in the art of war, and famed for his valor on the ever memorable heights of Abraham, where fell Wolfe, Montcalm, and since, our much lamented Montgomery, all covered with glory. In this fortunate interval, produced by his masterly conduct, our fathers, ourselves, animated by his resistless example, rallied around our country's standard, and continued to follow her beloved chief through the various and trying scenes to which the destinies of our Union led.

Who is there that has forgotten the vales of Brandywine, the fields of Germantown, or the plains of Monmouth? Everywhere present, wants of every kind obstructing, numerous and valiant armies encountering, himself a host, he assuaged our sufferings, limited our privations, and upheld our tottering republic. Shall I display to you the spread of the fire of his soul, by rehearsing the praises of the hero of Saratoga, and his much loved compeer of the Carolinas? No; our Washington wears not borrowed glory. To Gates—to Greene, he gave without reserve the applause due to their eminent merit; and long may the chiefs of Saratoga, and of Eutaw, receive the grateful respect of a grateful people.

Moving in his own orbit, he imparted heat and light to his most distant satellites; and combining the physical and moral force of all within his sphere, with irresistible weight he took his course, commiserating folly, disdaining vice, dismaying treason, and invigorating despondency; until the auspicious hour arrived, when, united with the intrepid forces of a potent and magnanimous ally, he brought to submission the since conqueror of India;

thus finishing his long career of military glory with a lustre corresponding to his great name, and in this, his last act of war, affixing the seal of fate to our nation's birth.

To the horrid din of battle, sweet peace succeeded; and our virtuous chief, mindful only of the common good, in a moment tempting personal aggrandizement, hushed the discontents of growing sedition; and surrendering his power into the hands from which he had received it, converted his sword into a ploughshare, teaching an admiring world that to be truly great, you must be truly good.

Were I to stop here, the picture would be incomplete, and the task imposed unfinished. Great as was our Washington in war, and as much as did that greatness contribute to produce the American republic, it is not in war alone his pre-eminence stands conspicuous. His various talents, combining all the capacities of a statesman, with those of a soldier, fitted him alike to guide the councils and the armies of our nation. Scarcely had he rested from his martial toils, while his invaluable parental advice was still sounding in our ears, when he, who had been our shield and our sword, was called forth to act a less splendid, but more important part.

Possessing a clear and penetrating mind, a strong and sound judgment, calmness and temper for deliberation, with invincible firmness and perseverance in resolutions maturely formed; drawing information from all; acting from himself, with incorruptible integrity and unvarying patriotism; his own superiority and the public confidence alike marked him as the man designed by heaven to lead in the great political as well as military events which have distinguished the era of his life.

The finger of an overruling Providence, pointing at Washington, was neither mistaken nor unobserved; when, to realize the vast hopes to which our Revolution had given birth, a change of political system became indispensable.

How novel, how grand the spectacle! Independent States, stretched over an immense territory, and known only by common difficulty, clinging to their union as the rock of their safety, deciding by frank comparison of their relative condition, to rear on that rock, under the guidance of reason, a common government through whose commanding protection, liberty and order, with their long train of blessings, should be safe to themselves, and the sure inheritance of their posterity.

This arduous task devolved on citizens selected by the people, from knowledge of their wisdom and confidence in their virtue. In this august assembly of sages and of patriots, Washington of course was found; and as if acknowledged to be most wise where all were wise, with one voice he was declared their chief. How well he merited this rare distinction, how faithful were the labors of himself and his compatriots, the work of their hands and our union, strength and prosperity, the fruits of that work, best attest.

But to have essentially aided in presenting to his country this consummation of her hopes, neither satisfied the claims of his fellow-citizens on his talents, nor those duties which the possession of those talents imposed. Heaven had not infused into his mind such an uncommon share of its ethereal spirit to remain unemployed; nor bestowed on him his genius unaccompanied with the corresponding duty of devoting it to the common good.

To have framed a constitution, was showing only, without realizing, the general happiness. This great work remained to be done; and America, steadfast in her preference, with one voice summoned her beloved Washington, unpractised as he was in the duties of civil administration, to execute this last act in the completion of the national felicity. Obedient to her call, he assumed the high office with that self-distrust peculiar to his innate modesty, the constant attendant of pre-eminent virtue. What was the burst of joy through our anxious land, on this exhilarating event, is known to us all. The aged, the young, the brave, the fair, rivalled each other in demonstrations of their gratitude; and this high-wrought, delightful scene, was heightened in its effect, by the singular contest between the zeal of the bestowers and the avoidance of the receiver of the honors bestowed. Commencing his administration, what heart is not charmed with the recollection of the pure and wise principles announced by himself, as the basis of his political life! He best understood the indissoluble union between virtue and happiness, between duty and advantage, between the genuine maxims of an honest and magnanimous policy and the solid rewards of public prosperity and individual felicity; watching, with an equal and comprehensive eye, over this great assemblage of communities and interests, he laid the foundations of our national policy in the unerring immutable principles of morality, based on religion, exemplifying the pre-eminence of a free government, by all the attributes which win the affections of its citizens, or command the respect of the world.

"O fortunatos nimium, sua si bona norint!"

Leading through the complicated difficulties produced by previous obligations and conflicting interests, seconded by succeeding Houses of Congress, enlightened and patriotic, he surmounted all original obstruction, and brightened the path of our national felicity.

The presidential term expiring, his solicitude to exchange exaltation for humility returned with a force increased with increase of age; and he had prepared his farewell address to his countrymen, proclaiming his intention, when the united interposition of all around him, enforced by the eventful prospects of the epoch, produced a further sacrifice of inclination to duty. The election of President followed, and Washington, by the unanimous vote of the nation, was called to resume the chief magistracy. What a wonderful fixture of confidence! Which attracts most our admiration, a people so correct, or a citizen combining an assemblage of talents forbidding rivalry, and stifling even envy itself? Such a nation ought to be happy, such a chief must be forever revered.

War, long menaced by the Indian tribes, now broke out; and the terrible conflict, deluging Europe with blood, began to shed its baneful influence over our happy land. To the first, outstretching his invincible arm, under the orders of the gallant Wayne, the American eagle soared triumphant through distant forests. Peace followed victory; and the melioration of the condition of the enemy followed peace. Godlike virtue, which uplifts even the subdued savage!

To the second he opposed himself. New and delicate was the conjuncture, and great was the stake. Soon did his penetrating mind discern and seize the only course, continuing to us all the felicity enjoyed. He issued his proclamation of neutrality. This index to his whole subsequent conduct, was sanctioned by the approbation of both Houses of Congress, and by the approving voice of the people.

To this sublime policy he inviolably adhered, unmoved by foreign intrusion, unshaken by domestic turbulence.

Justum et tenacem propositi virum,
Non civium ardor prava jubentium,
Non vultus instantis tyranni,
Mente quatit solida.

Maintaining his pacific system at the expense of no duty, America, faithful to herself, and unstained in her honor, continued to enjoy the delights of peace, while afflicted Europe mourns in every quarter, under the accumulated miseries of an unexampled war; miseries in which our happy country must have shared, had not our pre-eminent Washington been as firm in council as he was brave in the field.

Pursuing steadfastly his course, he held safe the public happiness, preventing foreign war, and quelling internal discord, till the revolving period of a third election approached, when he executed his interrupted but inextinguishable desire of returning to the humble walks of private life.

The promulgation of his fixed resolution stopped the anxious wishes of an affectionate people from adding a third unanimous testimonial of their unabated confidence in the man so long enthroned in their hearts. When before was affection like this exhibited on earth? Turn over the records of ancient Greece; review the annals of mighty Rome; examine the volumes of modern Europe; you search in vain. America and her Washington only afford the dignified exemplification.

The illustrious personage, called by the national voice in succession to the arduous office of guiding a free people, had new difficulties to encounter. The amicable effort of settling our difficulties with France, begun by Washington, and pursued by his successor in virtue as in station, proving abortive, America took measures of self-defence. No sooner was the public mind roused by a prospect of danger, than every eye was turned to the friend of all, though secluded from public view, and gray in public service. The virtuous veteran, following his plough, received the unexpected summons with mingled emotions of indignation at the unmerited ill-treatment of his country, and of a determination once more to risk his all in her defence.

The annunciation of these feelings, in his affecting letter to the President, accepting the command of the army, concludes his official conduct.

First in war, first in peace, and first in the hearts of his countrymen, he was second to none in the humble and endearing scenes of private life. Pious, just, humane, temperate, and sincere; uniform, dignified, and commanding, his example was as edifying to all around him as were the effects of that example lasting.

To his equals he was condescending; to his inferiors kind; and to the dear object of his affections exemplarily tender. Correct throughout, vice shuddered in his presence, and virtue always felt his fostering hand; the purity of his private character gave effulgence to his public virtues.

His last scene comported with the whole tenor of his life: although in extreme pain, not a sigh, not a groan escaped him; and with undisturbed serenity he closed his well-spent life. Such was the man America has lost! Such was the man for whom our nation mourns!

Methinks I see his august image, and hear, falling from his venerable lips, these deep sinking words:

"Cease, sons of America, lamenting our separation: go on, and confirm by your wisdom the fruits of our joint counsels, joint efforts, and common dangers. Reverence religion; diffuse knowledge throughout your land; patronize the arts and sciences; set liberty and order be inseparable companions; control party spirit, the bane of free government; observe good faith to, and cultivate peace with all nations; shut up every avenue to foreign influence; contract rather than extend national connection; rely on yourselves only; be American in thought and deed. Thus will you give immortality to that Union, which was the constant object of my terrestrial labors. Thus will you preserve, undisturbed to the latest posterity, the felicity of a people to me most dear: and thus will you supply (if my happiness is now aught to you) the only vacancy in the round of pure bliss high heaven bestows."

AFTERWORD

The Forgotten Character of George Washington

RICHARD BROOKHISER

George Washington, my psychoanalyst wife observes shrewdly, appeals to small children and to mature adults, but not to adolescents. Because he is neither crazy nor funny, the adolescent mind has trouble with Washington. Mature adults come to appreciate him again. That's why the made-up story about Washington and the cherry tree is unkillable. Parents like it, and so do their young children. But not adolescents. So how do we account for the fact that many of the men who revered him as their leader in war were teenagers? Perhaps teenagers were not adolescents then.

Today, on the other hand, even Americans well beyond their teenage years often remain essentially adolescent; so Washington's reputation does not shimmer as it once did. Therefore I want to emphasize some aspects of Washington's character that we moderns tend to forget or misunderstand. I'll discuss, in turn, Washington as a man of charisma, as a gentleman, as a hero, as a politician, as a thinker, and as a skeptic.

"Charisma" originally meant the qualities of saints. Now it refers to qualities that compel our attention. A charismatic man is someone to whom attention must be paid. Today we associate charisma with athletes and entertainers; the most charismatic man in America today is probably Michael Jordan—at least at the moment he retired from basketball. But we have to remember Washington had that kind of charisma throughout his life.

He was a person who drew the eyes of everyone in a room when he entered it. One of the doctors in the Continental Army noted that when Washington was riding with his staff, there could be no doubt who the commander in chief was, even to strangers at a distance.

In part, this charisma was a function of his stature. He was measured at 6'3" when he died. He also carried himself well. "Noble" and "commanding" are words that come up over and over in descriptions of him. John Adams grumped that the Continental Congress chose him as commander in chief because, like the ancient Hebrews, they wanted a leader who was a head taller than the other Jews. Abigail Adams, when she first met Washington, wrote to her husband, John: "You had prepared me to entertain a favorable opinion of him, but I thought the one *half* was not told me." She went on and on in this gushing tone, which could not have improved John Adams's frame of mind.

Washington was an excellent horseman. Thomas Jefferson said Washington was the best horseman of his age, and Jefferson was both an excellent horseman himself and a Virginian, which meant he took this kind of thing seriously. Washington also had an ability to use his appearance dramatically. He saw his first play when he was 19 years old, and whenever he had a chance, he went to the theater or any kind of performance, including the circus. He admired both Shakespeare and Joseph Addison's play *Cato,* and he once paid a man who was exhibiting an elk to come up to Mount Vernon to show it to him. Play-going shaped his notion of how he presented himself. He was always playing the role of George Washington. He was a character actor whose character was himself.

The most famous instance of his acting in real life was his performance at Newburgh in 1783. The officers in the Continental Army hadn't been paid, as usual. The war was now ending. An appeal went through the camp that said, in effect, if this is how you are being treated when you still have your swords, how will you be treated after peace is signed? If you want to be paid, you must threaten Congress.

Washington called a meeting of the officers, leaving it unclear whether he would attend. When the meeting began, he was not present. In due course he showed up as if on cue and proceeded to read an impassioned appeal to the officers' sense of duty, insisting they must not let themselves and their country down. When he was done, he took out a letter from Congress that would show that Congress, however slow, was not ill-willed. But he did not start reading immediately; he shuffled the paper. Then he took out his reading glasses and said, "Gentlemen, you will permit me to put on my spectacles, for I have not only grown gray but almost blind in the service of my country."

Washington did not stay for the vote. He knew you do not step on a line like that. After he left, the officers voted unanimously to do whatever he wished.

Washington as a gentleman is something we neglect, perhaps because so few of us are gentlemen ourselves. Washington had to practice gentlemanly behavior because he had a tremendous temper. We have forgotten this aspect of him, though anyone who knew him knew he could be testy, even as a teenager. Lord Fairfax wrote his mother that he was an excellent surveyor, but added, "I wish I could say that he governs his temper." When he was president, someone brought an anti-administration pamphlet to a cabinet meeting which described Washington's being guillotined. Jefferson recorded that Washington got into "one of those passions where he cannot contain himself" and quoted the rolling fury of his complaints.

The one time Washington lost his temper in public was at the Battle of Monmouth in 1778, when he rebuked General Charles Lee at a moment of maximum stress. All Washington's work over the last year in drilling his army and making it a professional force seemed to be at risk because of Lee's conduct, and the evidence suggests Washington exploded. Certainly Lee thought so.

Washington was capable of wrath, yet he almost always held it back. His first training in self-control came from *The Rules of Civility,* a collection of 110 rules for young gentlemen compiled by French Jesuit priests in the 1590s. The rules were translated into a number of European languages, and somehow an English copy got to Virginia in the 1740s. Washington copied them into a notebook, now in the Library of Congress, along with geography lessons and assorted legal forms. In part, writing them down was a penmanship exercise, but the main reason he copied the rules was to learn and internalize them.

These points of etiquette are not obvious moral precepts in the style of Benjamin Franklin's *Poor Richard's Almanac*. *The Rules of Civility* do not reveal what they're up to right away. They tell you how to walk, how to talk, how to dress, how to eat. But when you think about them, you realize they are exercises in attention. They tell you you are not alone in the world, but surrounded by people whose sensibilities you must consider. You cannot do the first thing that comes into your head. These are not guides for "self-expression" or "authenticity."

My favorite is rule 13, which starts off quaintly, but becomes very serious. "Kill no fleas, lice, ticks, et cetera, in the sight of others. If you see any filth or thick spittle on the floor, put your foot dexterously upon it. If it be upon the clothes of your companions, put it off privately. And if it be upon your own clothes, return thanks to him who puts it off."

Privately is a very important word. It means you do not go up in public to someone with filth or thick spittle on his clothes and say, "Oh, you've got filth on your clothing. Let me help you off with that." You do not do that, because it would embarrass him, and so you do it privately. On the other hand, if someone helps you, you may feel upset and embarrassed—but it doesn't matter. What you're feeling is not the most important thing. You have to thank the man who brushes your clothes off.

This rule was useful to Washington, apart from controlling his temper, because his range of acquaintance was wider than that of any other Founder. He knew officers, generals, and privates; Frenchmen and Englishmen; Yankees and Southern planters; frontiersmen and Quakers. He dealt with Indians who were enemies and Indians who were allies; with blacks who were slaves, who were freeman, and who were his own soldiers. His ability to deal with all of them was founded on his training in these rules.

Considering Washington as hero, I was struck by a lecture of John Keegan, the English military historian. Keegan said he thought there were four men who understood warfare in North America (which was different from warfare in Europe, because North America is larger, making the geographic points that control space more important). Keegan thought the four experts were Samuel de Champlain, Ulysses Grant, Benedict Arnold, and George Washington. Fortunately, Washington understood it better than Arnold.

It is often said against Washington that he lost more battles than he won. This is true. But war is not the World Series. It's not the best out of seven. You don't have to win every battle you fight or be the best general who ever lived. All you have to be is better than the generals you are facing. If you are better than they are, if you figure out sooner than they what the strategic situation is, you will win the war, and that is what Washington was able to do.

The other important thing about his generalship is the effect it had on his men. To understand the impact, we have to look at soldiers' memoirs. A lot of these were written in the 1830s when Congress offered bonuses to veterans, providing they first described what they had done in the war. So these old men wrote accounts of what they did, and Washington appears occasionally, sometimes in unexpected places.

The most moving vignette I have found is by an old man writing in a newspaper in the 1830s. He was in a Rhode Island unit that fought in the battles of Trenton and Princeton. Washington had won the Battle of Trenton, but the British were going to retake the town, which Washington anticipated. So he put most of his army outside town, across a stream, while he held Trenton with a small number of troops. Their job was to fire at the British when they came, then retreat across the stream back to the main army. The British came at dusk. A fighting retreat is a hard thing to do, because it's paradoxical. You are leaving the field, but you're still supposed to be resisting as you go—a psychologically delicate operation. This man, a teenager at the time, doesn't say he was panicked, but you can tell he was on the edge of panic.

There was only one bridge over the stream, and as his unit was hurrying across it, he saw that Washington had posted himself on the other side, to oversee the retreat. All the while there was an artillery duel going on between the British and the Americans on either side of the creek. As he crossed the bridge, he was jostled against Washington's boot and the flank of his horse. He remembered—50 years later—that the horse was as firm as the rider and seemed to know that he was not to quit his station. What the man did not say is that, at the moment of contact, he also knew this because Washington's presence gave him a sense that all was not chaos, that the battle was under control. And so he was able to escape with his unit and fight again another day.

Those little encounters mattered enormously to Washington's troops. Heroism is showing up, being where you ought to be. When you lose, which will happen much of the time, maybe most of the time, you keep showing up again and again and again, until you finally prevail. That was what Washington was able to do and to convey as commander in chief.

We don't like to think of Washington as a politician because we don't like our politicians, but Washington knew how the game was played and was quite good at it. When he was a teenager, his elder half brother Lawrence ran for the Virginia House of Burgesses, and George saved the vote count. He even alphabetized it. Why? So he could use it again next time. This shows a very precocious interest in politics. When he first ran for the House of Burgesses himself, the question of treating voters to drinks on election day came up. Although this was technically illegal, every candidate did it. Washington could not be at the polling place, but he had a friend who was, in effect, his campaign manager, and we have their correspondence. This is what Washington gave to the voters on election day: 28 gallons of rum, 50 gallons of rum punch, 38 gallons of wine, 46 gallons of beer, and two gallons of cider, probably hard. That adds up to 160 gallons of booze. Since there were 397 voters, that works out to a little less than two quarts per voter. Washington's only complaint to his friend was that he had not spent enough. Washington won.

Washington had a very practical understanding of office holding as well as elections. He spent sixteen years in the Virginia House of Burgesses. This is why, at Newburgh in 1783, he knew Congress should not be distrusted. Unlike many military men, he'd been on the other side. He knew how legislatures worked, and he knew that when they didn't work, it wasn't because of malice. Things take time. When he explained this to his men, he spoke with authority.

It is hard for scholars and intellectuals to appreciate Washington as a thinker. Washington makes it hard for us. In a letter to his aide David Humphreys, Washington called his own education "defective." Humphreys had gone to Yale, while Washington had never gone to college. He had the least formal education of any other president except Andrew Johnson.

Washington remedied the defect by reading all his adult life, particularly about politics and political controversy. This was at a time when writing on politics was the best it has ever been in this country, and some of it was among the best ever in the world. Washington read everything that came off the presses. He knew many of the authors; sometimes they were writing for him; and he had an ability to pick their brains and make use of their learning.

One intellectual politician he didn't resemble was Viscount Bolingbroke, an eighteenth-century English statesman responsible for many of the phrases still found in American politics. Bolingbroke's analysis of the checks and balances of the British constitution influenced the French thinker Montesquieu, who in turn influenced our Constitutional Convention. Bolingbroke also devised, for example, the "Patriot King," the leader above politics and parties who comes in and fixes everything—an idea invoked by Ross Perot and Colin Powell.

The only problem is, Bolingbroke didn't mean any of it. He was a scoundrel. He wanted some sovereign to hire him and was trying to "spin" himself a career. Washington was the opposite—not churning out journalism, but thinking seriously about the issues that confronted him.

Finally, Washington was a skeptic, something very hard for

Americans to accept, because we don't like to think of ourselves as skeptics. Washington saw a paradox in the doctrine of natural rights. He believed the rights of man had an eternal importance, but he did not believe founding a government based on those rights would be easy. He occupied an odd position, and you see this most clearly in his first farewell address, the "Circular to the States," which he sent to the governors in 1783. He was stepping down as commander in chief of the army, and as far as he knew, it was his farewell. He didn't know he would come back later as president.

There is a very arresting paragraph in the "Circular." It's only three sentences, describing the situation of America at the moment of its independence. The first sentence is a catalogue of blessings: natural resources, extent of territory—it goes on and on. The second sentence, also quite long, enumerates the blessings of the social situation: We have revelation, manners, science; we have access to the thoughts of previous philosophers. Once again, all these advantages pile up. If this were a convention speech or a Fourth of July speech, you would expect an uplifting send-off in the third sentence, but he doesn't give a send-off. The third sentence is a short one in which he says, if with all these advantages, the people cannot be "completely free and happy, the fault will be entirely their own."

That sentence is like hitting a speed bump. He is saying, I have done all I can; this generation will do all it can. But the rest is up to you. It's up to the American people. It's up to the future, and it's up to us.

NOTES ON CONTRIBUTORS

WILLIAM B. ALLEN is professor of political philosophy in the Department of Political Science at Michigan State University. He was director of the Council of Higher Education for the Commonwealth of Virginia, and he is editor of *George Washington: A Collection.*

VIRGINIA L. ARBERY is professor of politics at the Dallas Institute of Humanities and Culture. She has also taught at the University of Dallas, the Thomas More College of Liberal Arts in Merrimack, New Hampshire, St. Anselm's College in Manchester, New Hampshire, and with the National Center for America's Founding Documents at Boston University. Dr. Arbery recently contributed to *Invitation to the Classics,* edited by Louise Cowan and Os Guiness.

RYAN J. BARILLEAUX is a professor of political science at Miami University, Ohio. He is the author or editor of six books, including *The Post-Modern Presidency, The President as World Leader,* and *Presidential Frontiers: Underexplored Issues in White House Politics.* He has directed the graduate program in political science at Miami University, Ohio, and is the editor in chief of *Catholic Social Science Review*.

WILLIAM J. BENNETT is co-director of Empower America and is the John M. Olin Distinguished Fellow in Cultural Policy Studies at the Heritage Foundation. He served as secretary of education, director of the Office of National Drug Control Policy, and chairman of the National Endowment for the Humanities. His books include *The Death of Outrage*, *Our Sacred Honor: Words of Advice from the Founders in Stories, Letters, Poems, and Speeches*, and *The Book of Virtues*.

RICHARD BROOKHISER is senior editor of *National Review* and a columnist for the *New York Observer*. His books include *The Way of the Wasp*, *Founding Father: Rediscovering George Washington*, *Rules of Civility*, and *Alexander Hamilton, American*.

GARY L. GREGG II is Mitch McConnell Chair in Leadership at the University of Louisville and is the director of the McConnell Center for Political Leadership. He has served as the national director at the Intercollegiate Studies Institute, Inc. and is author of *The Presidential Republic: Executive Representation and Deliberative Democracy* and editor of *Vital Remnants: America's Founding and the Western Tradition.* He is an award-winning college teacher.

VICTOR DAVIS HANSON is a professor of Greek and director of the Classics Program at California State University, Fresno. He is the author or editor of nine books, including *The Other Greeks, Fields Without Dreams: Defending the Agrarian Ideal, Who Killed Homer? The Demise of Classical Education and the Recovery of Greek Wisdom* (with John Heath), and *The Soul of Battle*. In 1992 he was named the most outstanding undergraduate teacher of classics in the nation.

FORREST MCDONALD is Distinguished Research Professor of History at the University of Alabama and the author of fifteen books, including *Novus Ordo Seclorum: The Intellectual Origins of the Constitution, "We the People": The Economic Origins of the Constitution, E. Pluribus Unum: The Foundation of the American Republic, 1776–1790, The Presidency of George Washington*, and *The American Presidency: An Intellectual History*. He was named by the National Endowment for the Humanities as the sixteenth Jefferson Lecturer, the nation's highest honor in the humanities.

MACKUBIN OWENS is professor of strategy and force planning at the United States Naval War College, where he specializes in the planning of U. S. strategy and forces, the political economy of national security, and civil-military relations. From 1990 to 1997, he was editor in chief of *Strategic Review* and adjunct professor of international relations at Boston University. He is a regular columnist for *The Providence Journal,* and his essays on national security issues have been widely published in scholarly and popular journals.

MARK J. ROZELL is associate professor of politics and director of the graduate program in congressional studies at The Catholic University of America in Washington, D. C. He is the author or editor of numerous studies on the presidency and American politics, including *Executive Privilege: The Dilemma of Secrecy and Democratic Accountability* and *The Clinton Scandal and the Future of American Politics.*

MATTHEW SPALDING is director of the B. Kenneth Simon Center for American Studies at the Heritage Foundation, visiting assistant professor of government at Claremont McKenna College, and an adjunct fellow of the Claremont Institute. He is co-author of *A Sacred Union of Citizens: George Washington's Farewell Address and the American Character.*

MARK THISTLETHWAITE holds the Kay and Velma Kimbell Chair of Art History at Texas Christian University, where he has received the Chancellor's Award for Distinguished Teaching and Honors Program "Professor of the Year" Award. He has published widely on American history painting, with particular emphasis on images of George Washington.

BRUCE S. THORNTON is chair of the Department of Foreign Languages and Literatures at California State University, Fresno, and is the author of *Eros: The Myth of Ancient Greek Sexuality* and, most recently, *Plagues of the Mind: The New Epidemic of False Knowledge* (also published by ISI Books).

JOHN G. WEST, JR. is an associate professor of political science at Seattle Pacific University and a senior fellow of the Seattle-based Discovery Institute, where he runs the program on religion, liberty, and civic life. He is author of *The Politics of Revelation and Reason: Religion and Civic Life in the New Nation* and co-editor of *The Encyclopedia of Religion in American Politics* and *The C. S. Lewis Reader's Encyclopedia*.

NOTES

Introduction

GARY L. GREGG II AND MATTHEW SPALDING

1 The statements of the Senate and President John Adams are quoted in John Marshall, *The Life of George Washington,* Vol. 5 (Fredricksburg: The Citizens' Guild of Washington's Boyhood Home, 1926) pp. 368 and 369-70.

2 Henry Cabot Lodge, *George Washington* (New Rochelle: Arlington House), pp. 1-2.

3 Washington to Thomas Johnson, October 15, 1784, in John C. Fitzpatrick, ed., *The Writings of George Washington,* Vol. XXVII (Washington, D. C.: United States Government Printing Office, 1931-44), p. 481.

4 Henry Steele Commager, ed., *Documents of American History,* Vol. I (New Jersey: Prentice-Hall, 1973), p. 133.

5 Washington to James Madison, March 31, 1787, in Fitzpatrick, *Writings of Washington,* Vol. XXIX, pp. 191-2.

6 James Monroe to Thomas Jefferson, July 12, 1788, in Julian P. Boyd, ed., *The Papers of Thomas Jefferson,* Vol. XIII (Princeton, 1956), p. 352.

7 Thomas Jefferson, "Opinion on the Constitutionality of a National Bank," February 15, 1791, in Merrill D. Peterson, ed., Thomas Jefferson, *Writings* (New York: Literary Classics of the United States, 1984), pp. 416-21.

8 Alexander Hamilton, "Opinion on the Constitutionality of an Act to Establish a National Bank," February 23, 1791, in Morton J. Frisch, ed., *Selected Writings and Speeches of Alexander Hamilton* (Washington, D. C.: American Enterprise Institute, 1895) pp. 248-76.

9   James Madison, "Madison's Personal Memorandum Respecting Conversations With Washington About His Proposed Retirement," May 5, 1792, in Victor Hugo Palsits, *Washington's Farewell Address,* (New York: The New York Public Library, 1935), p. 215.

10 Written by Attorney General Randolph, the document did not include the word "neutrality" in deference to the sentiments of Jefferson.

11 The best study on this subject is Samuel Flagg Bemis, *Jay's Treaty: A Study in Commerce and Diplomacy* (New Haven: Yale University Press, 1962).

12 See Samuel Flagg Bemis, *Pinckney's Treaty: America's Advantage From Europe's Distress,* 1783-1800 (New Haven: Yale University Press, 1965).

13 Washington to Alexander Hamilton, June 26, 1796, in Fitzpatrick, *Writings of Washington,* Vol. XXXV, p. 103.

14 Douglas Southall Freeman, *George Washington: A Biography,* Vol. III (New York: Scribners, 1950), p. xiii.

15 James T. Flexner, *George Washington,* Vol. 1 (Boston: Little Brown, 1965), p. 5.

Two

"The Western Cincinnatus": Washington as Farmer and Soldier

BRUCE S. THORNTON AND VICTOR D. HANSON

1   See Garry Wills, *Cincinnatus: George Washington and the Enlightenment* (Garden City, N.Y.: Doubleday, 1984), 13.

2   Ibid., 35, 36, 13-14.

3   For agrarianism and its influence on the Founders and further bibliography, see my essay "The Founders as Farmers: The Greek Georgic Tradition and the American Founders," in *Vital Remnants: America's Founding and the Western Tradition,* ed. Gary L. Gregg II (Wilmington, Delaware: ISI Books, 1999), 33-69.

4   Meyer Reinhold, *Classica Americana: The Greek and Roman Heritage in the United States* (Detroit, Michigan: Wayne State University Press, 1984), 99.

5   Quoted in Carl J. Richard, *The Founders and the Classics: Greece, Rome, and the American Enlightenment* (Cambridge, Mass.: Harvard University Press, 1994), 165.

6   Aristotle, *Nichomachean Ethics* 1099a, trans. Martin Ostwald.

7   See Anthony Low, *The Georgic Revolution* (Princeton, N.J.: Princeton University Press, 1985), 117-54.

8   For Washington's early life, see Willard Sterne Randall, *George Washington: A Life* (New York: Henry Holt, 1997), 17-23.

9   Stephanie Wolf, *As Various as Their Land: The Everyday Lives of Eighteenth-Century Americans* (New York: HarperCollins, 1993), 141-42.

10   Washington to Arthur Young, 6 August 1786, *The Writings of George Washington. From the Original Manuscript Sources, 1745-1799*, ed. John C. Fitzpatrick (Washington, D.C.: Government Printing Office, 1931), 28:510. Subsequent references to Washington's letters and papers will be from this edition unless noted otherwise. Washington to Earl of Buchan: 4 July 1797, 35:487.

11   Washington to James Anderson, 24 December 1795, 34:406.

12   Washington to Alexander Spotswood, 13 February 1788, 29:414.

13   7 April 1797. Quoted in Richard Norton Smith, *Patriarch: George Washington and the New American Nation* (New York: Houghton Mifflin, 1993), 301.

14   Washington to Arthur young, 4 December 1788, 30:150.

15   See *The Papers of George Washington: Colonial Series*, ed. W.W. Abbot and Dorothy Twolig (Charlottesville, Virginia: University Press of Virginia, 1983), 7:344-48.

16   Washington to Cary & Company, 1 May 1759, 2:436.

17   Washington to Clement Biddle, 10 February 1786, 28.384; and 18 May 1786, 28:429.

18   Washington to George William Fairfax, 30 June 1785, 28.185; Washington to Arthur Young, 6 August 1786, 28:510.

19   Washington to Sir Edward Newenham, 2 March 1789, 30:217.

20   Washington to Theodorick Bland, 15 August 1786, 29:516-17; Metcalf Bowler, 19 August 1786, 29:524.

21   Washington to Samuel Chamberline, 3 April 1788, 29:455.

22   Washington to Henry Riddell, 22 February 1774, 3:187.

23   Washington to Timothy Pickering, 20 January 1791, 31:199.

24   Washington, "Talk to the Cherokee Nation," 29 August 1796, 35:193

25   Washington, "Address to Congress," April 1789, 38:305-7.

26   Washington to Thomas Jefferson, 1 January 1788, 29:350-51.

27   Washington takes command: Randall, *George Washington: A Life*, 282-6; L.C. Hatch, *The Administration of the American Revolutionary Army* (New York: B. Franklin, 1971), 6-8.

28 Washington's despair: Hatch, *Administration*, 15-16. For alternative voices calling for a permanent militia of amateur soldiers, see C. Royster, A *Revolutionary People at War: The Continental Army and American Army, 1775-1783* (Williamsburg, Virginia: University of North Carolina Press, 1979), 40-3, and cf. 62-126 for continuing problems of discipline.

29 Washington's acceptance of civilian authority: Wills, *Cincinnatus*, 21.

30 The New York controversy and fiasco: Randall, *Washington*, 306-25.

31 See Glenn A. Phelps, *George Washington and American Constitutionalism* (Lawrence, Kansas: University of Kansas Press, 1993), n. 38, 203-4.

32 On Benedict Arnold, see Royster, *Revolutionary People*, 289-94.

33 On the Conway cabal, see Randall, *Washington*, 352; Royster, *Revolutionary People*, 184-6; Hatch, *Administration*, 26-30.

34 Washington's reluctance to requisition: Hatch, *Administration*, 91; Washington and his officers' pay: Randall, *Washington*, 399.

35 Lost salary of Washington: Randall, *Washington*, 402-4.

36 Discharge: Hatch, *Administration*, 179-83; Washington's farewell: Randall, *Washington*, 409.

37 Washington's warning: Brookhiser, *Founding Father* (New York: The Free Press, 1996), 41.

38 The Society of the Cincinnati: Royster, *Revolutionary People*, 354-6; Washington's notes to the society: Wills, *Cincinnatus*, 140-3.

Three

General Washington and the Military Strategy of the Revolution

MACKUBIN OWENS

1 John Marshall, *The Life of George Washington* (1848; reprint, in 2 vols., New York: Walton Book Company, 1930) 2: 528-529.

2 Carl von Clausewitz, *On War*, ed. and trans. Michael Howard and Peter Paret (Princeton: Princeton University Press, 1976), 178.

3 Alexander Hamilton, James Madison, and John Jay, *The Federalist*, ed. Jacob E. Cooke (Middletown, Connecticut: Wesleyan University Press, 1961), 3.

4 Brevet Major General Emory Upton, United States Army, Military Policy of the United States (Washington, D. C.: Government Printing Office, 1904). See also Stephen Ambrose, *Upton and the Army* (Baton Rouge: Louisiana State

University Press, 1964) and Allan R. Millett and Peter Maslowski, *For the Common Defense: A Military History of the United States of America*, 2nd edition (New York: The Free Press, 1994), 271-274.

5   Don Higginbotham, "Introduction," *Military Analysis of the Revolutionary War* (Millwood, New York: KTO Press, 1977), 1.

6   Russell F. Weigley, "A Strategy of Attrition," *The American Way of War: A History of United States Military Strategy and Policy* (New York: Macmillan, 1971), 3-18.

7   Three excellent exceptions to this generalization are Dave Richard Palmer, *The Way of the Fox: American Strategy in the War for America, 1775-1783* (Westport, Connecticut: Greenwood Press, 1975); Millett and Maslowski, "The American Revolution," in *For the Common Defense.*; and Weigley, op. cit.

8   George Athan Billias, ed., *George Washington's Generals* (New York: William Morrow and Company, 1964), xvii.

9   Marcus Cunliffe, *George Washington: Man and Monument* (Boston: Little, Brown, 1958), 127.

10   Richard M. Ketchum, *The Winter Soldiers* (Garden City: Doubleday, 1973), 36.

11   John R. Alden, *A History of the American Revolution* (New York: Knopf, 1969), 185.

12   This is not true, but even if it were, the preponderance of means in favor of Great Britain was so great that even bad British generalship should not have reduced the odds against American independence.

13   Clausewitz, *On War*, 128, 177.

14   On the origins of modern strategy, see Azar Gat, *The Origins of Military Thought: From the Enlightenment to Clausewitz* (Oxford: Clarendon Press, 1989).

15   Mackubin Thomas Owens, "An Overview of U.S. Military Strategy: Concepts And History," in *Strategy and Force Planning*, 2nd edition, ed. Strategy and Force Planning Faculty, (Newport: Naval War College Press, 1997), 387.

16   Williamson Murray and Mark Grimsley, "On Strategy," in *The Making of Strategy: Rulers, States, and War,* ed. Murray et al. (Cambridge,: Cambridge University Press, 1994).

17   Clausewitz, *On War*, 177.

18   Ibid. p. 77. Cf. Mackubin Thomas Owens, "Technology, The RMA, and Future War," *Strategic Review* 26, no. 2 (spring 1998).

19   On the alleged transmission of republican "ideology" from Niccolo Machiavelli through James Harrington to the radical Whigs, see J.G.A. Pocock, *The*

Machiavellian Moment: Florentine Political Thought and the Atlantic Republican Tradition (Princeton: Princeton University Press, 1975). Cf. James Kirby Martin and Mark Edward Lender, *A Respectable Army: The Military Origins of the Republic, 1763-1789* (Arlington Heights, Illinois: Harlan Davidson, 1982), 6-15.

20	On the gap between republican theory and the American reality, see Charles Royster, *A Revolutionary People at War: The Continental Army and American Character, 1775-1783* (Chapel Hill: The University of North Carolina Press, 1979).

21	Clausewitz, *On War*, 131-132.

22	Palmer, *War of the Fox*, 74.

23	I follow Palmer in his division of the war. As he points out, however, these phases "were consciously recognized at the time by patriot leaders..." Ibid., xix.

24	General Orders, 2 July 1776, in *George Washington: A Collection*, ed. W.B. Allen (Indianapolis: Liberty Classics, 1988), 71.

25	General Orders, 9 July 1776, in Allen, *George Washington*, 73.

26	Washington to John Banister, 21 April 1778, *Washington's Writings*, ed. Jared Sparks (New York: Harper and Brothers Publishers, 1847), 5: 323.

27	Greene to Washington, 5 September 1776, cited in Palmer, *Way of the Fox*, 124.

28	Washington to the President of Congress, 8 September 1776, in Sparks, 4:81.

29	Palmer, *Way of the Fox*, 129-131.

30	Washington to Major General Schuyler, 12 March 1777, in Sparks, 4:358.

31	Palmer, 139.

32	Washington to Lt. Col. John Laurens, 15 January 1781, in Sparks, 7:371.

33	Robin Ranger, "The Anglo-French Wars, 1689-1815," in *Seapower and Strategy*, ed. Colin Gray and Roger Barnett (Annapolis: Naval Institute Press, 1989).

34	Clausewitz, *On War*, 81.

35	As the Admiralty observed, "England till this time was never engaged in a sea war with the House of Bourbon thoroughly united, their naval force unbroken, and having no other war or object to draw off their attention and resources." Quoted in Admiral Sir Herbert Richmond, *Statesmen and Seapower* (Oxford: Clarendon Press, 1946), 151. Or as a modern British historian has written, "England had allowed herself to slip into the situation which her statesmen had always dreaded, a war against the maritime powers of Europe with no Continental allies to impose a check on France's freedom to devote her resources to naval warfare." Piers Mackesy, "British Strategy in the War of American

Independence," *The Yale Review*, June 1963, 553. On overall British strategy, see Mackesy, *The War for America* (Cambridge: Harvard University Press, 1964).

36   Washington to Henry Laurens, 14 November 1778, in Sparks, 6:108

37   Washington to John Reed, 28 May 1780, in Sparks, 7:59.

38   Washington to the Marquis de Lafayette, 15 July 1780: "Memorandum for Concerting a Plan of Operations with the French Army," in Sparks, 7:509.

39   Greene to Henry Knox, 18 July 1781, quoted in Theodore Thayer, "Nathanael Greene: Revolutionary War Strategist," in Billias, *George Washington's Generals*, 109.

40   Cited in Palmer, *War of the Fox*, 175-176.

41   Washington to Lafayette, 15 November 1781, in Sparks, 8:205.

42   Washington to James McHenry, 12 September 1782, in Sparks, 8:344.

43   Washington to Joseph Jones, 14 December 1782, in Allen, 206-207.

44   "Speech to the Officers of the Army," 15 March 1783, in Allen, *George Washington*, 217-223.

45   Richard Brookhiser, *Founding Father: Rediscovering George Washington* (New York: The Free Press, 1996), 44.

46   "Circular to the States," 14 June 1783, in Allen, *George Washington*, 239-249. The quotation is at p. 241.

47   John Shy, "Charles Lee: The Soldier as Radical," in Billias, *George Washington's Generals*, 47.

48   John Shy, *A People Numerous and Armed: Reflections on the Military Struggle for American Independence* (Ann Arbor: The University of Michigan Press, 1990), 126-127.

49   Shy, "Charles Lee," 47-48.

50   Ibid., 47.

Four

George Washington and the Standing Oak

WILLIAM B. ALLEN

1   *The Collector Magazine*, July 1892, p. 171.

2   Barry Schwartz, *George Washington: The Making of an American Symbol* (New York: Free Press, 1987).

3   Forrest McDonald, *Novus Ordo Seclorum: The Intellectual Origins of the Constitution* (Lawrence, Kansas: University Press of Kansas, 1985).

4   Washington to LaFayette, January 29, 1789.

5   Washington to LaFayette, May 28, 1788.

6   John P. Kaminski and Gaspare J. Saladino, eds., *The Documentary History of the Ratification of the Constitution* (Madison, Wisconsin: State Historical Society of Wisconsin, 1981), vol. XIII, pp. 60-62.

7   Washington to David Humphries, July 25, 1785.

8   Washington to John Bannister, April 21, 1778.

9   Washington, General Orders, March 1, 1778, Valley Forge.

10 Washington to John Augustine Washington, May 31, 1776.

11 Washington to James Madison, March 31, 1787.

12 Henry Knox to George Washington, quoted in "Washington and the Constitution," David M. Matteson, #7 in *Honor to George Washington*, ed. by Albert Bushnell Hart for the George Washington Bicentennial Commission, Washington, D. C., 1931, p. 21.

Five

Washington and the Origins of Presidential Power

MARK J. ROZELL

1   Washington to James Madison, May 5, 1789, *The Writings of George Washington,* ed. John Fitzpatrick (Washington, D.C.: Government Printing Office, 1931-1944), 30: 311.

2   George Washington, "Queries on a Line of Conduct," May 10, 1789, *The Writings of George Washington*, 30: 321.

3   Willard Sterne Randall, *George Washington: A Life*, (New York: Henry Holt, 1997), 435.

4   Forrest McDonald, "Presidential Character: The Example of George Washington," in *The Presidency: Then and Now*, ed. Philip G. Henderson (Lanham, Maryland: Rowman & Littlefield, 1999).

5   See Charles E. Morganston, *The Appointment and Removal Power of the President of the United States* (Washington, D.C.: Government Printing Office, 1929).

6   See Henry J. Abraham, *Justices and Presidents: A Political History of Appointments to the Supreme Court*, 3d edition (New York: Oxford University Press, 1992); and

Henry J. Abraham, *Justices, Presidents, and Senators* (Lanham, Maryland: Rowman & Littlefield, 1999).

7   Sidney M. Milkis and Michael Nelson, *The American Presidency: Origins and Development* (Washington, D.C.: Congressional Quarterly Press, 1900), 75.

8   Edward S. Corwin, *The President, Office and Powers: 1787-1957.* (New York: New York University Press, 1957).

9   For an opposing view to my own, see Saikrishna Prakash, "A Note of the Constitutionality of Executive Privilege," *University of Minnesota Law Review* (May 1999).

10 *3 Annals of Congress* (1792), 493.

11 Paul Ford, *The Writings of Thomas Jefferson* (New York: Putnam, 1892) 1: 189-190.

12 Raoul Berger, *Executive Privilege: A Constitutional Myth* (Cambridge: Harvard University Press 1974), 167.

13 Abraham Sofaer, "Executive Privilege: An Historical Note," *Columbia Law Review* 74 (1975): 1319.

14 Ibid.

15 Ibid.

16 Ibid., 1320.

17 Ibid., 1321; Abraham Sofaer, "Executive Power and Control Over Information: The Practice Under the Framers," *Duke Law Journal* 1977 (March 1977): 8.

18 Quoted in Forrest McDonald, *The American Presidency: An Intellectual History* (Lawrence, Kansas: University Press of Kansas, 1994), 242.

19 James Richardson, *A Compilation of the Messages and Papers of the Presidents* (New York: Bureau of National Literature, 1897), 1:186-187.

20 *5 Annals of Congress* (1796), 771, 782-783.

21 Ibid., 773.

22 Ibid., 438.

23 Quoted in Gary Schmitt, "Executive Privilege," in *The Presidency in the Constitutional Order*, ed. Joseph Bessette and Jeffrey Tulis (Baton Rouge: Louisiana State University Press, 1981), 188 n.

24 Ibid., 187 n.

25 See Mark J. Rozell, *Executive Privilege: The Dilemma of Secrecy and Democratic Accountability* (Baltimore: Johns Hopkins University Press, 1994) Mark J. Rozell, "Executive Privilege and the Modern Presidents: In Nixon's Shadow," *University of Minnesota Law Review* (May 1999), 1069-1126.

26 Charles F.C. Ruff, "Ruff's Argument for Executive Privilege," unsealed May 27, 1998, available from <http://www.washingtonpost.com/wp-srv/politics/special/clinton/stories/ruff052898.htm>.

27 Milkis and Nelson, *The American Presidency,* xii.

28 The original "classic" version is Richard Neustadt, *Presidential Power* (New York: John Wiley and Sons, 1960). This book has now sold over one million copies and remains a standard in presidency courses. The editor of my publisher, The Johns Hopkins University Press, consulted me several years ago about the value of putting Clinton Rossiter's classic presidency text back into print. I enthusiastically endorsed the idea. My editor has since told me that the book barely sells 400 copies a year.

Six

Foreign Policy and the First Commander in Chief

RYAN J. BARILLEAUX

1 Marcus Cunliffe, *George Washington, Man and Monument* (New York: New American Library, 1958).

2 John Hart Ely, *War and Responsibility* (Princeton: Princeton University Press, 1993), 4.

3 Ibid., 3-4.

4 Louis Henkin, *Foreign Affairs and the Constitution* (New York: Foundation Press, 1972).

5 Dave R. Palmer, *1794: America, Its Army, and the Birth of the Nation* (Novato, California: Presidio, 1974), 241.

6 Ibid., 274.

7 Ibid., 273.

8 Ibid., 274-5.

9 See Forrest McDonald, *The American Presidency: An Intellectual History* (Lawrence, Kansas: University Press of Kansas, 1994), 236.

10 Quoted in Congressional Quarterly, *Powers of the Presidency* (Washington, D.C.: Congressional Quarterly, 1997), 127. Emphasis mine.

11 Ibid., 128.

12 Ibid.

13 Bas *vs.* Lingy., 4 US (4 Dall) 37, 1 L.Ed., 731.

14   Palmer, *America*, 268-9.

15   Ryan J. Barilleaux and Christopher Kelley, "The Other Side of War: Presidential Peace Powers," in *Presidential Frontiers: Underexplored Issues in White House Politics*, ed. Ryan J. Barilleaux. (Westport, Connecticut: Praeger, 1998), 119-34.

16   Palmer, *America*, 24.

17   Ibid., 24-5.

18   Ibid., 27.

19   Theodore Roosevelt, *The Works of Theodore Roosevelt* (New York: Charles Scribner's Sons, 1926), 13:501.

20   Roosevelt, *Works of Theodore Roosevelt,* 19:54.

21   Roosevelt, *Works of Theodore Roosevelt*, 13:182.

22   Ibid.

23   Roosevelt, *Works of Theodore Roosevelt*, 19:49.

Seven

The Symbolic Dimensions of the First Presidency

GARY L. GREGG II

1   Quoted in Herbert Storing, ed., *The Complete Anti-Federalists*, vol. 2, no. 8 (Chicago: University of Chicago Press, 1981), 178. John Adams makes a similar argument in his *Defence of the Constitutions of the United States in Works*, 285-292; 585.

2   Quoted in Clinton Rossiter, *The American Presidency*, rev. ed. (New York: Mentor, 1960), 16.

3   Quoted in Michael Novak, *Choosing Our King: Powerful Symbols in Presidential Politics* (New York: MacMillan, 1974), 21.

4   Richard Brookhiser, *Founding Father: Rediscovering George Washington* (New York: Free Press, 1996), 111.

5   Captain George Mercer, 1760, quoted in James Thomas Flexner, *George Washington* (Boston: 1965-1972), 1: 192.

6   Quoted in Barry Schwartz, *George Washington: The Making of an American Symbol* (Ithaca: Cornell University Press, 1987), 19.

7   Ralph Ketcham, *Presidents above Party: The First American Presidency* (Chapel Hill: University of North Carolina Press, 1984), 8.

8   The phrase is from Emmet John Hughes, *The Living Presidency: The Resources and Dilemmas of the American Presidential Office* (New York, 1973), 40.

9   Washington to James Madison, 5 May 1789, in *George Washington: A Collection*, ed. William B. Allen (Indianapolis: Liberty Fund, 1988), 531.

10   See Gary L. Gregg II, *The Presidential Republic: Executive Representation and Deliberative Democracy* (Lanham, Md.: Rowman & Littlefield, 1997), 19-26.

11   Forrest McDonald, *The Presidency of George Washington* (Lawrence, Kan.: University Press of Kansas, 1973), 25.

12   See Glenn A. Phelps, *George Washington & American Constitutionalism* (Lawrence, Kan.: University of Kansas Press, 1993).

13   See Max Farrand, ed., *The Records of the Federal Convention of 1787* (New Haven: Yale University Press, 1966), 1: 113, 2: 100-101. Such a notion of a plural executive that would represent rival sectional interests, see John C. Calhoun, *A Disquisition on Government and Selections from the Discourse*, ed. C. Gordon Post (1853; reprint, New York: Macmillan, 1953).

14   Washington to the Hebrew Congregation in Newport, August 1790, *George Washington: A Collection*, 548.

15   For more details on these attempts by Washington, see Phelps, *American Constitutionalism*, 160-189.

16   Ibid., 36-37.

17   See *The Writings of George Washington*, ed. John C. Fitzpatrick (Washington, DC: GPO, 1931-1944), 6:354 n.

18   Allen, *George Washington: A Collection,* 532.

19   Quoted in William J. Ridings, Jr. and Stuart B. McIver, , *Rating the Presidents: A Ranking of U.S. Leaders from the Great and Honorable to the Dishonest and Incompetent* (Secaucus, N.J.: Citadel Press, 1997), 4.

20   Quoted in Marvin Olasky, *The American Leadership Tradition: Moral Vision from Washington to Clinton* (New York: The Free Press, 1999), 17.

21   Quoted in Marcus Cunliffe, *George Washington: Man and Monument* (Mount Vernon, Va.: The Mount Vernon Ladies' Association, 1982), 134.

22   See Olasky, *American Leadership,* 22.

23   Allen, *George Washington: A Collection*, 462.

24   Quoted in James Thomas Flexner, *Washington: The Indispensable Man* (Boston: Little, Brown and Company), 218.

25   Allen, *George Washington: A Collection*, 521.

26   Ibid., 545.

27   Brookhiser, *Founding Father*, 77

28   Ibid., 76

29   GW to John Hancock, 26 October 1789, Writings, 30: 453.

30   Eric Voegelin, *The New Science of Politics* (Chicago: University of Chicago Press, 1952), 27-28.

31   Allen, *George Washington: A Collection*, 43.

32   Ibid., 521.

33   See George Washington to George Mason, 3 October 1785, in *George Washington: A Collection*, 312.

34   Allen, *George Washington: A Collection*, 403-404.

35   Ibid., 412.

36   According to a lecture delivered by Boston Clergyman Theodore Parker in 1858, the New York Indians held a tradition that "Alone among white men, he has been admitted to the Indian Heaven, because of his justice to the Red Men. He lives in a great palace built like a fort. All the Indians, as they go to Heaven, pass by, and he himself is in his uniform, a sword at his side, walking to and fro. They bow reverently. . . . He returns the salute, but says nothing." Quoted in Marcus Cunliffe, *Man and Monument*, 129.

Eight

Washington's Farewell Address and the Form of the American Regime

VIRGINIA L. ARBERY

1   The scale of the Republic was unprecedented. But Publius regarded this "enlargement of the orbit" as an addition to the science of politics" (*Federalist* 9). The teaching on the violence of majority factions in *Federalist* 10 argued that the largeness of the Republic would fragment passions before they could adversely affect "the permanent and aggregate good of the community." In *Federalist* 17, Publius argues that the new national government will earn popular support primarily through an administration superior to those of the state governments.

2   Alexis de Tocqueville, *Democracy in America*, trans. George Lawrence (New York: Anchor/Doubleday, 1969), 385.

3   For a historical treatment of how the solidity of the Constitution was related to

the person of Washington, see Marcus Cunliffe, *George Washington: Man and Monument* (New York: Mentor Books, 1958). "Indeed while Washington was venerated as one symbol of American union, the Constitution was likewise assuming an almost sacred character as a second and more permanent symbol of that union." Ibid., 131.

4   Ibid., 133–4, and Forrest McDonald, *The Presidency of George Washington* (New York: W. W. Norton & Company, 1974), 29–30.

5   All references to the Farewell Address are from *The Writings of George Washington,* ed. John C. Fitzpatrick (Washington, D. C.: United States Government Printing Office, 1934-40), 35:214–238.

6   Jefferson, *Selected Writings,* ed. Harvey C. Mansfield, Jr. (Arlington Heights, Illinois.: AHM Publishing Corporation, 1979), 62–66.

Nine

Making Citizens: George Washington and the American Character

Matthew Spalding

1   Thomas Jefferson to Washington, April 16, 1784, in Julian Boyd, ed., *The Papers of Thomas Jefferson*, Vol. VII (Princeton: Princeton University Press, 1953), p. 106.

2   *The Records of the Federal Convention of 1787,* ed. Max Farrand, (New Haven: Yale University Press, 1911), Vol. 3, p. 302. The delegate was Pierce Butler.

3   William B. McGroarty, *Washington: First in the Hearts of his Countrymen* (Richmond: Garrett & Massie, 1932), p. 29.

4   William B. Allen, *Washington: A Collection* (Indianapolis: Liberty Classics, 1988) pp. 8-13.

5   Washington to George Steptoe Washington, March 23, 1789, in John C. Fitzpatrick, ed. *The Writings of George Washington.* 39 vols. (Washington, DC: United States Government Printing Office, 1931-44), Volume 30, p. 248.

6   Washington to George Steptoe Washington, December 5, 1790, in *Writings of Washington*, Volume 30, p. 163.

7   Washington to Nicholas Pike, June 20, 1788, in *Writings of Washington,* Vol. 30, pp. 2-3.

8   Washington to George Washington Parke Custis, December 19, 1796, in *Writings of Washington*, Volume 35, p. 341.

9   Washington to Warner Lewis, August 14, 1755, in *Writings of Washington*, Volume 1, p. 162.

10   Washington to Alexander Hamilton, August 28, 1788, in *Writings of Washington*, Volume 30, p. 67.

11   Washington, First Annual Message to Congress, January 8, 1790, in *Writings of Washington*, Volume 30, p. 493.

12   Washington to John Armstrong, April 25, 1788, in *Writings of Washington*, Volume 29, p. 465

13   Washington, General Orders, January 1, 1776, in *Writings of Washington*, Volume 4, p. 202.

14   Washington to John Bannister, April 21, 1778 in *Writings of Washington*, Volume 11, p. 291.

15   Washington to the President of Congress, September 24, 1776, in *Writings of Washington*, Volume 6, p. 111. It was for this reason that Washington, despite the fears of many colonists, advocated a permanent military establishment instead of relying upon an untrained and undisciplined militia.

16   Washington, General Orders, July 4, 1775, in *Writings of Washington*, Volume 3, p. 309.

17   Washington, General Orders, July 9, 1776, in *Writings of Washington*, Volume 5, p. 245.

18   Washington, General Orders, January 1, 1776, in *Writings of Washington*, Volume 4, p. 202.

19   Washington, General Orders, July 2, 1776, in *Writings of Washington*, Volume 5, p. 211.

20   Washington, General Orders, 1 January 1, 1776, *Writings of Washington*, Volume 4, p. 203; Washington to Philip Schuyler, July 17, 1776, in *Writings of Washington*, Volume 5, pp. 290-1; Washington to Colonel William Woodford, November 10, 1775, in *Writings of Washington*, Volume 4, p. 80; Washington to the President of Congress, September 24, 1776, in *Writings of Washington*, Volume 6, pp. 108-10.

21   Washington, Farewell Orders to the Armies of the United States, November 2, 1783, in *Writings of Washington*, Volume 27, pp. 223-7. Emphasis added.

22   Washington to James Madison, March 31, 1787, in *Writings of Washington*, Volume 29, pp. 191-2. Madison replied by sending to Washington his outline of a new system based on the creation of a supreme national government and a change in the principle of representation.

23   Washington, Circular to the States, June 8, 1783, in *Writings of Washington*, Volume 26, pp. 483-96.

24   Washington to Marquis de Lafayette, February 7, 1788, in *Writings of Washington*, Volume 29, pp. 409-10.

25 Washington, Fragments of the Discarded First Inaugural Address, in Allen, *Washington*, p. 454.

26 Washington, First Inaugural Address, April 30, 1789, in *Writings of Washington*, Volume 30, pp. 291-6.

27 Washington, Fragments of the Discarded First Inaugural Address, in Allen, *Washington,* p. 458.

28 Washington, The Farewell Address, in *Writings of Washington*, Volume 35, pp. 214-38.

29 Alexander Hamilton, James Madison and John Jay, *The Federalist Papers,* ed. Clinton Rossiter (New York: New American Library, 1961) #10, p. 79.

30 Washington to George Chapman, December 15, 1784, in *Writings of Washington*, Volume 28, pp. 13-4.

31 Washington to the Commissioners of the District of Columbia, January 28, 1795, in *Writings of Washington*, Volume 34, p. 106.

32 Washington, Eighth Annual Message, December 7, 1796, in *Writings of Washington*, Volume 35, pp. 316-7.

33 Washington, Circular to the States, June 8, 1783, in *Writings of Washington*, Volume 26, pp. 483-96.

34 Washington to John Banister, April 21, 1778, in *Writings of Washington*, Volume 11, p. 286. Banister was a Virginia delegate to the Continental Congress.

35 John Marshall, *The Life of George Washington* (1801-1805; reprint, Fredricksburg, Va.: The Citizens' Guild of Washington's Boyhood Home, 1926), Volume 5, pp. 374-5.

36 Jefferson to Dr. Walter Jones, January 2, 1814, in Merrill D. Peterson, ed. *Thomas Jefferson, Writings* (New York: Literary Classics of the United States, 1984), p. 1319.

37 Edwin P. Whipple, ed., *The Great Speeches and Orations of Daniel Webster* (Boston: Little, Brown & Co., 1894), p. 150. (emphasis added)

Ten

"Our Illustrious Washington": The American Imaging of George Washington

MARK THISTLETHWAITE

1 Washington Goff, "Oration on the Anniversary of General George Washington delivered in the city of New York, February 22, 1859," in

Goff's Book of American Constitutions, containing the Declarations of Independence...the Farewell Address of General Washington ...and Goff's Oration on the Character of Washington (New York: Washington Goff, 1859), 1.

2   For recent in-depth and specific studies of Washington imagery, see Mark Edward Thistlethwaite, *The Image of George Washington: Studies in Mid-Nineteenth-Century American History Painting* (New York and London: Garland Publishing, 1979); Patricia A. Anderson, *Promoted to Glory: The Apotheosis of George Washington*, exh. cat. (Northampton, Massachusetts.: Smith College Museum of Art, 1980); Wendy C. Wick, *George Washington, An American Icon: The Eighteenth-Century Graphic Portraits*, exh. cat. (Washington, D. C.: Smithsonian Institution Traveling Exhibition Service and the National Portrait Gallery, 1982); Garry Wills, *Cincinnatus: George Washington and the Enlightenment* (Garden City, New York: Doubleday, 1984); Barry Schwartz, *George Washington: The Making of an American Symbol* (New York: Free Press, 1987); Karal Ann Marling, *George Washington Slept Here: Colonial Revivals and American Culture, 1876-1986* (Cambridge: Harvard University Press, 1988); Barbara J. Mitnick, *The Changing Image of George Washington*, exh. cat. (New York: Fraunces Tavern Museum, 1989); Ellen G. Miles, *George and Martha Washington: Portraits from the Presidential Years*, exh. cat. Washington, D.C.: Smithsonian Institution, National Portrait Gallery, 1999); William M. S. Rasmussen and Robert S. Tilton, *George Washington: The Man Behind the Myth* (Charlottesville and London: University of Virginia Press, 1999); and Barbara J. Mitnick, ed., *George Washington: American Symbol* (New York: Hudson Hills Press, 1999).

3   George Lippard, *Blanche of Brandywine* (Philadelphia: T. B. Peterson and Brothers, 1846), 172.

4   For detailed discussions of the icon in connection with Washington imagery, see Eugene F. Miller and Barry Schwartz, "The Icon of the American Republic: A Study in Political Symbolism," *The Review of Politics* 47, no. 4 (October 1985), 516-543; and Barry Schwartz and Eugene F. Miller, "The icon and the word: A study in the visual depiction of moral character," *Semiotica* 61 no. 1/2 (1986), 69-99.

5   Pavel Petrovich Svinin, *Picturesque United States of America: 1811, 1812, 1813, Being a Memoir of Paul Svinin, Russian Diplomatic Officer, Artist, and Author, Containing Copious Excerpts from His Account of His Travels in America, with Fifty-two Reproductions of Water Colors in His Own Sketchbook, by Avrahm Yarmolinksy* (New York: William Edwin Rudge, 1930), 34.

6   "Washington," *American Magazine of Useful and Entertaining Knowledge* 2 (March 1836), 266.

7   George B. Forgie, *Patricide in the House Divided: A Psychological Interpretation of Lincoln and His Age* (New York: W. W. Norton & Co., 1979), 121.

8   Quoted in Harold Edward Dickson, ed., *Observations of American Art: Selections from the Writings of John Neal (1793-1876)* (State College, Pennsylvania: Pennsylvania State College, 1943), 3.

9   Ibid.

10 Michael Pollak, "A Gallery of Memories," *New York Times*, January 7, 1996, sec. 4A, 28-29.

11 Karal Ann Marling, *George Washington Slept Here: Colonial Revivals and American Culture, 1876-1986* (Cambridge: Harvard University Press), 337-345.

12 "Washington," *American Magazine of Useful and Entertaining Knowledge* 2 (March 1836), 266.

13 Robert C. Winthrop, *An Address Delivered in Aid of the Fund for Ball's Equestrian Statue of Washington* (Boston: Little, Brown & Co., 1859), 57.

14 Martin Scorsese, "Sacred Images," *Civilization* 5, no. 1 (February/March 1998), 70.

15 "The Fine Arts," *Gleason's Pictorial Drawing-Room Companion* 5 (August 25, 1853), 14.

16 W. W. Abbot and Dorothy Twohig, eds., *The Papers of George Washington*, Confederation Series, (Charlottesville: University Press of Virginia, 1992), 2: 561.

17 Grant Wood, "A Statement from Grant Wood Concerning His Painting 'Parson Weems' Fable'," January 2, 1940, unpaginated typescript, curatorial files, Amon Carter Museum, Fort Worth.

18 Thomas Woodson, ed., *The French and Italian Notebooks*, vol. 14 of *The Centenary Edition of Works of Nathaniel Hawthorne* (Columbus, Ohio: Ohio State University Press, 1980), 281.

19 Quoted in Charles Coleman Sellers, *Portraits and Miniatures by Charles Willson Peale*, Transactions of the American Philosophical Society, vol. 42, part 1 (Philadelphia: American Philosophical Society, 1952; reprint, 1968), 225.

20 Allan Nevins, ed, *The Diary of Philip Hone 1828-1851*, (New York: Dodd, Mead and Company, 1952), 2: 694.

21 Quoted in Natalie Spassky, *American Paintings in the Metropolitan Museum of Art* (New York: Metropolitan Museum of Art, 1985), 18.

22 "Facts and Opinions," *The Literary World* 7 (August 31, 1850), 174.

23 "Opening of the Art-Union," *Evening Post* [New York] (September 23, 1851), 2.

24 "Fine Arts. Washington Crossing the Delaware: By Leutze," *Albion* 10 (October 1, 1851), 525.

25 L. Carroll Judson, *The Sages and Heroes of the American Revolution* (1851; reprint, (Port Washington, New York: Kennikat Press, 1970), 368.

26 C. Edwards Lester, "Washington," in *The Odd-Fellows' Offering, for 1851* (New York: Edward Walker, 1851), 9.

27 The compass held by the boy reminds viewers of Washington's early years as a surveyor.

28 Reverend Henry F. Harrington, "Anecdotes of Washington," *Godey's Lady's Book* 38 (June 1849), 427.

29 [H. Hastings Weld], *The Life of George Washington* (Philadelphia: Lindsay and Blakiston, 1845), 146.

30 "Washington's Marriage," *The Ladies' Repository* 9 (January 1849), 4.

31 Mason Locke Weems, *The Life of Washington*, ed. Marcus Cunliffe (Cambridge: Harvard University Press, 1962), 128.

32 A provocative aspect of Stearns's painting is the prominent inclusion of slaves at a moment when the slavery question was becoming ever more dominant and divisive. Both Northerners and Southerners offered arguments justifying Washington's ownership of slaves. More recently, his role as a slaveholder became the subject of much discussion and controversy, when, for example, the New Orleans School Board adopted a policy of changing any school named for a slaveowner. In 1997, the board voted to rename an elementary school that bore Washington's name.

33 See William Ayres, "At Home with George: Commercialization of the Washington Image, 1776-1876," in *George Washington: American Symbol*, ed. Barbara J. Mitnick (New York: Hudson Hills Press, 1999), 91-107.

34 The painting was commissioned by The Hotel George in Washington, D. C. The hotel's motto is "on a first-name basis with Washington." The 1990s also witnessed the publication of *George*, a popular magazine inspired by Washington.

35 Quoted in Andrew Ross, "Poll Stars: Komar & Melamid's 'The People's Choice'," *Artforum* 33, no. 5 (January 1995), 74-75.

36 Ibid., 75.

37   Ibid.

38   For an excellent theoretical discussion of this point in regard to Abraham
     Lincoln imagery, see Barry Schwartz, "Postmodernity and Historical
     Reputation: Abraham Lincolon in Late Twentieth-Century American
     Memory," *Social Forces* 77 no. 1 (September 1998): 63-103.

Eleven

George Washington and the Religious Impulse

JOHN G. WEST, JR.

1   Washington, Farewell Address, September 19, 1796, *The Writings of George
     Washington*, ed. John Fitzpatrick (Washington, D. C.: Government Printing
     Office, 1931-1944), 35: 229.

2   Washington, quoted by Beecher, *The Practicality of Suppressing Vice by Means
     of Societies Instituted for That Purpose* (New London, Connecticut: Samuel
     Green, 1804), 18.

3   Petition from citizens of Castleton and vicinity, Vermont, received on
     February 22, 1830, Petitions received by the House Committee on the
     Post Office and Post Roads, RG 233, National Archives.

4   See Paul F. Boller, *George Washington and Religion* (Dallas: Southern
     Methodist University Press, 1963), 15-16.

5   Wright, quoted in Boller, *George Washington and Religion*, 15. Even in some
     evangelical pulpits, Washington's orthodoxy came under suspicion; in
     Albany, Episcopal divine Bird Wilson lamented that Washington "was a
     great and good man, but he was not a professor of religion." Wilson, quot-
     ed in Boller, *George Washington and Religion*, 15.

6   E. C. M'Guire, *The Religious Opinions and Character of Washington* (New
     York: Harper and Brothers, 1836).

7   William J. Johnson, *George Washington the Christian* (New York: Abingdon
     Press, 1919); Boller, *George Washington.*

8   Walter Berns and Harry Jaffa, "Were the Founding Fathers Christian?"
     [Debate in the Correspondence section], *This World,* Spring/Summer 1984,
     7.

9   Berns, in Edward R. Norman, "Christians, Politics, and the Modern State
     (with a comment by Walter Berns)," *This World*, Fall 1983, 98.

10 Tim LaHaye, *Faith of Our Founding Fathers* (Brentwood, Tenn.: Wolgemuth and Hyatt, 1987), 113.

11 See discussion in Boller, *George Washington and Religion*, 24-25.

12 Washington, Farewell Orders to the Armies of the United States, in *George Washington: A Collection*, ed. W. B. Allen (Indianapolis: LibertyClassics, 1988), 267.

13 Washington, First Inaugural Address, *George Washington: A Collection*, 460-1.

14 Washington, Thanksgiving Proclamation, October 3, 1789, *George Washington: A Collection*, 535.

15 Washington to William Pearce, May 25, 1794, *Writings*, 33: 375.

16 Washington to Henry Knox, March 2, 1797, *Writings*, 35: 408-409.

17 See Benson J. Lossing, *The Pictorial Field-Book of the Revolution* (New York: Harper and Brothers, 1859), 2:215 n. 2; Boller, *George Washington and Religion*, 26-27.

18 Boller, *George Washington and Religion*, 68; Washington, Circular to the States, June 8, 1783, *Writings*, 26: 496.

19 See Boller, *George Washington and Religion*, 24-44.

20 Washington to Marquis de Lafayette, August 15, 1787, *Writings*, 29: 259.

21 James Hutson, *Religion and the Founding of the American Republic* (Washington, D. C.: Library of Congress, 1998), 81.

22 Washington, First Inaugural Speech, *George Washington: A Collection*, 462.

23 Washington, First Annual Message, *George Washington: A Collection*, 469.

24 Washington, Farewell Address, *Writings*, 35: 229.

25 Alexander Hamilton, John Jay, and James Madison, *The Federalist* (New York: New American Library, 1961), 322.

26 George Will, *Statecraft as Soulcraft* (New York: Simon and Schuster, 1983), 133 .

27 Benjamin Franklin to Messrs. The Abbe's Chalut and Arnaud (April 17, 1787), *Writings of Benjamin Franklin,* ed. Albert Henry Smyth (New York: Macmillan, 1905-1907), 9: 569.

28 Nathanael Emmons, "The Evil Effects of Sin," *Works of Nathanael Emmons*, ed. Jacob Ide (Boston: Crocker and Brewster, 1842), 2: 47. See also John M. Mason, "Divine Judgments," September 20, 1793, *Complete Works of John Mason*, ed. Ebenezer Mason (New York: Baker and Scribner, 1849), 2: 59-60; Bishop James Madison, "Manifestations of the Beneficence of Divine Providence Towards America," (1795) in *Political Sermons of the*

Founding Era, 1730-1805, ed. Ellis Sandoz (Indianapolis: LibertyPress, 1991), 1319-1320; Zephaniah Swift Moore, "An Oration on the Anniversary of the Independence of the United States of America," (1802) in *American Political Writing during the Founding Era, 1760-1805* (Indianapolis: LibertyPress, 1983), ed. Charles S. Hyneman and Donald S. Lutz, 2: 1212-1213; Samuel Kendal, "Religion the Only Sure Basis of Free Government," (1804), *American Political Writing*, 2: 1241-1263; Nathaniel Bouton, *Christian Patriotism* (1825), 6; Phinehas Cooke, *Reciprocal Obligations of Religion and Civil Government* (Concord: Jacob B. Moore, 1825), 13; Nathaniel Bouton, *The Responsibilities of Rulers* (Concord: Henry F. Moore, 1828), 24-27; Daniel Dana, *An Election Sermon* (Concord: J.B. Moore, 1823), 17-18; *Sermon* (1822), 20-21; Nathan Lord, *A Sermon Preached at the Annual Election* (Concord: Hill and Barton, 1831); Lyman Beecher, "Reformation of Morals," *Works of Lyman Beecher* (Boston: Jewett, 1852), 2: 79-80, 99-101; Francis Wayland, *The Elements of Moral Science*, ed. Joseph L. Blau (Cambridge, Massachusetts: Belknap Press, 1963), 320-321.

29   Washington, Farewell Address, *Writings*, 35: 229.

30   Washington, General Orders, July 4, 1775, *Writings*, 3: 309.

31   Washington, General Orders, July 9, 1776, *Writings*, 5: 245.

32   Washington, General Orders, August 3, 1776, *Writings*, 5: 367.

33   Washington, General Orders, July 29, 1779, *Writings*, 16: 13.

34   See, for example, Washington's appointment of a day of thanksgiving after America's victory in the battle of Monmouth. Washington, General Orders, June 30, 1778, *Writings* 12:131.

35   Washington to Reverend John Rodgers, June 11, 1783, *Writings*, 27: 1.

36   Washington to George Mason, October 3, 1785, *Writings*, 28: 285.

37   Washington, Thanksgiving Proclamation, October 3, 1789, *Writings*, 30: 427-428; Washington, A Proclamation, January 1, 1795, *A Compilation of the Messages and Papers of the Presidents*, ed. James D. Richardson (Washington, D. C.: Bureau of National Literature, 1897), 1: 171.

38   Washington, General Orders, July 29, 1779, *Writings*, 16: 13.

39   See, for example, Washington, General Orders, July 4, 1775, *Writings*, 3: 309; Washington to Major and Brigadier Generals, Sept. 8, 1775, *Writings*, 3: 483; Washington, General Orders, July 9, 1776, *Writings*, 5: 245; Washington, General Orders, August 3, 1776, *Writings*, 5: 367; Washington, General Orders, July 29, 1779, *Writings*, 16: 13; Washington to General Assembly of the Presbyterian Church (May, 1789), *George*

Washington on Religious Liberty, 15; Washington to the Religious Society Called Quakers, October, 1789, *George Washington on Religious Liberty*, 11; Washington to the Roman Catholics in the United States, December, 1789, *George Washington on Religious Liberty*, 10; Washington to New Church, Baltimore, January 27, 1793, *Writings*, 32: 315; Washington , A Proclamation, January 1, 1795, *Compilation of Messages of the Presidents*, 1: 171.

40 Adams, "A Dissertation on the Canon and the Feudal Law, No. 2," August 1765, *Papers of John Adams*, ed. Robert Taylor (Cambridge: Belknap Press, 1977-), 1: 115.

41 Adams, "A Dissertation," August 1765, *Papers*, 1: 116.

42 Ibid.

43 Adams, "Discourses on Davila," (1790), *Works of John Adams*, ed. Charles Francis Adams (Boston: Little, Brown, 1856), 6: 397.

44 Jay, Address to the American Bible Society, May 8, 1823, *Correspondence and Public Papers of John Jay*, ed. Henry Johnston (New York: Putnam's Sons, 1890-93), 4: 488.

45 Madison, "James Madison's 'Detached Memoranda,'" *William and Mary Quarterly* 3 (1946), 560-561.

46 Hamilton, *The Farmer Refuted* in *Papers of Alexander Hamilton*, ed. Harold Syrett (New York: Columbia University Press, 1961-79), 1: 87.

47 Jefferson to James Fishback, September 27, 1809, *Jefferson's Extracts from the Gospels*, ed. Dickinson Adams (Princeton: Princeton University Press, 1983), 343.

48 See discussion in John G. West, Jr., *The Politics of Revelation and Reason* (Lawrence, Kansas: University Press of Kansas, 1996), 75.

49 Washington to different denominations residing in and near Philadelphia, March 3, 1797, *Writings*, 35: 416.

50 Washington to Henry Knox, March 2, 1797, *Writings*, 34: 409.

51 Washington, General Orders, July 29, 1779, *Writings*, 16: 13.

52 Washington to Benedict Arnold, September 14, 1775, *Writings*, 3: 492.

53 Washington, Farewell Address, *Writings*, 35: 229.

54 Washington, First Inaugural Address, *George Washington: A Collection,* 462.

55 John Witherspoon, *An Annotated Edition of Lectures on Moral Philosophy*, ed. Jack Scott (Newark, Delaware: University of Delaware Press, 1982), 64.

56 Ibid.

57 For good introductions to the Christian natural law tradition, see J. Budziszewski, *Written on the Heart: The Case for Natural Law* (Downers Grove, Illinois: InterVarsity Press, 1997) and Michael Cromartie, ed., *A Preserving Grace: Protestants, Catholics, and Natural Law* (Grand Rapids: Eerdmans, 1997).

58 See Washington's letter to the Religious Society Called Quakers, October, 1789, *George Washington on Religious Liberty*, 11.

59 Berns, "Religion and the Founding Principle," in *The Moral Foundations of the Republic*, ed. Robert Horwitz, 3rd ed. (Charlottesville: University Press of Virginia, 1986), 215.

60 See Anson Phelps Stokes and Leo Pfeffer, *Church and State in the United States* (Westport, Conn.: Greenwood, 1964), 11-19; Perry Miller and Thomas Johnson, *The Puritans: A Sourcebook of their Writings*, rev. ed. (New York: Harper Torchbooks, 1963), 2: 219-224. Of course, the fact that most supporters of religious liberty in America were Christians does not mean that there were no American defenders of this concept who were hostile to traditional Christianity. Clearly, figures such as Thomas Jefferson and Thomas Paine linked their support of religious liberty to a hostility toward revealed religion. However, they were far from representative of the Founding generation in this area.

61 See, for example, the role of evangelicals in arguing against the establishment of religion in Virginia. Thomas Buckley, *Church and State in Revolutionary Virginia, 1776-1787* (Charlottesville: University Press of Virginia, 1977); Levy, *The Establishment Clause: Religion and the First Amendment* (New York: Macmillan, 1986), 55-58; Thomas Curry, *The First Freedoms: Church and State in America to the Passage of the First Amendment* (New York: Oxford University Press, 1986), 143-146.

62 Washington to the United Baptist Churches in Virginia, May 10, 1789, *George Washington: A Collection*, 532.

63 Washington to the Roman Catholics in the United States of America, March 15, 1790, *George Washington: A Collection*, 547.

64 Washington to the Hebrew Congregation in Newport, August 1790, *George Washington: A Collection*, 548.

65 Harry Jaffa, "Crisis of the Strauss Divided," (unpublished paper, April 22, 1987), 23, 26.

66 Washington to General Assembly of the Presbyterian Church, May, 1789, *George Washington on Religious Liberty*, 15.

67 Washington to the Religious Society Called Quakers, October, 1789, *George Washington on Religious Liberty*, 11.

68 Ibid.

69 See, for example, *West Virginia State Board of Education v. Barnette*, 319 U.S. 624 (1943); *Sherbert v. Verner*, 374 U.S. 398 (1963); *Gillette v. United States*, 401 U.S. 437 (1971); *Wisconsin v. Yoder*, 406 U.S. 205 (1972); *Hobbie v. Unemployment Appeals Commission of Florida*, 480 U.S. 136 (1987). The Supreme Court abandoned this approach for free exercise claims in *Employment Division, Department of Human Resources of Oregon v. Smith*, 110 S. Ct. 1595 (1990).

70 Washington to George Mason, October 3, 1785, *Writings*, 28: 285.

INDEX

Abraham, Henry, 128

Adams, Abigail, 25, 186, 300

Adams, John, 30, 182, 197; crisis with France and, 186; revelation and reason and, 279; royalty in office and, 166; tensions with France and, 13; Washington's character and, 184, 300; Washington's death and, 2; Washington's example and, xiii–xiv; Washington's presidential election and, 9

Addison, Joseph, 27, 301

agrarianism: Jefferson and, 48; republicanism and, 40; utilitarian aspect of, 41–42; virtues in, 40–41. *See also* farming

Agricultural Revolution, 42

agriculture. *See* farming, agrarianism

Alden, John, 64

Alexander Hamilton, American (Brookhiser), 310

Alexandria Conference, 1785, 7, 114

Allen, Ethan, 73

Allen, William B., 15, 309

America: British relations with, 11–12; character of, x; culture of, 241; foreign policy of, 10; French relations with, 11, 121–22, 151–52; independence of, 62, 98; military policy of, 144; modern army of, 62–63; provincialism and, 96–97; religion in, 192, 194; republicanism and, 25; role of military in establishment of, 62; security of, 148–49; strategic goals of, 69–72; Washington's example and, xii

American Founding: character and, 218; *The Federalist* and, xi; Jefferson's presidency and, 212; liberty and, xi–xii, 23; Washington's Farewell Address and, 17; Washington and, ix–xi, 23, 120

American Presidency (McDonald), 36, 311

American Revolution: Britain and, 70–73, 76, 82–83, 89; Congress and, 31, 78–79; Continental Army and, 24, 53–55, 76, 79, 82, 92; debt incurred by states in, 9; First Inaugural Address and, 37; first phase of, 72–76; France and, 84–90, 102; George III and, 92–93; independence and, ix; liberty and, ix; peace treaty negotiations after, 32,

Britain: American opposition to, 5–6; American relations with, 11–12; American Revolution and, 70–73, 76, 82–83, 89; Continental Army and, 97; encroachments of, 30; foreign policy of, 158; Franco-American treaties and, 11; French and Indian War and, 29; Jay's negotiations with, 133; problems of, 68; provincialism and, 96–97; queen as symbol in, 166; sea power of, 67, 85; Seven Years' War and, 85; strategic goals of, 67–69; Suez Canal and, 155; Virginia military and, 5; war with France of, 102, 127, 151

British Channel Fleet, 2

Brookhiser, Richard, 20, 250, 310

Brooklyn Heights, 80

Brownsecombe, Jennie, 261

Buchan, Earl of, 43

Bull Run, Battle of, 147

Bunker (Breed's) Hill, 73, 84, 107

Bunker Hill monument, xii

Burgoyne, John, 68, 83, 84

Burke, Aedanus, 58–59

Bush, George, 150, 155

Butler, Pierce, 143

Byron, Lord, 39

The C. S. Lewis Reader's Encyclopedia (West), 313

cabinet government, 127–29

Caesar, 24, 59

Calvert, Cecilius, 282

Calvin, John, 281

Cambodia, 155

Camden, 89

Camelot, 170

Canada: British soldiers sent to, 79; expedition against, 74, 75; French and American invasion of, 87–88; French claims to, 86; French expedition from, 4; threat of British forces in, 156

Canova, Antonio, 39

Capes, Battle of the, 91

Carroll, Daniel, 110, 111

Castro, Fidel, 24

Catholic Social Science Review, 310

Cato (Addison), 27, 301

Chamberline, Samuel, 46

Champlain, Samuel de, 304

character: national, x; politics and, 218–19, 221

character, American: divisions between states and, 7; establishment of, 109; habits of the people and, 236–37; history and, 141; Washington and, 222, 238–40

Charleston, 89, 92

Chatham, Earl of, 68

Cherokee Nation, 46

cherry tree story, 3, 23

Chesapeake Bay, 7

Christ, 272

Church of England, 196

Cincinnatus, 14, 59, 60

"Cincinnatus" (Freneau), 39

Circular Address, 113, 115, 119

Circular Address to the Governors of the Thirteen States, 108–9

Circular to the States, 95, 272

citizens: character of, 18; government and, xi; habits of, 200; love for liberty of, 203; piety of, 203; self-government and, 18

Civil War, 58, 63, 70, 146

Clark, George Rogers, 88

Clausewitz, Carl von, 62, 64–66, 67, 72, 86